ANNE
The Working Princess

Paul James is in his late 20s and has a lifelong interest in royalty – an interest fuelled in his formative years by his aunt who was lady in waiting to the Queen Mother.

After taking his degree he became a full-time writer in 1980, since when he has completed many books, both fiction and non-fiction, for adults and children. In 1983 he compiled a book with HRH The Duke of Edinburgh and has written numerous articles on the Royal Family and a number of royal books. Throughout 1986 he followed Princess Anne's progress closely in preparation for writing Anne: The Working Princess.

ANNE
The Working Princess

Paul James

Pan Books
London, Sydney and Auckland

First published 1987 by Judy Piatkus (Publishers) Ltd
This edition published 1988 by Pan Books Ltd,
Cavaye Place, London SW10 9PG
9 8 7 6 5 4 3 2 1
© Paul James 1987
ISBN 0 330 30480 1

Printed in Great Britain by
Richard Clay Ltd, Bungay, Suffolk

For
DAVID and BARNABY JAMES

ILLUSTRATIONS

Princess Anne, aged 7, with her mother (*Camera Press*)
On her way back to school (*Radio Times Hulton Picture Library*)
Bridesmaid again (*Radio Times Hulton Picture Library*)
Galloping on High Jinks (*Camera Press*)
Confrontation with the press (*Radio Times Hulton Picture Library*)
Norman Parkinson's photograph, prior to the wedding (*Camera Press*)

Michael Noakes' portrait of the Princess (*Camera Press*)
Captain Mark Phillips (*Camera Press*)
The Sound of Music Gala (*J. S. Library*)
The Cavalry Old Comrades parade (*J. S. Library*)
Princess Anne with the Children of Courage (*J. S. Library*)
The President of the Save The Children Fund on tour in
Bangladesh (*both J. S. Library*)
As Chancellor of the University of London (*J. S. Library*)
Off-duty with her children (*J. S. Library*)
With Mark Phillips in Dubai (*J. S. Library*)
At a leper colony in the Sudan (*J. S. Library*)
Discussing the problems of India (*J. S. Library*)

Ninth wedding anniversary portrait by Norman Parkinson
(*Camera Press*)
At work on the farm (*Camera Press*)
Meeting the travellers (*Topham Picture Library*)
A visit to a sausage factory (*Topham Picture Library*)
Glamour at the première of *A Passage To India* (*Camera Press*)

Contents

Acknowledgements

Writing the biography of a member of the Royal Family is akin to writing of the dead. You cannot communicate easily with your subject. Fortunately for me, Princess Anne is very much alive and I owe an enormous debt of gratitude to all those who have allowed me to attend many of Her Royal Highness's engagements and observe her work at first hand. For enabling me, in the Princess's words, to 'tag along' I am deeply grateful to John Haslam, the Assistant Press Secretary to the Queen, who has guided me throughout my research, has generously assisted, and where necessary curbed my impetuosity. I must also thank Princess Anne's Private Secretary, Lieutenant Colonel Peter Gibbs.

My gratitude goes to Chris Thornton, Press Officer for the Save the Children Fund, and the staff of the Fund, including Jane Button and Sara Wingfield, who enabled me to watch the Princess at work and discover more about her achievements; the staff of Dillons Bookshop; Madame Tussauds; Andrew Lownic, David Horne, Diane James, John Lawton, Peter Russell; those around the world who kindly wrote to me, including Kimberlea Tracy and Bridie Chambers, and all those too numerous to mention who have helped me to get close to my subject and better understand the Princess. Finally, thanks to the members of my family and household who, for the past eighteen months, must have felt as if they were living with Princess Anne.

In any book of this nature there are invariably anecdotes and stories which are apocryphal and open to conjecture. This is unavoidable when the only person who knows the truth is Princess

Anne. I have tried, therefore, only to include facts that I personally have been able to verify. Any opinions expressed are my own, as are any unwitting errors or omissions.

Having the opportunity to accompany Princess Anne on various functions, to watch the working royal in action, has been a rewarding experience, enlightening and always fun. That is the key to Princess Anne, she enjoys what she is doing and this is passed on to those with whom she comes into contact. My greatest thanks must, therefore, go to the Princess herself.

PAUL JAMES
London

*I*ntroduction

Princess Anne is a phenomenon. Like her or loathe her, there can be few who cannot admire her stamina, her achievements, her sheer guts. For ten years, however, from the time of her marriage until her outstandingly successful Save the Children Fund tour of Africa in 1982, there were few good words spoken about the Princess, dubbed 'Sourpuss' by the world media.

Today she remains unchanged, but the public conception of her, the media cliché 'image', has altered. Biographers, like myself, who in recent years have studied her in depth, who watch the Princess from close quarters, confess that they fall just a little bit in love with their subject. Those who meet Princess Anne during the course of her work find it difficult not to become over-enthusiastic.

Princess Anne is an enigma. Born into one of the richest families in the world, her mother is the Queen, her father a Duke, she is Princess Royal. She could also call herself Lady Anne Phillips, or equally Dame Anne Phillips, as a Member of the Royal Victorian Order, yet she happily takes tea in gypsy caravans and forsakes tiara and pearls to don T-shirt and jeans for visits to some of the poorest regions in the world.

When you meet Princess Anne for the first time you are struck by her beauty. 'Beauty' is a word that one associates with the Princess of Wales, Princess Michael of Kent or the Duchess of York, but would not instantly apply to Princess Anne. 'You expect her to be big and horsey,' said a close friend of mine, yet in the flesh she is nothing less than petite. She fits comfortably into a size 10 dress, with a size 8 waist, and a model figure of 35–24–35, the same today as when she was 21. Unphotogenic, when you look closely her skin is clear and fresh, her hair thick and glossy, and she is shorter in height than one would imagine, at 5 feet 6½ inches, nearly four inches shorter than the Princess of Wales.

Yet forget the physical appearance and dig deeper into her character and you feel that she is someone you would want to be your friend. Princess Anne would be practical and clear-headed in a crisis; get things out of perspective and she would bring you back down to earth to face reality; experience true hardship and she would be sympathetic, but display self-pity and her patience would snap. Forget the 'jolly hockey-sticks' approach that five years at Benenden instilled and you find a sharp, wry sense of humour and a down-to-earth approach to life. One Save the Children Fund organiser said, 'She can still put you down pretty sharply, even if it is just in fun. You can bounce in and say, "It's lovely to see you again, Ma'am," and she will turn round and say "Oh, really – why?" It can floor you until you realise that she is joking.'

Princess Michael believes that 'people don't want to see me doing the washing-up in my Carmen rollers'; the Princess of Wales would not be seen dead wearing a headscarf; the Queen would never appear in public wearing trousers, but The Working Princess undoubtedly places a higher value on the quality of human life than on the designer labels in her wardrobe, or indeed on what the public's opinion of her may be. Like the Duke of Edinburgh, Princess Anne speaks her mind, leaves you in no doubt how she feels, and if she fails to match up to the expected image of a member of the Royal Family, then it's *your* problem, not hers.

When she is working abroad often the people she meets have no conception of who she really is. 'She looks very young to be a Queen,' came a comment in Beirut. 'Is this the wife of Charles?' came another. The way her image is projected comes very low on Princess Anne's list of priorities. After falling from a horse in Russia an attendant radiologist asked the Princess to lie on her right side. 'Not bloody likely!' came Princess Anne's reply. 'That's the side that hurts.' Loyal to her favourite hat-designer, John Boyd, when one of her dress designers asked if he could create a hat to match one of his outfits Princess Anne looked him straight in the eyes and said 'Cobblers!' People appreciate her earthy honesty, but they are sometimes surprised at the language of the Queen's only daughter. 'That's school, not Palace or even horsey circles,' she confesses. 'I learned to swear at Benenden.'

There have been times when criticism of Princess Anne has been justified. It took a long time for her to find her feet, draw an adequate line between private and public life, and to come to terms with her position. The *paparazzi* were, in her father's terminology, 'bloody vultures', but irritating though they may be to the Royal Family she has learned to accept the press as a necessary evil that must be endured. Just as the critics in New York can make or break a Broadway show, the popularity and effectiveness of what Malcolm Muggeridge in 1955 dubbed the 'Royal Soap Opera' relies very heavily on positive publicity. In 1985 much media-hype ensured the success of Band Aid and Live Aid, with Bob Geldof as figurehead. Geldof's intentions were no greater than Princess Anne's. Her work continues quietly and in 1986, through her inspiration, the Save the Children Fund received a record £43.4 million. When she became President the annual income was less than £4 million. Princess Anne has now emerged through the battlefield as a philanthropic figure, and press support is undoubtedly useful. It took time, effort and compromise but her dedication and hard work have won the day.

Princess Anne attends over 500 different engagements every year, even working through the summer when the rest of the Royal Family are at Balmoral. It has been a working life that on 1st March 1989 will have spanned two decades, taking her to remote and diverse areas of the globe, travelling over one million miles. One day she can be taking part in a high level meeting to discuss grain distribution in Somalia, the next she can be seen riding at Epsom to raise funds for charity.

The door of Princess Anne's second-floor office at Buckingham Palace is noticeable by a small white pasteboard plaque bearing the words: HRH The Princess Anne. It is practical, unassuming and to the point; that is her style. In any single working week she can spend 80 hours fulfilling 15 official engagements. She will travel over 2000 miles, shake 500 hands, change clothes 30 times, and in the process meet thousands of people once and only once. It is a strange and lonely existence for, although rarely alone, she is yet in constant isolation.

The circumstances of her birth may have set her on this pedestal but Princess Anne has an enquiring mind, and has turned her duties into opportunities. A look at the following pages which detail her engagements for the first three months of 1987 will give a good sense of the breadth and variety of the job she takes on with dedication rather than as drudgery.

JANUARY 1987

20   Attended a gala performance of *The Voyage of the Dawn Treader* at Sadler's Wells Theatre, London.

27   As President of the British Knitting and Clothing Export Council, visited Astraka Limited, Blyvoor Works, County Durham.
Evening: Attended the Scottish Sportswoman of the Year 1986 dinner at the Albany Hotel, Glasgow.

29   Morning: As Master of the Worshipful Company of Carmen, attended a Court Meeting of the Company at Carpenter's Hall, London.
Evening: As President of The British Knitting and Clothing Export Council, attended a banquet given by the Council at the Mansion House, London, during which she presented the Council's Export Awards.

FEBRUARY

1–9   Visited Western Australia for the closing stages of the America's Cup.

10–21 Visited the United Arab Emirates, Qatar, Kuwait and Jordan.

24   Morning: Visited Stockport Grammar School, Greater Manchester.
Afternoon: As President of the Save the Children Fund, visited ASHA Neighbourhood Project at 43 Stratford Street, Leeds.
Evening: As President of the Save the Children Fund, attended a preview of a sale of work at Hugh Ripley Hall, Ripon, Yorkshire.

25   As Chancellor of the University of London, attended the Senior Student's Dinner at Hughes Parry Hall, London.

MARCH

2   As President of the Save the Children Fund, visited the Burdett Matchbox Community Centre, London.
Attended the Spring Luncheon of the City of London Police Senior Officers Dining Club, Wood Street Police Office, London.

2–4   Visited the International Lowlanders Cross Country Ski Championships at Isny, Bavaria, West Germany.

4   Evening: As Chancellor of the University of London, presided at a dinner for major benefactors and fund raisers, Senate House, London.

5   As President of the Riding for the Disabled Association, attended a council meeting followed by luncheon at Saddlers' Hall, London.
Evening: Attended a dinner given by The Royal Cruising Club at the Naval and Military Club, 94 Piccadilly, London.

7   As Patron of the All England Women's Lacrosse Association, attended a match against Scotland to celebrate the 75th Anniversary of the Association, at Queen's Park Rangers Football Club, London.

9   As Honorary President of the Chartered Institute of Transport, attended the Institute's Annual Philip Henman Overseas Lecture at the Institute of Civil Engineers, London, and attended a dinner after the lecture.

10   Morning: As Patron of the British Executive Service Overseas, visited their offices at 10 Belgrave Square, London SW1.
Visited Douay Martyrs' Roman Catholic Comprehensive School, Uxbridge, in celebration of the School's Silver Jubilee Year.
Afternoon: Opened the new hydrotherapy unit at the London Hospital, London E1.
Opened the new Homerton Hospital, Hackney, London.

Evening: Attended a Livery Banquet of the Worshipful Company of Carmen at Mansion House, London.

11   As Chancellor of the University of London, presided at the University Presentation Ceremony at the Royal Albert Hall.

12   Attended *Equitana* the World Fair for Horse Sports in Essen, West Germany.

13   Attended a dinner given by the National Council for Carers and their Elderly Dependants before their National Conference at Cobden Hotel, Birmingham.

15   As President of the British Academy of Film and Television Arts, attended the Craft Awards at Granada Studios, Manchester.

16   As Patron of the Butler Trust, presented their awards at Lambeth Palace, London, and was afterwards entertained to luncheon.

17   12 noon: Rode Aldaniti over one mile at Cheltenham Racecourse, Gloucestershire in aid of the Bob Champion Cancer Trust.

18   As President of the Royal Agricultural Society of England, attended a council meeting at Belgrave Square, London.

19   As Master of the Worshipful Company of Carmen, attended the Foundation Day Service at St. Michael Paternoster Royal. Attended the Company's luncheon in Whittington Hall, London.
Opened the new City of London School, Queen Victoria Street, London.
Evening: As Master of the Worshipful Company of Carmen, attended a dinner with the Director General of Transport and Movements and Officers, Aldershot, Hampshire.

20   Opened the Glen Hospital, Durdham Down, Bristol.
Opened the extension to Westfield House of St. Monica's Home of Rest, Westbury-on-Trim, Bristol.

21   As Patron, Scottish Rugby Union, attended the Scotland versus Wales match at Murrayfield, Edinburgh.

23   Opened Greendown Community School, Swindon, Wiltshire.
Visited Tredworth Junior School, Gloucester.
Visited the School's Language Unit for children with special educational needs.
Visited Robinswood School and Family Centre, Gloucester.

24   As President of the Save the Children Fund, attended a Dinner and Fashion Show at the Banqueting Room, Guildhall, Bath.

25   Attended the Clothworkers' annual Charities Luncheon at Clothworkers' Hall, London.
Evening: As President of the Save the Children Fund, attended the Mayfair Diamond Jubilee Ball at the Mayfair Hotel, London.

26   Visited North Humberside.
Opened Tharos Hydrotherapy Pool at Frederick Holmes School for physically handicapped children, Hull.
Opened the East Riding Institute's Beech Holme Court Flats.
Opened the new health centre, Hull.

31   Attended a luncheon and visited the factory of Swaine Adeney Brigg and Sons Limited at Great Chesterford, Essex.

APRIL

2   Morning: Visited the Allergy and Environmental Medicine Department at Lister Hospital, London.
As President of the Save the Children Fund, attended a Council Meeting of the Fund, Mary Datchelor House, London, followed by luncheon.
Afternoon: Visited the Ladywell Centre for Physically Handicapped People, Brockley, London.

3   As President of the Riding for the Disabled Association, visited the Strang Riding Centre at Washington, Tyne and Weir.
Evening: As Honorary President, the Chartered Institute of Transport, attended the Conference and Dinner of the Yorkshire Section, College of Ripon and York St. John, Lord Mayor's Walk, York.

8   Undertook engagements in Birmingham.

9   As Vice-President, the Royal Bath and West and Southern Counties Show, visited 'Muck South West' at the Showground, Somerset, followed by luncheon.
Afternoon: Opened the new offices of the Mendip District Council.
Planted a tree in Collett Park, Shepton Mallett.

12   As President of Federation Equestre International, attended the Volvo World Cup Final for Jumping Riders, Paris.

14   Attended the Point-to-Point Owners' Association Meeting, Ashborne, Warwickshire.

20   As Patron of the Royal Lymington Yacht Club, attended the Club's Easter Dinghy Meeting, Lymington, Hampshire.

23   As Master of the Worshipful Company of Carmen, attended the Court Meeting and the Court Dinner with the Royal Corps of Transport at Clothworkers' Hall, London.

24   As President of Federation Equestre International, attended an IOC Executive Committee Meeting, Lausanne, Switzerland.

25   As Colonel-in-Chief, The Worcestershire and Sherwood Foresters Regiment (29th/45th Foot), took the Salute at the Ceremony of Trooping the Colour by the 3rd Battalion, Newark, Nottinghamshire.

27   Opened the new laboratories at ICI's Plant Protection Division, Jealott's Hill Research Station, Bracknell, Berkshire.

Evening: Attended the Annual Dinner of the Freight Transport Association, London Hilton, Park Lane.

28   Morning: Attended the Centenary Annual Meeting of the Church of Scotland Woman's Guild in the Assembly Hall, Edinburgh.
Evening: As Colonel in Chief, the Royal Corps of Signals, attended a band concert and reception at Goldsmith's Hall, London, and had dinner with members of the Corps.

29   Morning: As Chancellor of the University of London, visited the Institute of Archaeology during their Jubilee Celebrations.
As Honorary President of the Chartered Institute of Transport, visited the offices of the Institute, Portland Place, London.
Afternoon: As President of the Save the Children Fund, visited Hampton Court House, Surrey, the Fund's centre for Vietnamese children.

30   Opened the new Rehabilitation Unit at the Mayday Hospital, Thornton Heath, Surrey.
Evening: Attended the Annual Dinner of the Grain and Feed Trade Association at the Grosvenor House Hotel, London.

Chapter 1

The changing image of a Princess

Spectators at the 1985 Olympia Horse Show watched in uncomfortable silence as a gun was aimed directly at Princess Anne's head. Seconds later shots reverberated throughout the stadium and the Princess disappeared from view. When the King's Troop fired at the Royal Box for a second time, Princess Anne emerged waving a white handkerchief. The 6000-strong audience erupted into enthusiastic applause at the spontaneous humour of the once most unpopular member of the Royal Family.

Princess Anne is only too aware of her reputation. Earlier in the year she had surprised journalists, and her husband, by arriving at the Gatcombe Park Horse Trials wearing a Mr. Grumpy costume from the Mr. Men cartoon series. Honest, forthright, independent, she has never fitted the image of a fairy-tale princess, has refused to be trapped in a regal cage, and has seldom conformed to the mould of the archetypal daughter of a monarch. Conscious from a very early age that she would have to take second place to her brother, and would forever be overshadowed by the heir to the throne, Princess Anne turned into a royal rebel.

Saddled with a bad-tempered image – in 1982 she told a journalist at the Badminton Horse Trials to 'Naff off!' – whatever Princess Anne did used to be bad news. Confrontations with the press have always been fraught, and more so if any recalcitrant photographer attempted to take a picture of the Princess off duty. She accepts that interest in her is part and parcel of her position, reluctantly acknowledges the media as a necessary evil on official engagements, but refuses to 'act' in front of the cameras. The Queen Mother will go down in history for giving the public what they expected and never failing to perform, even the Queen will on occasions alter a grim expression to satisfy a photographer, but the working Princess goes about her business without pandering to the press. 'I didn't ask to be born a Princess!' she snapped at television interviewer Alastair Burnet on the eve of her wedding, when even the unenthusiastic media were attempting to show her in a kind light. She was still kicking back at centuries of tradition, social barriers and expectations that no amount of aggression could remove.

Princess Anne's position can be likened to that of Princess Margaret. Both stood in the shadow of a future monarch. Both rebelled against being royal and found themselves inadvertently victimised as the 'baddies' in the Windsor soap opera that the media have created. At the age of 15 Princess Margaret encountered false reports in the newspapers that when out sailing with the Sea Rangers at Frogmore she had pulled the bung out of the bottom of the boat, causing it sink. Princess Anne's first attack came at the age of 13 when, on a tour of Australia, the ribbons of her hat blew constantly in her eyes and she was heard to exclaim loudly, 'I can't see a thing in this bloody wind!' Dubbed 'Princess Sourpuss', the battle with the press had begun. She delighted in putting her nose six inches from an offending cameraman's lens and saying, 'Is this close enough for you?' When one photographer said that he hoped he wasn't being a pest, the Princess responded, 'You *are* a pest by the very nature of that camera in your hand.'

At 37 Princess Anne has mellowed and would be the first to admit that her 'image' has changed, while insisting that she is still the same. With the advent of the Princess of Wales, and more recently the Duchess of York, she has been relieved of the pressures of media attention and carried on with business as usual. So today Princess Anne is good news. She has given highly entertaining interviews on both television and radio, for which the once acid press lauded her with such comments as 'She has the timing and confidence of a professional performer . . . The Princess revealed an engaging sense of humour and a razor sharp wit . . . Much of the humour was used by the Princess to send up one person – herself.'

Having drawn a very definite line between her working and private life, Princess Anne is now more settled than ever before. She became the first princess in over 900 years to marry the man she loved without having to consider his social position or title. And she has been adamant that her children, Peter and Zara, will live as normal a life as is possible having the Queen as a grandmother; putting paid to any suggestion that they or her husband should be titled.

In her working life she personifies the theory that if you are going to support something, you should take an active role and not be a mere figurehead. In February 1986, as Colonel-in-Chief of the 14th/20th King's Hussars, she visited the regiment in sub-zero temperatures in northern Germany where she took control of a 52-ton Chieftain tank and sped across the snow-covered battlefield in an army exercise, something she has done many times. The following day she was spotted on the forecourt of a garage changing the wheel of her own car. When not undertaking official duties she can be seen on the farm at Gatcombe Park driving a tractor or ploughing a field.

If she visits India it is not as a sight-seeing VIP boosting Britain's fashion houses with high couture, meeting only the *crème de la crème*. Instead she ventures where only the bravest and most unsqueamish dare to tread, witnessing at first hand the real problems of the world, never wishing to be sheltered from the horrors of the starving and the dying. Perhaps, as a royal, she is even more aware than most of the appalling contrasts that exist within cultures. In 1984 Princess Anne visited the Upper Volta, the poorest region in the world, on what the press then described as the 'toughest tour ever undertaken by a member of the Royal Family.' Those who have travelled the thousands of dusty miles with the Princess reiterate the words of one of her aides: 'What she has is grit, guts and staying power. She also has a lot more charm and compassion than people realise . . .'

Later that same year her Save the Children Fund tour of India and Bangladesh was brought to a hasty conclusion when a sudden burst of gunfire shattered the tranquil peace of the clear, bright October morning, and brought an unexpected end to the long political rule of one of the world's legendary leaders. India's Prime Minister, Mrs. Indira Gandhi, slumped to the ground in the garden of her home under a hail of assassins' bullets – fired by her own bodyguards. Within hours the streets of Delhi were torn apart by riots. For her own protection Princess Anne was rushed to the relative safety of the British High Commissioner's residence in Delhi. She was flown home immediately after Mrs. Gandhi's funeral. 'Don't worry, I'm coming back at the first possible opportunity,' she told distressed field workers, and it was a promise she kept.

More recently the Princess undertook one of her most gruelling trips, visiting Ethiopia, Tanzania and famine stricken areas of the Sudan. As always, her priority was to witness the reality of the situation at first hand. Within minutes of stepping off the plane the Princess was inspecting a fleet of specially-built lorries and trucks which provide a vital link between food suppliers and the starving. This was no cursory glance. The Princess swung herself up into the cab of the largest vehicle, the Leyland 'landtrain', for closer scrutiny, and taking advantage of her HGV licence was soon driving it for herself.

Ignoring the 90°F heat, Princess Anne visited 20,000 refugees from Chad, her energy apparently inexhaustible while several of her accompanying aides and journalists were on the verge of collapse. Throughout, her wry sense of humour remained. 'Did you bring any creature comforts with you?' asked a reporter. 'Yes, I brought my torch,' she laughed. Comfort, however, is not high on the agenda, in fact it scarcely enters into it, and Princess or not there are no concessions made simply because she is the Queen's only daughter or President of the Save the Children Fund. Here she is a worker and must muck in with the rest of them.

No cosy hotel room is available with bathroom *en suite*. Instead Princess Anne slept in a mud hut with a thatched roof, containing little more than a bed and a chair. One luxury was that a lavatory had been freshly dug for her own private use, and a shower was created out of two empty oil drums. With everyone living in the same conditions Princess Anne can talk freely and as an equal with relief workers. They all know the stark realities of famine, drought, overcrowding, disease and death and understand the problems on the same level. The answers may not be instantly forthcoming, but Princess Anne is characteristically practical and realistic about the situation: 'I'm probably a natural pessimist,' she says, 'but I don't regard the prospects for Africa in that sense. I'm sure it would be a mistake for anybody to think like that. I think the problems at the moment are solvable. It will require a much greater co-ordinated effort and it will be expensive to reverse some of the particular environmental trends that have been happening. The political will and the ability to overcome the sort of internal security problems that have exacerbated the problems in some of these areas is beyond the ken certainly of the voluntary agencies. Even the Government has its hands tied in the same respect. Whatever you may *think* you want to do, they are sovereign states that you are dealing

with and they have their own pride. They don't want to be over-
taken and run by other people, however you put it and whatever
sort of guise you run it under. Aid is fine, but it has to be really
understood and controlled from the country in which you're working, and that's got to come with time. That level hasn't really been
reached, I don't think yet. It works well in some places and a great
deal less well in others. That's got to come.'

After nearly two decades as the Save the Children Fund's President, Princess Anne confesses that she still has one ambition to
fulfil – to set up a branch in Moscow. 'I only hope that I live long
enough!' she remarks.

Tireless in campaigning for the Third World, she still adheres to
the adage that charity begins at home, showing the greatest concern for the social, economic and medical problems in Great
Britain, particularly where young people are concerned. She man-
ages to remain unemotionally involved and able to look clearsight-
edly at the causes and effects of today's situations. When she
comments, it is with insight and understanding that many members of the Royal Family in the past have lacked. Princess Anne and
her elder brother were the first of a new generation of royals to
experience the harsh realities of the twentieth century from which
the monarch's family had previously been shielded. Edward VIII
deplored the poverty of South Wales; had his reign continued
perhaps he would have preceded Princess Anne into the Third
World. It is said that when Queen Mary was driven to Badminton
during the war, by which time she was in her seventies, she pointed
to a field of hay and asked what it was. 'So *that's* what hay looks
like!' she exclaimed. Queen Elizabeth the Queen Mother once
admitted that her favourite radio programme was *Mrs. Dale's
Diary*, revealing 'I try never to miss it because it is the only way of
knowing what goes on in a middle-class family.' Even the Queen,
who has travelled further than any other monarch before her, is
sheltered from the harshness of reality. On many of her tours there
will be few places that are not smartened up for her visit. One
notable exception was in 1983 when Her Majesty paid a State visit
to India and Bangladesh. The Queen seemed close to tears when
confronted with the starkness of dying children. The richest woman
in the world gazed into the calm vacant eyes of those suffering
from severe malnutrition. It was a contrast the press could not
ignore.

Thanks to Princess Anne's patronage, the Save the Children

Fund brought the starving back from the brink of death and, exactly one year later, the Princess met the same children, now progressing well and living in a family unit. Had Princess Anne been confronted with the same vision of death as her mother had she would not have flinched visibly. Inwardly perhaps; outwardly she has to control her emotions. 'You have to switch off,' she says philosophically, 'because you know that in six months that child in front of you could be dead. You'd go nuts if you took every case personally.'

One reason for this enlightenment, which is bringing the monarchy into the realities of the twentieth century, is the fact that Princess Anne and Prince Charles broke out of the confines of the Palace nursery and individual tutorage and became the first heirs to the throne to attend boarding schools. At Benenden, Princess Anne, nicknamed 'P.A.', was treated like any other pupil. She had to satisfy the Headmistress that her work was of a satisfactory standard before she was accepted and there no special privileges.

Anne was to become, in a word, unconventional. At three she was introduced to riding. At five, not content with ponies, she bravely climbed on to a hunter at a meet of the West Norfolk foxhounds. At nine, under the Duke of Edinburgh's supervision, she could drive a car around the Windsor estate. On her first royal tour abroad with the Queen, noticing a small boy lost in the crowd, she stopped the procession until his parents were found.

From Princess Anne we began to see numerous examples of humour, which had previously been denied to members of the public. Britain gripped tightly to the austere face of the monarchy, revelling in the 'We are not amused' image of Queen Victoria, respecting the severity of Queen Mary's matronly air, reverencing the shy King George VI's memory, and loyally supporting the young Queen Elizabeth. However, these daunting figures of the Royal Family were not associated with laughter and familiarity.

In his study at Buckingham Palace Prince Philip has a photograph of his daughter wearing a cheeky grin and an equally cheeky straw hat. He and Princess Anne are kindred spirits and, like many father-daughter relationships, theirs is particularly close. Neither are afraid of being outspoken, occasionally at the risk of causing upset. Equally, they share the quality of being able to send themselves up in public when permissible.

Relaxing in a Sydney restaurant on a visit to Australia, Princess Anne joined in with the cabaret by singing Shirley Bassey numbers.

'I love music,' she admits, 'but I was forced to give up the oboe because my teeth got in the way!'

At an award ceremony, televised live, the Princess began by deliberately reading the wrong speech in a stilted mechanical way. The audience and award winners shuffled nervously until she grinned broadly and announced: 'Sorry, that was yesterday's!' and launched into a witty, off-the-cuff speech without notes. It is the kind of practical joke that Prince Philip would not only enjoy but admire – he himself once having set fire to Sir Harry Secombe's speech with a candle while the former 'Goon' was still reading it! Of Prince Philip, his equerry, Michael Parker, says 'No one has a kinder heart, or takes more trouble to conceal it.' The same could be said about Princess Anne.

Princess Anne has a uniqueness among the new generation of Princesses in being the last of the genuine breed. She was brought up as a 'royal', giving her a distinction, fascination and remoteness that has set her apart from any princess since 1950. The Princess of Wales, the Duchess of York, Princess Michael of Kent, the Duchess of Gloucester have all experienced a 'normal' working life, albeit with aristocratic backgrounds. They have savoured the freedom of living their lives unrecognised and unhampered by security.

Yet being denied liberty has given Princess Anne the edge because she has in turn been saved from the transition period that anyone entering royal life must undoubtedly go through. The young Lady Diana Spencer at 21 found the loss of independence particularly painful to come to terms with. The Queen had to take the unprecedented step of calling a press conference to ask newspaper editors to leave the young Princess alone and allow her time to adjust.

Princess Anne is intelligent enough to realise that she *is* different, and has the ability to draw a dividing line between public and private life; the latter will never be that of a non-royal as the Princess is only too aware, but unlike some royal ladies she attempts to play down her position. It would be all too easy to take advantage of one's birth and accept that people are fully prepared to treat you as a superior being *if you let them*. Princess Anne's cliché 'I didn't ask to be born a Princess' gains credence and sympathy through her efforts to remain unassuming and utilitarian in domestic issues. That is not to say that she is an easy employer: more cooks and nannies have passed through Gatcombe Park in the last ten years than through any other royal household. Yet if staff are competent, intelligent and compatible in working standards to those of their employer, then life is harmonious. Princess Anne is impatient if forced to suffer inefficiency, but in turn does not create unnecessary obstacles for her household. Princess Michael of Kent, who has stepped into Princess Anne's shoes as the most controversial member of the Royal Family, has a much smaller staff but is said to treat them with an attitude bordering on contempt.

Princess Anne's children have benefited from their mother's down-to-earth approach and have avoided the glare of publicity that the sons of Prince Charles have attracted. When photographer 'Gypsy' Joe Andrews gave Peter ten pence for posing at the Badminton Horse Trials in 1984, the six-year-old boy made the error of boasting to his mother about the extra pocket money he had received. Shocked by this incident, Princess Anne admonished her children and quickly confiscated the money before launching into the lesson of never taking money from strange men. It was an early warning and now the children are seldom troubled by the press.

The Princess' practical approach to her own children is also reflected in the dealings she has with children in her public life. She treats them like adults, dealing with them totally on an equal footing. When meeting the physically and mentally disabled, it is difficult not to change one's tone to a more sympathetic level. But on her 1982 tour of Africa she visited the Allatentu Leper Camp where in the 112°F heat she laughed and joked with the leprosy victims and shook the stumps of children's withered limbs as if they had been able to stretch out a strong five-fingered hand. A simple act perhaps, but for the victims of leprosy it was a heartfelt greeting of total acceptance. In these far-off regions of the world, surrounded by poverty and disease, the Princess must be aware of her good fortune and feel gratitude for the good health of her own offspring. It is something she can never take for granted, and this may well account for her continual insistence that work takes priority over private affairs. In 1981 when she could have been celebrating her eighth wedding anniversary and her son's fourth birthday, she was visiting a medical team in the Himalayas. Typically, she slipped away to buy some local handcrafted toys for Peter and Zara as a consolation. When the Princess later arrived in Katmandu she was greeted by a notice which said, 'Welcome Zara's Mother'.

At the wedding of the Duke and Duchess of York, Zara and Peter

Phillips were bridesmaid and pageboy. Whilst the other six children fidgeted throughout the service, and the Princess of Wales kept a nervous eye constantly on four-year-old Prince William, Princess Anne scarcely glanced at her children and they behaved impeccably throughout. Was this because of their training and upbringing or, as the *Daily Mail* put it the next day, because Princess Anne had 'put the fear of God into them first'? Either way, her disciplinarian approach to motherhood appears to have had first rate results.

Princess Anne's own childhood and upbringing provide an insight into her character. She has the reserved and cool exterior that is instilled into children of royal birth almost as if it were mother's milk. Throughout their lives royalty can offer friendliness but rarely find true friendship. They always have to hold back, can never reveal their inner self, will only ever have a few close friends in fear that trust will be betrayed and confidences abused. It is impossible to appreciate that the freedom most children experience is denied the daughter of a monarch. Whenever contemporaries chatted about their home life in the classroom, Princess Anne could only smile and listen. No anecdotes about the Queen could ever be bandied around the dormitory at night, no gossip from behind the scenes at Buckingham Palace could ever pervade the playground. Such pressures on one so young inevitably leave their mark, and the caring and sympathetic side of Princess Anne was lost to sight behind her austere exterior. Her greatest quality is undeniably compassion. Unable to relax totally in public and express her true sentiments, Princess Anne can compensate by pouring love into her work. In contrast to the reserve she must show emotionally, she can give to the limits of her stamina in public duties. Ask personal questions and you are greeted with a frosty reply.

'How does it feel to be an aunt?' shouted a journalist when Prince William was born. 'That's my business, thank you,' retorted the Princess. This was dangerous ground. Ask about work, the latest projects in Bangladesh, the achievements of the Save the Children Fund or the Missions to Seamen, and you will have her undivided attention. Talk about her pet subject, horses, and she will give you her time, but encroach once on personal territory and you will lose her trust for ever.

Behind the royal princess façade is a wife and mother that only the closest friends and family appreciate. Rumours have frequently dominated foreign publications of the imminent collapse of her marriage, yet the partnership is extremely successful. Despite Princess Anne's apparent toughness she draws very much on the strength and support of her husband. Mark Phillips' role as 'consort' is not an easy one and he is the one that has suffered through marrying a public figure. Anyone who marries an outwardly dominant woman risks being branded a 'wimp', but their marriage thrives on hard work.

Unfortunately work keeps them apart, adding fuel to the fire that their marriage is crumbling. In fact it is work that binds them together. Princess Anne undertakes a punishing schedule to justify her annual Civil List income. Mark Phillips has his own career to pay off a very hefty mortgage. Gatcombe Park was originally purchased for £300,000 with money loaned by the Queen. A sound investment as it is now estimated to be worth in the region of 3½ million pounds. Mark Phillips had little money of his own at the time of his marriage and now boosts his income as a farmer by lecturing at equestrian weekends around the world. For around £300 for three days you can spend the weekend in the luxury of a hotel, like Gleneagles in Scotland, and lectured by Captain Phillips on the techniques of equestrian events, advanced dressage and show-jumping. 'Anyone who knows Princess Anne must also know that she would never have married a doormat. The fact is she turns to him for everything,' says father-in-law Major Peter Phillips. This may be an overstatement, but the couple certainly work as a team.

Princess Anne was not impressed by Mark's plan to open Gatcombe Park for one day annually for a horse trial. It is, after all, her home, a haven of privacy, and the Royal Family are not generally disposed to allowing members of the public on to their private property when in residence. Nevertheless, the scheme went ahead, first in September 1983 and each year since, charging £7 a car and £50 a coach. Despite any misgivings, the Princess was up at dawn hammering posts into the ground and attaching ribbons to control the crowd. Late that evening after the crowds had left, she was to be seen again pulling up the posts and winding up the tape for another year. 'She does it for him,' says a close friend. 'She may seem sharper and tougher than he does in public, but privately she leans on him. It's a bit like Margaret Thatcher and Denis.' This year Princess Anne's wicked sense of humour was apparent at the now firmly established sporting event, when she dressed her daughter in a bright red T-shirt bearing the logo: 'Gatcombe Park Horse Trials – Menial Tasks Division.'

Knowing that one day the fact that Peter and Zara are the Queen's grandchildren will catch up with them and intrude into their privacy makes Princess Anne possibly a little over-protective towards her children. Time and again she has been drawn into the question of titles for these heirs to the throne, still branded 'commoners' when her brother's children have royal prefixes. Deep down Princess Anne yearns for her children to have opportunities that she never had. As seventh and eighth in line to the throne, and soon to be pushed even further down the line of succession by the children of Charles, Andrew and Edward, it would take a catastrophe of cataclysmic proportions wiping out a large proportion of the Royal Family before Peter Phillips could inherit the throne. Neither Peter nor Zara will receive an income from the Civil List and it is unlikely that they will undertake royal duties, certainly not in this century, so royal titles seem superfluous. Princess Anne would like both her children to have careers of their own choosing, an option she was herself denied, where the title Mr. and Miss will have a distinct advantage. Mark Phillips, for this reason, declined any offer of a title from the Queen at the time of his marriage. Princess Margaret's former husband accepted an earldom in 1961 resulting in titles for their children, Lady Sarah Armstrong-Jones and Viscount Linley. It has taken David Linley a long time to establish his own furniture-making business in the King's Road, hampered by the media interest in the woodworking lord. Given the anonymity of Master and Miss Phillips pressures would have been less. 'They have to know that the limelight is there,' says Princess Anne, 'otherwise the shock when it arrives is going to be awful,' but at present she will shield them from the glare until she feels the time is right. She herself was less fortunate: from the moment of her birth it was Hobson's choice.

Chapter 2

Childhood and early learning

Even before Princess Anne was born interest in the forthcoming royal baby was intense. At 24 Princess Elizabeth was first in line to the throne, though none could foresee how soon the burden of sovereignty was to weigh down upon her, and public attention bordered on adulation. The memories of the dark oppressive days of war had only recently begun to diminish and the wedding of Princess Elizabeth of York to the dashing young naval lieutenant, Philip Mountbatten, had done much to bury the haunting spectre of battle. The first major royal event since the War was symbolic of hope for the future.

The wedding took place at Westminster Abbey on 20 November 1947. On the previous day Philip had been granted royal status and on the wedding day itself the King made him Baron Greenwich, Earl of Merioneth, Duke of Edinburgh and Knight of the Garter. Princess Elizabeth became known as the Duchess of Edinburgh. With clothes rationing still in force the Duchess was subject to a clothing allowance like everyone else, but the ever resourceful Queen Mary had some material locked away in readiness, and endless parcels of silk and lace arrived from around the world, but not from enemy countries, the public were informed. Silk bought in by Norman Hartnell came from Nationalist China.

By the time Princess Anne was born to the couple three years later it was the dawning of a new decade. The Duchess of Edinburgh had been delivered of a baby prince and heir two years earlier, and now the public waited in eager anticipation that the second child would be a girl. It was an age of hope. Clement Attlee headed a Labour government, having won the February General Election with a narrow majority. Food rationing ended in Britain after eight years, and petrol rationing was abolished two weeks later. Donald Peers became the first pop singer to be screamed at by adoring female fans and was mobbed at stagedoors by 'Bobby-soxers'. The Duke and Duchess of Edinburgh had only recently moved into the newly renovated Clarence House and in May the expectant mother withdrew from all public engagements.

Royal confinements have considerably changed in the past 60 years, for when the Queen Mother, as Duchess of York, was expecting her first child few people other than close family or friends were even aware that she was pregnant. Throughout the entire pregnancy her public appearances were curtailed. The Queen withdrew almost completely from official life during the later months, but today's royal mothers by contrast continue with engagements up until a few weeks before the birth and speculation as to possible pregnancy begins within months of the wedding. So fanatical is the interest in royal mothers-to-be that the tabloid newspapers even sank to the depths of photographing the Princess of Wales on a beach wearing a bikini whilst expecting Prince William.

Princess Anne's birth had been treated with greater dignity. The only one of the Queen's children to be born at Clarence House, Anne arrived just before Big Ben struck twelve noon on Tuesday 15 August 1950. Crowds had gathered daily in The Mall in anticipation, and this day they were rewarded for their efforts. It had been a long hot summer, but on this morning it rained, leaving the ardent royalists in the right place at the right time, albeit wearing raincoats. King George VI was holidaying at Balmoral, recovering from his first serious illness, but Queen Elizabeth had remained in London for the birth of her second grandchild and, although always notoriously late, she left Buckingham Palace with impeccable timing at 11.45 am, just before the baby was born.

With equally auspicious timing, the skies cleared and a 41-gun salute by the King's Troop, Royal Horse Artillery, rang out across Hyde Park. Simultaneously guns fired at the Tower of London, church bells pealed and flags fluttered in the breeze. Returning to Buckingham Palace, Queen Elizabeth (the Queen Mother) had mouthed to the waiting crowds 'It's a girl', uncharacteristically releasing news before an official announcement. Shortly afterwards the official announcement was posted on the gates of Clarence

House in the handwriting of Martin Charteris. The baby had been born at 11.50 am and weighed six pounds. Prince Philip telephoned the King at Balmoral and his own mother at Kensington Palace with the news.

Although the still unnamed baby was blissfully unaware of the situation, there had been fewer pressures surrounding this royal birth. The birth of Prince Charles had been of greater significance for, as the first child of the heir, it seemed essential that he was male. Had Princess Anne been the first born she would automatically have lost her rights to succession in favour of any subsequent males. Possibly there would have been an outcry if this had happened, and the laws of succession might have been changed, but Princess Elizabeth produced her heirs in a comfortable order. Newspaper editors had time to fill the following days' pages with extraordinary details of the new Princess's expected lifestyle and ancestry. Had she been born at midnight rather than midday the press would not have had such a field day. Amid the obvious joy the inevitable sour note crept in, Princess Anne's first bad press. Columnists speculated and commented on this very privileged baby, who would never experience hardship, who was already third in line to the throne, and whose parents had an income of £50,000. It was noted that 'as this is their second child the couple will now be entitled to the five-shilling family allowance'.

It was an auspicious day for the Duke of Edinburgh, for he not only gained a daughter but also naval promotion, becoming Lieutenant-Commander of HMS *Magpie*, a frigate in the Mediterranean Fleet. Two weeks later, on 29 August, Prince Philip officially registered the birth before Mr. Boreham, the Westminster Registrar and the world learnt that she was to be given the names ANNE ELIZABETH ALICE LOUISE. The name Anne naturally has many royal connections, but although it was suggested that there was a Stuart revival using the names 'Charles' and 'Anne', the baby was named after one of Princess Elizabeth's closest friends, Lady Anne Nevill. Elizabeth is the name of her mother and grandmother, and Alice that of her paternal grandmother. Louise was given to Princess Anne in honour of her 'Uncle Dickie', Lord Louis Mountbatten, Louise being the feminine form. She was to be known as Her Royal Highness Princess Anne of Edinburgh. The prefix used today which now makes her *The* Princess Anne was not used until 1952 when her mother became Queen. As daughters of monarchs only Princess Anne and Princess Margaret are entitled to use this distinction today. The sons of the Prince and Princess of Wales, for example, should not be called The Prince William as occasionally appears on even the most official of documents. This subtle change will occur when King Charles III inherits the throne. The practice stems back to the age of large royal families, when intermarriage between royals resulted in scores of princes and princesses and it was quite possible to have a number of Prince Alberts or Princess Charlottes in the family. To distinguish the sons and daughters of the monarch, and give them marginally higher rank, they became 'The' princes.

On signing the National Registration Form 33/31, Prince Philip made an interesting omission. The entry required the name and maiden surname of the mother, which was completed as 'Her Royal Highness The Princess Elizabeth Alexandra Mary, Duchess of Edinburgh', therefore omitting the surname 'Windsor'. Titles of the Royal Family invariably cause confusion, unexpected when one considers the accuracy with which protocol insists on correct forms of address. For a number of years there was confusion as to whether or not the Queen and her family were Mountbattens or Windsors. Her Majesty is undoubtedly from the House of Windsor, yet through her legal marriage contract she is a Mountbatten. To clear up any misunderstanding, ten days before the birth of Prince Andrew in 1960 the Queen announced that the Royal Family would henceforth be called in future generations Mountbatten-Windsor, and it was this surname that was entered on Princess Anne's marriage certificate.

Royalty always sign with their first Christian name only, thus when Princess Anne signs a visitors' book today she is given a completely new page and will put simply 'Anne'. In Newhaven, Edinburgh, the Church of Scotland Children's Home has a unique signature in its carefully preserved book. Signing the book in her customary fashion was insufficient for the children she had visited. They eyed her up and down suspiciously as if she were an imposter. 'You haven't signed your *other* name,' they complained indignantly. 'You haven't put Princess!' Amused by this protest she added 'Princess' in brackets to appease them.

When Donald Boreham had signed Princess Anne's birth certificate, he presented the Duke of Edinburgh with a green ration book and yellow identity card, a grim reminder that the War had ended just a few years earlier and austerity prevailed. The identity card, number MAPM/396, is preserved in the Royal Archives at

Windsor Castle; the ration book was used to obtain cod liver oil and orange juice for the baby.

As with all royal infants the Princess was kept well out of the public eye and under the protective care of a strict Scottish nanny, whose early influence was to have a lasting effect on the Princess's discipline and perhaps planted the seeds of a rebellious nature. More used to dealing with boys, Nurse Helen Lightbody stood no nonsense from her young charge. She had worked for the Duke and Duchess of Gloucester, so was no stranger to the task and certainly not in awe of royalty. It was at the age of four weeks that Princess Anne made her public debut when Princess Elizabeth took her new daughter to Balmoral for the usual family holiday. Hundreds lined the route to King's Cross Station to see the baby for the first time, along with her two-year-old brother. It was Princess Anne's first confrontation with press photographers and the following day photographs of the tiny white bundle in her mother's arms were syndicated around the world.

On 21 October 1950, having returned to London, the royal baby was christened in the Music Room at Buckingham Palace (the Chapel having been bombed during the War and never rebuilt) wearing the now familiar Honiton Lace christening gown that had originally been made for Queen Victoria's eldest daughter in 1840. The same silk and lace gown was to be worn by Princess Anne's own children, Peter and Zara, nearly 30 years later and is still being used for royal christenings today. At almost 150 years old the christening robe is kept in a special room at Windsor Castle. The ceremony was performed by the then Archbishop of York, Dr. Garbett, using Holy Jordan water from the silver gilt font, another heirloom from Queen Victoria. The five sponsors were Queen Elizabeth and Princess Alice, the baby's two grandmothers, Princess Margarita of Hohenlohe-Langenburg (Prince Philip's sister), Earl Mountbatten of Burma (Uncle 'Dickie'), and Andrew Elphinstone (Princess Elizabeth's cousin). By tradition the ceremony was private, with members of the Royal Family, close friends and some of the Household present, but we are told that the baby behaved 'impeccably'. The same cannot be said for Prince Charles, who at two years old became easily restless. With the baby as the centre of attention, the young Prince danced around the gentle Cecil Beaton as he attempted to take the photographs, in much the same way as Prince William of Wales did at Prince Harry's christening in December 1984. Just as at Prince Harry's baptism there were four generations of the Royal Family present, so Princess Anne was photographed with her mother, grandmother and great-grandmother, Queen Mary, then 83 years old.

The Princess of Wales has today set a precedent of taking her children abroad on state visits, but this was unthinkable in the 1950s, and when Princess Elizabeth set off for Malta to join her husband for Christmas shortly after the baptism she was forced to leave Prince Charles and Princess Anne behind. The delight at being with her husband can have compensated only in part for the disappointment of missing her daughter's first Christmas. This was only the first of many separations. The following year, 1951, Princess Elizabeth began to undertake even more duties as heir presumptive owing to her father's increasingly poor health, and in the summer she set out with the Duke of Edinburgh on a lengthy tour of America and Canada; Princess Elizabeth was visibly fighting back the tears as she waved goodbye to her two children once again. It is a hard fact of royal life that duty must come before emotion.

Much is spoken today of the bond that exists between mother and baby during the early months. Physical contact and inter-action play an important role in the child's development. Arguably one could say that Princess Anne was too young to miss her mother, she had the comfort of Palace life, the constant attention of Nurse Lightbody, and the love of her grandparents, we can only speculate as to the lasting effect that separation from her mother can have left. Talking recently about her Commonwealth tour after the Coronation, which lasted for six months, the Queen has said that on being reunited with her children she is sure that they had no idea who she was. 'They were very polite,' she joked, but thereafter she spent every possible spare moment with her son and daughter in an attempt to make up for the loss.

On 31 January 1952, King George VI stood in the bitter cold of London Airport and waved farewell to his daughter and son-in-law as the Duke and Duchess of Edinburgh embarked on a lengthy tour of East Africa, Australia, New Zealand, Kenya and Ceylon. It was to be a final farewell. Less than a week later, in the early hours of Wednesday morning, 6 February 1952, King George VI passed away and the mother of 18-month-old Princess Anne became Queen, the forty-second Sovereign of England since William the Conqueror. Princess Anne automatically became second in line to the throne, blissfully unaware of the dramatic changes that were happening within her family. Possibly she realised that her surroundings altered when the family moved further down The Mall to Buckingham Palace. After barely three years in the chintzy comfort of Clarence House, the Queen was reluctant to move to the gloomy Palace that felt like 'a museum'. It had been her home from the time of her father's accession until 1949 when she moved away with her young husband. The first 15 months of marriage had been spent in the austere Belgian Suite at the rear of the Palace whilst Clarence House was made habitable and the bomb damage repaired, and it had been with relief that they had been able to leave this formidable building behind.

Initially it was suggested that the new Queen might retain Clarence House as her home and let Buckingham Palace serve a formal function as a government department and a venue for constitutional duties and affairs of state, but the Prime Minister, Winston Churchill, was fiercely opposed to this proposal. For 115 years Buckingham Palace had been the home of the monarch; four kings had followed Queen Victoria into this gloomy mansion and for Queen Elizabeth II there was to be no escape. In a life dictated by tradition she had to retrace the footsteps of her predecessors. As Queen she should be seen to live in a palace; to relegate the building to a mere office would demean the Crown. It was one battle that the Queen could never win and, forced to concede, she left the only real home she had ever known and returned to Buckingham Palace.

To ensure that her children would settle, Queen Elizabeth II had the nursery of Clarence House expertly copied, down to the last detail, so that only the most discerning eye would appreciate the change of location. Naturally, where the Princess went, Nanny Lightbody went too, and life carried on as normal.

As she grew older it was apparent that Princess Anne was very much a tomboy. Her doll's pram remained in pristine condition while she played with her brother's toys. Once when she was asked the name of one of her dolls she said, quite matter-of-factly, 'No name.' Yet these were the days when she did appear outwardly to fit the fairytale image. She grew thick golden curls and inevitably she was photographed dressed in frilly feminine clothes, with bows and lace. It is said that while many girls dream of becoming a princess, Anne wanted to be a boy. She preferred playing with jigsaw puzzles (something she still enjoys today) and any game where she had to use her brain. Her favourite toy was a rocking horse, which had once belonged to the Queen.

Princess Anne's earliest recollections are of her mother's Coronation in June 1953. At less than three years old she was considered too young to attend the long ceremony in the Abbey; even Prince Charles at five found the strain of sitting just too great and had to be led out before the end. Although she remembers little about the day and obviously understood even less about the importance of the celebrations, Princess Anne vividly recalls the 'sense of being left out of something' and 'the normal sisterly fury at being left behind'. Left alone with Nanny Lightbody, she jokes, 'I was probably tied to the rocking horse.' Even a Coronation party later with young friends could not appease her, playing with cousins 'for whom I couldn't have cared less.' Eventually she was allowed to join her brother and the rest of the family to give her first royal wave from the balcony of Buckingham Palace to the jubilant cheering crowds below.

Although it was obviously impractical to include Princess Anne in the Coronation proceedings, for a child of an impressionable age her exclusion from this event was the dawn of a gradual realisation that she was not quite as important as her brother, that he gathered greater attention and she seemed always to be cast in his shadow. If at times she appeared pushy or rebellious, it was a perfectly natural reaction, nothing more than a young child's craving for attention. A three-year-old could have no real understanding that her brother would one day be King, and would be aware only that she was forced to take second place. When great-grandmother Queen Mary insisted that Anne should curtsey out of respect for her position, Princess Anne refused to oblige. It did not matter that 'Gan-gan' was annoyed for it made sure Princess Anne's presence was felt. Queen Mary scoffed that she was 'as stubborn as a mule', unaware of the childish plea to be recognised. If out in public, Princess Anne would thrust herself in front of her brother in order to be noticed. When the children's heads appeared on stamps the Princess would no doubt have been annoyed had she realised that her picture appeared on a lower denomination.

It was at this time that Princess Anne's lifelong love of horses was encouraged. One morning she was taken to the Royal Mews to meet her first pony, William. Part of the joy of horseriding, the Princess was later to explain, is that a horse has no respect for royalty and treats everyone alike – an ideal companion for someone battling against protocol throughout their life. William was meant to be a pony for Charles and Anne to share, but the more timid

Prince hardly stood a chance when his younger sister took control of the creature. Barely three years old she proved a natural in the saddle, and when most people are quite happy to canter slowly the first time they sit on a horse Princess Anne wanted speed, she wanted to gallop, holding on to the reins with the expertise of an experienced horsewoman. Nobody present could fail to see the potential in the young Princess.

Although a marvellous introduction to the world of equestrian sports, William was also partly a bribe, for he occupied Anne's time when her parents were abroad or committed to formal functions. A lot of time was spent with the Queen Mother, for whom playing with her grandchildren was undoubtedly therapeutic in overcoming the grief of widowhood. With the constant attention of Helen Lightbody and her assistant, Mabel Anderson, Princess Anne hardly had time to miss her parents. She knew of no other life and accepted the situation without question. At five years old Prince Charles had begun lessons with a private tutor at Buckingham Palace, a strict Scottish governess called Miss Catherine Peebles, and Princess Anne tagged along too. The children were never spoilt or mollycoddled simply because they were royal; if Charles or Anne misbehaved they were smacked.

The Queen and the Duke spent as much time with their children as possible, and when they were at the Palace, Nanny Lightbody would bring the children down at around 9.30 every morning so that Prince Philip could play with them in the Grand Corridor. The Duke's love of gadgetry is well known and he would frequently amuse Princess Anne with ingenious toys that he had collected on foreign tours, a favourite being a mechanical grasshopper. Each evening the Queen would spend an hour with her children before their nightly bath, often dismissing the maid and bathing them herself. If a state banquet or formal function prevented this nightly ritual, the Queen would visit the nursery in full evening dress,, much to the children's delight. Originally the Queen's weekly audience with the Prime Minister took place at 5.30 every Tuesday evening, but because it interfered with 'play hour' the then head of the government, Winston Churchill, agreed to delay the audience until 6.30. There can be few children who can boast that they have kept a prime minister waiting an hour, but if your mother happens to be the Queen of England you can get away with almost anything.

When Princess Anne reached the age of five it was felt that she should begin her education. Early observation of the Princess when she sat in on her brother's lessons proved that she was of above average intelligence and frequently had to be admonished for not giving Prince Charles a chance to answer. As Charles was going away to boarding school at Cheam, an austere Victorian institution, it was decided that other children should join Princess Anne in the Palace schoolroom as added stimulation and to fill the gap left by the absent Prince. So the Princess was joined by two girls of her own age Caroline Hamilton and Susan Babington-Smith, her first real companions from outside the Royal Family. It was to be a relationship that was to last for seven years until the three girls were 12 years old, then, just as suddenly as they had come into Princess Anne's life, they departed. The Royal 'system' decreed that the two girls had served their purpose, and they had no contact with the Princess again.

This was a time of study for Princess Anne. She was seldom included in any official functions and was rarely seen by the public. She did attend the Royal Maundy service with her mother, and gained experience in being a bridesmaid at the weddings of her cousin Lady Pamela Mountbatten to David Hicks, her aunt Princess Margaret to Anthony Armstrong-Jones, and again when the Duke of Kent married Miss Katherine Worsley in York Minster. But life at the Palace followed a very strict educational routine of three terms a year, with the autumn term beginning during the family's annual holiday at Balmoral, which necessitated the transportation of Miss Peebles and the two girls, Susan and Caroline, to Scotland for four weeks. Every morning the girls would study general education, mathematics, geography, history, and English with Miss Peebles and in the afternoons there would be more specialised subjects with private tutors – French, music or gymnastics. Time would also be set aside for educational visits to museums, galleries, churches, exhibitions, and tourist attractions. The fact that she was with the other two girls allowed Princess Anne to mingle with the public unnoticed. They could visit the ice rink at Richmond or go to the cinema without attracting any attention. Very occasionally the Queen would visit a cinema or theatre with her daughter, and they would slip unobtrusively into their seats just as the lights dimmed.

With Princess Margaret's encouragement Anne's social circle was extended with the formation of the 'B'hams' (the Buckingham Palace Brownie Pack) made up of girls from Holy Trinity in Knightsbridge and the young daughters of the senior Household staff. With no daughter of her own at this time Princess Margaret had a very soft spot for Princess Anne, perhaps able to identify more than anyone with the young Princess's position. She knew what it was like to take second place always, to be the sister of the heir to the throne, and she had suffered the kind of bad press that Princess Anne was later to receive.

Fully appreciating Princess Anne's position, Princess Margaret knew that the discipline of the Brownies was character building and an ideal organisation for an intelligent and energetic girl. From the comfort of Palace splendour Princess Anne also learnt what it was like to rough it under canvas, was able to take part in team games and experience new outdoor pursuits such as sailing and fishing. She amazed the 17-year-old Prince Michael of Kent when at nine she took control of his yacht! The Queen was horrified when she discovered that her only daughter, always keen on new and exhilarating experiences, had been mountain climbing and she quickly put a stop to any further death-defying plans.

At the age of nine Princess Anne first took control of a car. Prince Philip gave his speed-loving daughter early driving lessons on the private roads on the Windsor estate where she could come to no harm. This early encouragement meant that she was a proficient driver by the time she was seventeen and passed her driving test at the first attempt. Going on to obtain her Heavy Goods Vehicle licence, she quickly progressed to driving large horseboxes and once, when visiting a road transport training centre, she needed little encouragement to get behind the wheel of a double-decker bus.

As the Princess grew older horses began to play a more important role in her life. After the first pony, William, came Greensleeves and Mayflower now that Anne began taking her first riding lessons from a professional. In 1958 she presented her first trophy at the Royal Windsor Horse Show and was due to visit the Badminton Horse Trials but contracted chicken-pox from Prince Charles who had returned from Cheam for Easter. It would have been her first association with the three-day event that was to play such a major part in her life in the years ahead.

On the morning of 19 February 1960, Princess Anne was restless. A frustrated Miss Peebles attempted to interest her in the geography lesson, but found it impossible to hold the Princess's attention. Eventually Miss Peebles gave up and cancelled the rest of the day's work. Later that afternoon the Queen gave birth to Prince Andrew.

Princess Anne's excitement was intense. She had spent a great deal of time on her own since Prince Charles' departure to Cheam, and now she had a replacement brother. Subconsciously too Princess Anne may have realised that she had an ally. She was no longer 'second' to Prince Charles. Prince Philip took her to see the new-born baby less than an hour after he was born, and within weeks she was helping Prince Andrew's nanny to bath him, feed him, change him, and at the earliest opportunity began pushing her new brother around the gardens of Buckingham Palace.

Inevitably it was not many months before duty called and the Queen found a state visit to India and Pakistan beckoning, but in her ten-year-old daughter she had a surrogate mother to Prince Andrew to keep her informed of his progress. Princess Margaret had recently married photographer Anthony Armstrong-Jones, who had introduced Princess Anne to photography, and Prince Andrew became the subject of her first pictures. Through these black and white photographs the Queen was able to follow her son's progress.

As the Princess grew into her teens, lessons with Miss Peebles were considered insufficient and it was time for Princess Anne's education to develop further. Having closely followed Prince Charles' exploits at boarding school she was eager to enter the 'real' world herself, to venture amongst ordinary girls of her own age and escape from the closeted security of the Palace walls. The prospect of escaping from a private tutor, with whom she had never quite seen eye to eye, into a class with 30 other girls seemed an exciting prospect. It was to mark a new chapter in Princess Anne's life and introduced major changes that she had not expected. Soon she said goodbye to Susan and Caroline for the last time; the Buckingham Palace Brownie Pack disbanded and has never been re-formed. Dressed in a regulation blue uniform, Princess Anne left the cosy surroundings of Buckingham Palace and set out for a new life at Benenden. Only years later after Miss Peebles had died in her Palace room did Princess Anne feel any slight nostalgia for the passing of those early years.

Chapter 3

*B*enenden and early
working life

The decision to send Princess Anne to Benenden was a momentous one for the Queen. It meant that Princess Anne, third in line to the throne, would be educated with the discipline necessary for any schoolgirl, and would have to cope with the inevitable questions that would be asked by classmates. Survival would depend ultimately upon her ability to ignore her royal status for five years and fall in line with any other upper-middle-class student.

It was a prospect that Princess Anne looked forward to. When interviewed in 1985 on television by Terry Wogan, Princess Anne quickly quashed any suggestion that she had been dragged off to Benenden against her will. It was, she insisted, through choice. She wanted to go. Private education 'requires an awful lot of concentration' and she relished the thought of having 30 other pupils to ease the pressure and enable her to blend into the background.

Benenden School for Girls is set in the heart of the Kent countryside. The large Victorian mansion surrounded by some 200 acres of secluded parkland was chosen by the Queen for the privacy that it offered as much as its high academic standards. By coincidence, it was a school that Queen Elizabeth, the Queen Mother, had visited on 15 July 1950, exactly one month to the day before Princess Anne was born, and had reported on favourably. It was geographically close to family friends, the Nevills at Uckfield and the Brabournes near Ashford, to give the Princess a means of escape at weekends.

The headmistress, Miss Elizabeth Clarke, studied the Princess's work and abilities very closely before agreeing to accept her. Having the Queen's only daughter as a pupil was one thing, but it would have been acutely embarrassing for all concerned if Princess Anne had failed to keep up with the rest of the girls. Fortunately the intelligent 13-year-old presented no problems. No problems academically, that is. For the Princess there were greater social adjustments to make, far greater than those encountered by the 300 other girls. From the regal serenity of Buckingham Palace with servants to cater for every need, suddenly she found herself having to share a dormitory with four other girls and pull her weight when it came to laying tables for meals. It was a life dominated by bells and rigid timetables, and the Queen's wishes that her daughter should have no special concessions and be treated as any other girl were strictly adhered to, even to the extent of Miss Clarke actually refusing the Queen permission to excuse her daughter for one day's lessons for a family occasion. It would have been all too easy to concede, but the Princess's credibility as a pupil, as 'one of the girls' would have been destroyed. Princess Anne put on a brave face, but it took time to settle into her new surroundings and come to terms with her situation.

On 20 September 1963, shortly after her thirteenth birthday, the Princess was driven with the Queen from Balmoral to Benenden, staying overnight at Buckingham Palace on route, for her first day at school. It was a daunting prospect, and the Princess's calm exterior when she arrived to be greeted by the entire school lining the drive belied the intense fear that she felt inside and the fact that the royal car had been forced to stop on the way so that she could be physically sick. After the initial introduction to quell the girls' curiosity, Princess Anne quickly became accepted as one of the girls and her royal status was soon ignored, although it could never quite be forgotten. Lurking unobtrusively in the background was Perkins, her personal detective, the inevitable cross that had to be borne throughout her stay at Benenden. Once when out horse riding she was asked who was the man watching her. Princess Anne felt obliged to explain why a detective was guarding her, only to find herself totally disbelieved.

The greatest problem was making friends. Friendships are never easy for any member of the Royal Family and even today Princess Anne has few really close friends. It is impossible to know who can be trusted, whose friendship is genuine and based on personal admiration rather than a boast of a royal connection, and throughout the Benenden years Princess Anne remained very discreet, never once letting slip the slightest detail or gossip about her

parents or brothers that could so easily fall into the wrong hands.
Friends that Princess Anne made at school have remained loyal
confidantes since, and one of the first friends she made at Benenden, Victoria Legge-Bourke, later went on to become the Princess's
lady-in-waiting.

Eager to be accepted by the other girls, Princess Anne quietly
fitted into the often difficult routine and traditions of Benenden,
which began with an early morning run, whatever the weather. For
those of us outside Palace life it is hard to realise exactly how
difficult this adjustment must have been for the Princess. Those
entering the Royal Family from the outside, like the Princess of
Wales, have had problems adjusting to the new status. Equally it is
difficult to enter the real world from royal life. At Benenden the
Princess had to help lay tables and 'muck in' with the others.
Perhaps today she is much better adjusted as a woman, having sat
on both sides of the fence.

The pattern of the working day at Benenden followed the timetable that she had been used to at Buckingham Palace with formal
lessons in the classroom every morning and recreational activities
in the afternoon. Here the options covered a much wider span than
Miss Peebles and colleagues could ever have offered and Princess
Anne quickly seized the opportunity to participate in as many
activities as possible. She soon proved that she was an expert
dancer, and outshone all the other girls with her Highland dancing
after a few tips from the Queen Mother and the Household at
Balmoral. The Princess is also a competent ballroom dancer. In
1985 the National Hunt jockey Steve Smith-Eccles found himself
partnering the Princess. Jokingly he complained that every woman
he danced with was always taller than him. Immediately Princess
Anne kicked off her high-heeled shoes, bringing her down to his
height, and danced barefoot.

Discovering that she possessed a rich contralto voice, Princess
Anne became a leading light in the Benenden choir. In an attempt
to further her artistic talents she took up pottery. Prince Charles's
early clay models are still on display in the Queen's study at
Buckingham Palace, including a fruit bowl. Princess Anne on the
other hand donated her works of art to the school fêtes and bazaars
to raise money for charity, and not surprisingly became known for
modelling clay horses. For identification in the kiln the girls used to
score their initials in the clay, which meant that any object bearing
the letter 'A' always sold first. This greatly amused the discreet

Princess, obviously not the only girl in the school with the initial 'A' or even the name Anne.

Socially Princess Anne fitted in quickly and began to use Benenden's own unique nicknames. 'Dead man's leg' (jam roll), 'Ganges mud' (chocolate pudding), 'Bones and barley' (Irish stew), 'the honk' (lavatory) which would never have been bandied around the Buckingham Palace schoolroom.

Princess Anne's accommodation throughout the Benenden years was as unlike a palace as any environment could be. Bare green and white walls surrounded her dormitory in Bachelor's Wing, no sumptuous paintings or wallcoverings, no historic carpets handed down through the generations, just polished floor boards, and her only furniture was a bed, dressing-table, a not-too-comfortable chair, and a wardrobe. The novelty of having the Queen's daughter as a pupil quickly wore off from the other girls and Princess Anne was able to blend in with them. The greatest adjustment she had to make, she admits, was to the noise. The corridors of Buckingham Palace have a certain tranquility found in large museums. Servants move silently, even members of the family outside their own apartments talk in hushed tones. Dignity, however, does not appear in the vocabulary of schoolgirls clamouring along Benenden corridors, and Princess Anne found the constant clanging of bells, clattering of footsteps and giggling girls, difficult to accept initially.

Loss of privacy was equally hard to come to terms with. At Buckingham Palace she had been able to put pop posters on the walls of her room and play records in her spare time, and frequently the room became 'out of bounds' even to her mother. 'There'll be a "Private" notice on it next,' confided the Queen to a close friend. At Benenden, if Princess Anne went to her room one of the other girls would be there; records could only be played at specific times, in the music room. To compensate, the Princess used to go for long walks in the countryside in her free time to be alone.

Other pupils had equal problems coming to terms with the discipline of boarding school, the long hours of waking at 7.00 am, breakfast at 7.40 am, lessons, sports, and homework, finishing at 7.20 pm, nearly always a 12-hour day filled with an enforced rota of activities, academic and social. This was one aspect of school that Princess Anne *could* accept. The key word in royal life is duty, and the Princess had learnt from an early age to be disciplined in every aspect of life, putting duty before emotion. At times she rebelled, as any normal, energetic girl would have done, but it was a lesson she had learnt.

The Benenden years probably made the Princess much tougher as a person. With an obvious indomitable spirit it would have been too easy for her, as the only girl in the family, to have been spoilt and received too much of her own way. Benenden thrust her in at the deep end. At first she was shy, nervous of the effect her presence would have on other people, afraid of pushing herself forward too far in case she appeared to be pulling rank on the others, frightened also of letting the Queen down or embarrassing the Royal Family. An enormous responsibility for a 13-year-old, constantly pursued by the media who attempted to catalogue every aspect of the Princess's life. When she considered taking up judo, journalists had a field day, and her greatest sense of achievement in any sport was not having won or obtained high scores, but having got through the game without being recognised.

The fees when Princess Anne first attended Benenden were £175 a term, and included many extra-curricular activities which she was keen to involve herself in. Given a choice, Princess Anne said, 'I'll try the lot!' This over-ambitious approach was quickly curbed, nevertheless she did try roller-skating, rock climbing, ballet, fencing, speech and drama (she appeared in a number of school plays, notably in male roles, playing Alfred in *The Boy With A Cart* and a drunken sailor in *Dido and Aeneas*), cookery, lacrosse, netball, and tennis, as well as more academic studies. With history, geography and English literature her favourite subjects, Princess Anne proved to be well above average also in mathematics and French, and undertook courses in physics, chemistry, art, needlework, German, Latin, Greek. All Benenden girls also have to attempt public speaking.

For someone on the verge of entering public life the breadth of subjects which the Princess studied were to stand her in good stead for her future working life. Whereas any other girl, choosing a career, would specialise in one particular field, Princess Anne has needed knowledge of every area of human life.

It was also a time of adventure. With above-average intelligence Princess Anne would be the first to admit that she did not work quite as hard as she might have done where exams were concerned. As a blossoming teenager she was discovering new and unexpected delights. She tasted fish and chips, something that had never appeared on a Palace menu, she travelled in buses and coaches,

A seventh birthday portrait of Princess Anne with her mother in the gardens of Buckingham Palace.

*On her way to school,
Princess Anne dressed
à la mode.*

*Below: bridesmaid again.
This time at the wedding of
Princess Alexandra to Angus
Ogilvy in 1963.*

At 19, indulging in her favourite sport, Princess Anne gallops through Windsor Great Park on High Jinks.

An early confrontation with the press: the Princess is obviously angry at being photographed with friends.

Fairy tale photography from Norman Parkinson prior to the wedding.

and saw for the first time the inside of an airport lounge, very ordinary activities that this extraordinary girl had never experienced.

Physical activities seemed to be her forte. A keen swimmer, she achieved a standard in life-saving high enough to qualify in the Duke of Edinburgh Award Scheme, but was too modest to accept a medal from her own father, no doubt realising that she would be ribbed mercilessly if she did. For A-level geography she studied agriculture and farming on a practical level, little realising the benefit that the knowledge would be in future years at Gatcombe Park and in contributing some ideas to the Save the Children Fund's land useage programmes. Of all activities, it was the sport most recently added to Benenden's curriculum that attracted her most – riding.

Princess Anne's early aptitude for riding was encouraged under the supervision of Cherry Kendall, herself a successful competitor in the Three-Day Event at the Badminton Horse Trials. She did much to stimulate the Princess's interest in competitive sports. For her twelfth birthday the Princess had been given a pony called High Jinks and was granted permission to keep him at the Moat House stables near Benenden where girls went every afternoon for a 75-minute lesson.

Having ridden from an early age, Princess Anne had already won first prize in a jumping event at an Ascot gymkhana, and she perhaps felt that she knew more about riding than the other girls. Here was something that she felt confident in. But at 13 she needed bringing down to earth, and this happened (often quite literally) under Cherry Kendall's guidance, although at times it was a battle of wits between the two of them. One teacher recalls that the Princess would deliberately pinch her horse if she was bored so that he bucked and disrupted the lesson. One of the Princess's weaknesses was, and still is to some extent, impatience. Like her father she does not suffer fools gladly. She is a quick learner, today on public engagements she will ask very direct questions, and cannot understand why others with apparently the same intelligence and initiative can be slower to comprehend. Whatever the lesson, speed was the essence. In essays her teachers noted that she would quickly grasp all the main and pertinent points of any argument, but in her haste to complete the work she would omit the small basic facts that would back up her point of view. Her style of writing was individual too: down to earth and colloquial. This is one of the main reasons why she composes all her own speeches today, so that they can be delivered in her own way. 'I would sound very pompous if I spoke someone else's words,' she says and feels that her sincerity and credibility would be lost if someone else did all the research and she produced a ready-prepared speech. Another skill that Benenden taught her that was to prove invaluable in later life. Twenty years on, the Princess does do her homework today and fully researches any project in which she is involved so that she can talk confidently. It is not an aspect of the work that she particularly enjoys, but she has come to realise the importance of careful planning.

In her final year Princess Anne was made Captain of her House and a Benenden 'House Mother'. Each new pupil at the school is allocated a guide to show them around and settle them in. Whether she would have attained these posts had she not been the most famous pupil has been debated. Many believe that the House Captaincy was inevitable and predictable. Headmistress Elizabeth Clarke insists that she was considered as a pupil and not a princess, that she had worked hard to achieve the distinction. Those close to Princess Anne agree that, as with her patronage today, she will only accept something in which she can be fully involved and offer a significant contribution to the task. Any suggestion that it was a concession would have resulted in her swift refusal. And this is confirmed by her subsequent refusal of the idea of going to university. She achieved low grades in Geography and History A levels, which would at that time have attained a University place, not Oxford or Cambridge, but Princess Anne was adamant that she did not want to go. Her education had lasted 15 years and she did not relish the thought of another three or four years' study to attain academic qualifications which she would never need in her working life.

'Many of my contemporaries were going to University simply because it was "university", not for any real reason,' she explains. She agreed to undertake an intensive six-week course in French language, involving up to ten hours a day of study. The Queen and Prince Philip both spoke fluent French and were insistent that it was an essential requirement for the future. After the course Princess Anne was determined to leave the closeted academic world behind and step forward into the adult world which beckoned.

So, in 1968, she left Benenden, after five of the most character building years of her life to date. Having arrived at the school as a plump 13-year-old she had blossomed into a tall, slim 18-year-old. Horse-riding and team games had removed the puppy fat and as a mature teenager on the brink of womanhood she was considered ready to undertake her first official duties as a member of the Royal Family. The Benenden years brought the Princess's compassion to the fore. The role of 'House Mother' taught understanding and sympathy with other girls, displaying a skill and inherent calmness during a crisis if one of her colleagues was ever injured during sport or taken ill, compassion that was to be seen publicly on her later Save the Children Fund tours. Having taken part in practical studies of environmental town planning, nursing, sociology, and occupational therapy, she had a greater insight into the charities and organisations that she would eventually work for. She became aware of financial reality for the first time in her life, having had an allowance of two-pounds a term like all the other girls. Unlike the others, due to what she calls a natural 'meanness', she always had some money left at the end of term.

Surprisingly, having been born into one of the world's richest families, Princess Anne is extremely thrifty with money and conscious always of keeping her expenses to a minimum. This quality may well also have been learnt from her mother. As a child when Prince Charles lost a dog lead the Queen made him go and look for it. 'Dog leads cost money,' she scolded. Today at Buckingham Palace the Royal Family always have cheaper cuts of meat whenever possible, the horses in the Royal Mews sleep on shredded newspaper rather than straw, and no unnecessary lights are ever allowed to blaze away. Princess Anne is equally mindful of waste at Gatcombe Park. While the Queen has many of her clothes redesigned, hats retrimmed, sequins used again and again, frequent changes of accessories to make an old outfit appear new, Princess Anne is content to be seen wearing exactly the same outfit time and time again. Initially this produced media criticism, but 'if you go on doing it long enough they have to give up in the end'. Once when someone commented that a dress she was wearing had been seen six months earlier, she laughed, 'Oh, it's a lot older than that!'

Other aspects of the Princess's character also became apparent at Benenden. On one notorious occasion she was taking part in an Elizabethan pageant at school and was required to play the part of a messenger. In full Elizabethan costume she was to gallop on her horse High Jinks and announce the arrival of Elizabeth I, and for the sake of her own safety the producer of the pageant requested that the Princess wear a modern hard hat underneath her Tudor bonnet. No other girl was wearing two hats and Princess Anne refused to look ridiculous. The producer begged, Cherry Kendall pleaded, even her house-mistress attempted to make her see reason. Princess Anne stamped her foot, pouted her lips, and insisted that she was not going to wear two hats. This was meant to be an Elizabethan pageant and she refused to wear a twentieth-century riding hat. For the first time in her years at boarding school she decided to use her royal status to overrule the authorities and announced that she was going to telephone the Queen. A daunting prospect for the producer and the headmistress. If the Queen sided with her daughter they would have no control, yet they could not prevent *any* daughter from telephoning her parents. After a short time Princess Anne returned looking distinctly dispirited. There were to be no special favours, the Queen had insisted, and so for her own protection the Princess reluctantly wore two hats.

When the time came for Princess Anne to leave Benenden, she left with a degree of sadness. At school she had discovered the pleasure of anonymity that is rare for someone of royal birth. Friends she made then have remained loyal, but reunions are difficult to arrange because of Princess Anne's working schedule.

The departure from Benenden was a progression back into the royal limelight. Yes, it meant a certain amount of independence, at last she was treated as an adult, and she no longer had to abide by strict dictatorial rules, but at the same time it created pressures. Gone was the leafy rural security of school, the careless world of giggling teenagers, now there was the glare of publicity, speculation about boyfriends and the inevitable question of a possible husband.

The first 12 months after leaving Benenden were exacting and exciting. The fashion-conscious took notice for the first time when she wore blue and white polka dots at a Buckingham Palace garden party, although the reports were far from favourable. 'Frumpy, dumpy and grumpy,' declared one leading fashion expert, but by the end of the year she was hailed as 'the wittiest, gayest, and most natural member of the Royal Family'. During this period of blossoming she could really do no wrong. When the initiation period had ended and Anne had bloomed, it was not to be long before the press began firing verbal pellets.

One great boon, however, was that the Princess could now

indulge herself unashamedly in the equestrian world, and at a quiet dinner party one evening she engaged herself in conversation with a pleasant young man who shared her love of horses. His name was Mark Phillips.

This was the year of the Mexico Olympics in which the British Equestrian Team won a gold medal for their country. Although not required to take part, Mark Phillips was a reserve rider for the team. Princess Anne followed the Olympic Games with interest, and delighted in meeting the British athletes at a reception given by the Queen later in the year. She particularly sought out the handsome reserve rider to chat to.

Having reached the age of maturity it was time for Princess Anne to undertake certain responsibilities within the Royal Family, and it was a prospect that she looked forward to. It would give her a function and purpose in life. No longer a mere privileged daughter, but someone who could be of benefit to the nation. In the sixties the popularity of the Royal Family had reached an all time low, and suffered bitter attacks as their relevance began to be questioned. Did the Queen really play a significant role or was she now merely an anachronism, MPs asked? Consciously, Princess Anne felt that she must prove that royalty can be worldly, she was determined never to be a mere figure-head. She was not just going to plant trees, lay foundation stones and engage in smalltalk on official functions. She intended to *work*.

Unobtrusively the Palace machinery was set in motion. First the Queen included the Princess on official banquets and state dinners. Later she was included in film premieres and informal luncheons at Buckingham Palace, giving her an opportunity to test the water and experiment with her 'image' – a word she detests. She sought professional advice about make-up and began to experiment with hairstyles. Since the advent of the Princess Diana mania in 1981 people have forgotten the influence that Princess Anne once had on fashion. In a recent interview she joked that it takes people time to find a style that suits them, 'it's just taken me longer than most', yet when she discovered a talented young designer called Mary Quant in the sixties, it wasn't long before everyone was wearing miniskirts. If Princess Anne could show off her legs then it seemed acceptable for every teenage girl to do likewise, although the Queen quickly rejected any suggestion from her daughter that she should adopt the fashion too. 'I am not a film star,' declared the Queen, but even our monarch's hemline rose discreetly to knee-level in the late sixties. When Princess Anne wore a cheeky cowboy hat there was a boom in the millinery trade; when she wore white boots a new footwear fashion began.

Tentatively she looked forward to her first solo engagement. She had presented prizes at the Windsor Horse Show when she was eight, had accompanied the Queen on a number of foreign visits, but she had never undertaken any official engagement entirely alone. The extrovert side of her nature responded with excitement, but fear caused mounting tension. 'I think that if you didn't feel nervous about anything you probably wouldn't do it very well,' she says philosophically. Her introduction to working life was 'gentler' than she had expected.

Knowing of Anne's love of the countryside and knowledge of agriculture, the Queen had chosen a small and simple task for her daughter's debut. It was to perform the opening ceremony of a Young Farmer's Club in the Midlands at the end of April. There was, however, a conspiracy at the Palace. Prince Philip was to present leeks to the Welsh Guards on St. David's Day, 1 March. As Colonel-in-Chief the Prince agreed to undertake the usual duty, until the opportunity to visit Ethiopia occurred. In Princess Anne he had the perfect understudy, and at the last minute it was decided that she should deputise for her father, so her first solo engagement came two months earlier than expected. With little time to worry, the Princess was driven to Pirbright in Surrey to present the Welsh leeks. She performed this strange duty with dignity and confidence and impressed the regiment with her ready wit and engaging sense of humour. We cannot know how she really felt, but outwardly she appeared confident and relaxed, enjoying the media attention that surrounded her, for once legitimately. Dressed in bright green, one of the Welsh colours, and a stylish almost Dickensian cap, her undoubted success boosted the Princess's spirit and made her feel 'a hundred times better!'

Soon, like a performer with good notices, Princess Anne was in demand by everybody. After that significant date of 1 March 1969, the engagement diary was quickly filled. On 25 April she undertook the opening of the Young Farmers' Club centre at Kenilworth, and a visit to the Equestrian Centre at Stoneleigh Abbey, Warwickshire. For good measure, and as a foretaste of the packed programme she was later to undertake, the Princess was shown around the Rover Car Works at Solihull on the same day. This was of particular interest as she had been given a blue Rover 2000 as an eighteenth birthday present the previous year, shortly after passing her driving test.

Thirty engagements were to follow. She launched a ship, paid a state visit to Vienna, attended the FA Cup Final at Wembley, presented a gold trophy for the Ladies' Singles Championship at Wimbledon, attended a mass meeting of the Scotland Women's Guild in Edinburgh, opened a new hospital at the Animal Health Trust's Centre in Suffolk, made a very witty speech at a luncheon for the opening of the Festival of London Stores ('Selfridges supplied me with what an outraged woman described as a "Zebra" coat. I've never seen a blue and white zebra – she must have confused me with a zebra crossing!'), launched a hovercraft named *The Princess Anne*, attended the Bath and West Agricultural Show, held a press cocktail party at Buckingham Palace (it was noted that she made one glass of Coca-Cola last all evening), and, strangely, inspected some land drains in Shepton Mallet!

What emerged was an active Princess. When she opened the Road Transport Industry Training Board's education and training centre at High Ercall in Shropshire on 10 September she drove a 9-ton, 79-seater double-decker bus. When she visited the Rover car factory she took control of the latest model; when taken to a Spanish riding school she appeared in full riding kit and displayed her unique skills as a horsewoman by riding a stallion, putting him expertly through his paces. In the same year she was appointed Colonel-in-Chief of the 14th/20th King's Hussars, who presented her with a personalised number plate for her car, 1420 H, which she still uses. Later she was amused to discover that it had originally adorned a United Dairies milk float in Ealing. Through her sheer professionalism the Princess quickly endeared herself to the regiment and on a visit to them in Germany proved that she was 'one of the boys' by donning army uniform and taking command of a 52-ton tank, and at a later regimental dinner complied with the tradition of drinking champagne out of a chamber pot that had belonged to Napoleon. The Queen would have refused, Prince Charles might have blushed, but Princess Anne did not bat an eyelid.

On 1 July 1969, one of the most spectacular royal ceremonies since the Coronation took place at Caernarvon Castle when Prince Charles was invested as the Prince of Wales. This had been planned since 1958, when at the British Empire and Commonwealth Games in Cardiff the Queen had made her wishes known via a tape recorded message because she was ill at the time. Princess Anne had listened to the recording privately just a few hours before, delighted as an eight year old to be let in on a secret, but it must have crossed her mind that yet another honour was being bestowed upon her elder brother, already Duke of Cornwall and heir apparent, pushing her even further into the background.

As plans were made for the impending ceremony the question was raised as to whether Princess Anne should also be honoured with a title – the Princess Royal. The title had, after all been vacant for over four years since the death of Princess Mary, Countess of Harewood. It had been the longest period this century without a Princess Royal, and it seemed an ideal opportunity. Yet it was felt that because it had been common knowledge for ten years that Prince Charles was to be created Prince of Wales it would appear very much an afterthought if such an announcement were to be made at the last minute. The ceremony was also seen as being particularly pertinent to Wales, whereas Princess Anne had no obvious connection with the region, having only briefly been to Milford Haven to board the Royal Yacht *Britannia*. Also, with only a few months experience of official engagements behind her it was eventually considered that she lacked the necessary standing. Princess Mary had given the title an unprecedented significance and Princess Anne, still six weeks short of her nineteenth birthday, appeared unready to step into those shoes. So the idea was shelved at least until she was 21, when once again the idea was dismissed. Every New Year since, when the Honours List is due for publication, speculation about the title is mooted. 'Anne Set To Become Princess Royal' blazed the headlines in January 1987. A year earlier she had informed a leading newspaper editor, 'I would be a very anonymous Princess Royal, it is as Princess Anne that I will be remembered . . .'

Although it was Prince Charles' day, the Princess certainly did not go unnoticed at the investiture ceremony. In an outfit of pale blue she was applauded warmly by the crowds. Princess Anne admits to having been deeply moved at the response from the people of Wales as the Queen presented her son to them, and years later expressed a sense of isolation. As the only girl in a family of four children it is understandable that there were occasions when she felt alone, perhaps in need of a girl of her own age and in the same position to unburden her heart to. Yet there was nobody to fill that void.

Princess Alexandra took Princess Anne under her wing, and Princess Margaret was always ready to lend a sympathetic ear, but Princess Anne found her main solace in horses. Her early enjoyment of riding had never faltered. Undaunted even when thrown off, breaking her little finger and nose on separate occasions, she saw the great challenge that lay ahead in the sport of three-day eventing. With the tough combination of dressage, cross-country riding and show jumping, if she could succeed it would be an achievement of her own. Not because she was royal but because of her merits as a rider.

This became Princess Anne's goal in all things, that achievements in all walks of life should be through her own endeavour and determination, not because of the privileges of birth. If she could have chosen any career in life it would have been something ambitious, and her commitment would have been total, her aim high. After launching the SS *Esso Northumbria* from the Swan Hunter yard on Tyneside, soon after her solo debut, she remarked 'I have had the honour of launching the largest ship ever built in this country, and, for a starter, that's not bad . . .'

The working princess had arrived.

Chapter 4

*H*orses and a special friend

Think of Princess Anne and horses immediately spring to mind. Had she not immersed herself totally in royal duties, she may well have taken up horses as a full-time career, as a rider and breeder. Horses have become synonymous with the Royal Family. In 1965 the Queen Mother had a 'blower' installed at Clarence House to receive the racing results; the Queen is an expert breeder, rider and racing devotee; Prince Charles plays polo; the Duke of Edinburgh enjoys the sport of carriage driving, and in every type of royal ceremony the family are surrounded by horses. It was natural that Princess Anne should be attracted to the animals, but, typically, her goals were higher than mere occasional riding for pleasure. It was a sport at which she could work, a hobby in which she could actually achieve results. Her sights were set on the three-day event European championships and the Olympic Games.

Eventing is said by many to be the most difficult of all equestrian sports because of the variety of skills necessary to compete. Princess Anne modestly disagrees, 'There are two different ways of looking at it: if you do it you regard it as an ultimate test of horsemanship because you have to do three rather separate disciplines, and if you're almost anybody else, you say you're not good enough to be a proper dressage rider, you're not good enough to be a proper race jockey, you're not good enough to be a proper showjumper, so you do them all within three days of each other and make the best of it. It is still just about amateur enough that I can keep up.'

The sport dates from 1902 when the French army devised the competition to test the speed and skills of their horsemen.   Called

58

the *Championnat du Cheval d'Armes* it was comprised of the three exercises that form eventing today. Up until the Second World War only military men could compete, and in England the Duke of Beaufort encouraged the sport by building a course at his Badminton home where horse trials have been held since 1949. In 1961 an international course was constructed at Burghley. It has been an Olympic sport since 1912. Many say that Princess Anne took up the sport because it is an individual sport, not a team effort, and that she could succeed in her own right as a horsewoman, not as a member of the Royal Family. 'When I'm approaching a water jump with dozens of photographers waiting for me to fall in, the horse is the only one who doesn't know I'm royal.'

Today millions of people take an interest in the Badminton or Burghley horse trials and go along as spectators or sit captive in their armchairs in front of the television, but in 1969, when Princess Anne began training, three-day eventing was very much a minority sport open only to the privileged classes bred on country estates, and today's enthusiasm for the sport is due almost entirely to Princess Anne's patronage. The first step for the Princess was to find a suitable trainer, which was no easy task. It was not merely a case of finding a competent trainer, but it was important to find someone who would accept her for her abilities as a rider and not because of who she was. She visited Alison Oliver, then one of the country's most celebrated riding instructors, who only agreed to take on Princess Anne after witnessing her skills on horseback, her ability to learn, and her potential as a three-day eventer. Only when the Princess had proved to Mrs. Oliver that she was up to it, did intensive training begin. Reaching the required standard is a full-time occupation, but there was no way the Princess could escape her ever-increasing list of royal duties, so she would get up at the crack of dawn to practise for three hours every morning, bath and change in preparation for a full day of functions, and then return to her horses in the early evening. Only through sheer dedication and love of horses could she adapt herself to the long and often arduous hours.

Princess Anne had three first class horses – Doublet, Purple Star and Royal Ocean – and more than enough determination to succeed. Three-day events are a test of both rider and horse, both need to be incredibly fit and have to work as a team if they are to be placed at all. Princess Anne and Doublet proved to be a magic combination that was to have the whole nation on the edge of their seats, but it was on Royal Ocean that Princess Anne successfully competed in the Windsor Horse Trials in April 1969 and found herself in the lead. Although this early triumph made the equestrian world sit up and take notice, non-sporting journalists dipped their pens in vitriol and hinted that Princess Anne had an unfair advantage because she was riding on home ground. It was over 12 months since the Princess had ridden the course and it was her first attempt at three-day eventing in competition with experienced riders. The snide remarks, aimed at her private life, were to sour her relationship with the press from then onwards. Yet the professionals took little notice of the media, and instead took note of the potential new champion.

After a gruelling 12 months of travelling the length and breadth of Britain, taking part in various competitions, Princess Anne and Doublet faced the most challenging event of their career – the Badminton Horse Trials. These brought together the best riders in the world, 47 top men and women, to compete over the country's most difficult course, including the famous lake which has been the downfall of even the most experienced riders. While the country and the entire Royal Family held their breath in support of her, Princess Anne rode as if for her life and after three exacting days managed to come fifth in her first major international event. It was nothing short of a triumph, the sporting world now began to take her seriously, and the press meekly congratulated her, whilst the harder journalists secretly wished she had fallen in the lake. Pictures like that sell more newspapers. They would have done better to have printed a photograph of the Princess congratulating the winner, one Mr. Mark Phillips . . .

Princess Anne set her sights firmly on the 1972 Olympic Games in Munich. It seemed too much of a dream for someone who had only been training for little more than a year, yet within a few weeks of Badminton Princess Anne was selected to ride at the European Championships in September at Burghley, although as an individual rider and not a member of the team.

After weeks of rigorous training Princess Anne collapsed with severe stomach pains and was rushed to hospital where she underwent an operation for the removal of an ovarian cyst. Although a minor operation in itself, any surgery requires a period of convalescence and the muscle control needed for riding is certainly not something doctors would recommend after an abdominal operation. When members of the Royal Family visited the hospital they went prepared to commiserate with the Princess, expecting to find her depressed at this setback in her career. They should have taken into account the indomitable spirit of Princess Mary inherited by Princess Anne, for they found the Princess walking around the ward, helping out wherever possible, and planning her fitness routine like a military manoeuvre, determined to be back on Doublet in time for the European Championship. She joined the Family at Balmoral, took lots of long walks through the Highlands, and before long was back with Alison Oliver training harder than ever.

On 5 September 1971, just weeks after leaving hospital, Princess Anne faced the final day of the European Championships, having found herself in the lead on the two previous days. It was a tense time. The Queen and the Duke of Edinburgh sat nervously in the stands, Alison Oliver stood anxiously on the sidelines, and Princess Anne and Doublet rode calmly on to the course to thunderous applause. If she could jump ten of the 12 fences on the show-jumping course she would be not only European Champion but at that time World Champion too. In silence the Princess set out on what must have been the most nerve-racking ride of her life. Excitement mounted as she approached the tenth fence, Doublet cleared the eleventh, and the crowds went mad as Princess Anne landed safely over the final fence, a clear round making her European Champion. She had achieved her goal of proving her skills as an individual, and received international acclaim through her own merit and determination, not because she was a princess. No mother could have been as proud as the Queen as she presented her daughter with the trophy and medal. Princess Anne went on to be voted Sports Personality of the Year by millions of viewers who had 'ridden' with her over every step of the triumphal way, she won the Sportswriters' Award, and was declared Sportswoman of 1971 by the National Press.

After an outstandingly successful career, Princess Anne could easily have retired while at the top, and contented herself with her royal duties but she still dreamt of winning a gold medal at the Olympic Games, and with her track record she had every chance of being picked for the Olympic team. But just before the Badminton Horse Trials the following April, Doublet sprained a tendon and the Princess was forced to withdraw. It was a bitter blow after the sweet taste of success. Sadly, Doublet's competitive career was at an end, and Princess Anne began working with one of the Queen's horses, Goodwill. There was no chance of taking part in the Olympic Games, but there were the usual three-day events and the following year's European Championships to aim for. In 1974 Princess Anne was riding Doublet through Windsor Great Park when suddenly she heard a cracking noise. Immediately she dismounted, realising to her horror that the horse had broken a leg. She watched, helpless and numb with shock, as a vet gave Doublet a painless injection that was to bring to an end a long, affectionate partnership. Calmly the Princess made her way back to Windsor Castle where she broke down with grief. Members of the Household admitted they had never seen her so dispirited, it was as if part of her had died with Doublet. He had been her escape from the confines that her birth had imposed upon her, he allowed her to forget who she was and what she was, and spurred her on to victory and glory in her own right. She described the day as the worst in her entire life. She had lost a friend.

Goodwill proved a good substitute but was never to bring her the memorable successes of Doublet. The European Championships in Kiev are today remembered not because of the Princess's outstanding achievements, but for the dramatic events of the second day. The cross-country course proved to be one of the toughest ever constructed, and on the most difficult jump riders began to fall like flies. Over 30 horses went down, including Goodwill. Princess Anne landed on her side chipping her shoulder blade, dislocated her collar bone and suffered severe bruising. Typically she went to the stables to check that Goodwill was unharmed before receiving treatment herself. The photographers had a field day snapping the sporting picture of the year. 'I hope you've got your money's worth now,' snarled the Princess, angry not so much with the press as with herself. 'At the start of the cross-country I'm usually a bit jazzed up; it's a mistake if you aren't. But on this occasion I didn't feel anything, which is a bad sign and usually means that something may go wrong.'

The jump that was to be her downfall, quite literally, had been of Russian construction, and the Princess had been advised how to tackle the very narrow approach. At the actual event she ignored the advice, attempted to tackle the jump her own way, and in her words, 'Quite simply, I got it wrong, putting in two and a half strides instead of three. Goodwill almost made it, nevertheless. I think he thought he had, but his back toes, which were tucked right under him, caught the pole and he pitched on to his nose.' Describing how she felt, Princess Anne says, 'It was like hitting tarmac as far as I was concerned. I had never hit the ground as hard or as fast. The main impact was on the side of my leg and, when I got up, it was numb from mid-thigh to mid-calf; I couldn't feel a thing. I wasn't, at that stage, aware that there was anything wrong with my shoulder – but I couldn't walk – I could stand on one leg, that was about all. I didn't think I'd broken anything, but Goodwill looked completely stunned and I couldn't walk, so I decided that there wasn't a great deal of point in going on. I was only riding as an individual, so there didn't seem to be a great deal of honour at stake.'

This was a character-forming lesson for the Princess whose early success had caused over-confidence in her own abilities, perhaps a certain unconscious feeling of superiority over her trainers. Although having the greatest respect for Alison Oliver, Princess Anne was still only 24, had been used to falling off and bouncing back on again. Of Doublet she says, 'He was undoubtedly the quickest stopper I'd ever come across. I'd disappear over his head so frequently that people used to say to Alison: "Why is she riding that dangerous horse when she keeps falling off it?" ' The incident at Kiev, which put her out of action in a public and undignified manner, gave the Princess time for reflection, and the pain, it seems, brought a closer understanding of what is one of her favourite charities – the Riding for the Disabled Association.

As much as she enjoys riding the Princess is only too aware of the privilege of being able-bodied, and the obvious joy that riding brings to the physically and mentally handicapped; the freedom that being on horseback can give to someone who is otherwise wheelchair bound, the comforting rocking sensation that even severely mentally handicapped children can appreciate. Much of the Princess's spare time, as well as part of her working life, is devoted to teaching disabled children to ride.

Throughout the late sixties and early seventies, much was made of the Princess's riding 'career' as if it were a full-time occupation. It was, and is, a very important hobby, but one which still comes second place to work. Princess Anne likes to ride every day, but it must be fitted in during her non-working hours. Mark Phillips confesses that this is one of the problems of being married to Princess Anne, the fact that she rises at six to fit in an hour's riding. 'She pulls all the bedclothes off me,' he says. 'She keeps getting up at some ungodly hour to go training, while I just want to go back to sleep. But she is off and out of the door before I have a chance.'

The early seventies heralded the beginning of Princess Anne's royal duties. With a change in the law in 1970 when the coming-of-age was lowered to 18, the Princess began to receive an allowance from the Civil List, and for the first time had money in her own right in a bank account at Coutts. Previously she had received little money of her own other than a dress allowance from her parents. Even when she began winning prize money at eventing she discovered that cheques she received were made out to the Queen as the owner of the horses. 'I didn't see a penny,' wailed Princess Anne. When she did eventually receive a Civil List income (£6000 a year in 1970) she had to begin paying administrative staff, contributing towards official cars, and generally covering expenses incurred on royal duties. Although the income has increased over the last 20 years, it has done so below the current rate of inflation, and there are now a far greater number of expenses to be met.

One of the most important decisions that Princess Anne made was to accept the presidency of the Save the Children Fund. It was to be over a decade before the public and the Princess were to realise exactly how important the decision was, but from the very start the Princess's involvement was enormous. On 6 February 1971, 19 years to the day since her mother acceded the throne, the Princess flew out to Nairobi with a film crew and presenter Valerie Singleton from the popular children's television programme *Blue Peter*, to see at first hand the conditions that prevailed. This was a unique venture for a member of the Royal Family, to bring a cause to the public's attention through television. Aimed at children, the programme brought the royal patronage down to the level of accessibility and brought the Fund more publicity than any campaign of their own could ever have funded. Two months later she paid a Save the Children visit to Norway. By the age of 21 she became the most travelled member of the Royal Family and an opinion poll voted her the third most popular woman in the world. (The Queen came first and Israel's Mrs. Golda Meir second.) With her obvious maturity and inceasing experience, Princess Anne was created by the Queen a Counsellor of State to represent the Sovereign whenever she was absent from the country. It was an honour King George VI had bestowed on his sister, Princess Mary, the Princess Royal. Interest in the Princess's work there may have been, but after a visit to Egypt looking at irrigation schemes and calmly ignoring any terrorist threats to assassinate her, the Prin-

cess caused the biggest stir of her short life when she landed at
Heathrow airport early one February morning in 1973. Instead of
driving to Windsor Castle or Buckingham Palace as expected, she
drove to Wiltshire. To the home of a Major and Mrs. Phillips. By
coincidence their son Mark was home on leave from his regiment.
Fleet Street began to buzz.

The paths of Princess Anne and Mark Phillips, a lieutenant in
the Queen's Dragoon Guards, had frequently crossed when they
found themselves competing at equestrian events. Mark had won
at Badminton three times on his horse Great Ovation and as a
result had the Princess's admiration. The only year she was placed
ahead of him on Goodwill was when Great Ovation went lame. At
first the media took little notice of the time they spent together, they
were after all expert riders vying against each other, but when any
unattached princess gives a man apparently more than a second
glance there is bound to be speculation. From the age of 14 Princess
Anne had been forced to suffer the linking of her name with eligible
males from an Austrian prince to an ex-pageboy of the Queen.
Amusing in retrospect but 'intensely irritating' at the time. The
press came very close when they claimed one of the country's finest
riders as her suitor, but they picked the wrong one by choosing
Olympic Gold Medalist Richard Meade. Princess Anne was much
too discreet for the media and was quite prepared to play a game of
cat and mouse with them. It was far more of a game than the press
realised and many newspaper editors seethed at the skill with
which they had been duped by the couple hiding in horseboxes to
avoid detection.

At first it appeared purely coincidental that Mark Phillips and
Princess Anne were frequent guests at the same house parties. They
were colleagues and there were family connections since Mark's
uncle had married the Duke of Norfolk's sister, and the Duke's
eldest daughter, Lady Anne Fitzalan-Howard, was a close friend of
the Princess's. On her twenty-second birthday, however, in 1972,
family and friends could not fail to notice the starry-eyed look in the
couple's eyes as they spent the entire evening dancing together, and
for the whole summer they embarked on a series of secret rendez-
vous. Meeting in horseboxes, stables, at the Phillips' home, Mount
House, secretly holding hands on a picnic when nobody was looking, and once the Princess even disguised herself with a wig and
glasses so that she could escape reporters. She joked afterwards
that even Mark didn't recognise her. For the first time in her life she

was in love, and enjoying the game. They attended hunt balls together in the autumn, but it was when Mark was invited to join the Royal Family at Sandringham in the New Year that everyone knew that he was more than just a friend, and when he later departed to Harwich to return to his regiment in Germany Princess Anne accompanied him to the dockside and kissed him goodbye in public. The Buckingham Palace switchboard was inundated with calls as the Press Office attempted to deny that there was any romantic attachment. No, the couple were not engaged, and Princess Anne, when questioned, snapped, 'All we want to do is to get on with training our horses in peace.'

It was at the Badminton Horse Trials that spring when Mark Phillips proposed to Princess Anne and she agreed immediately to become his wife. For six long weeks all rumours of an engagement were scotched, until 29 May 1973, the Spring Bank Holiday weekend, when the following announcement was made from Buckingham Palace:

> It is with the greatest pleasure that the Queen and the Duke of Edinburgh announce the betrothal of their beloved daughter The Princess Anne to Lieutenant Mark Phillips of The Queen's Dragoon Guards, son of Major and Mrs. Peter Phillips.

It was clear to all that this was a love match and no marriage of convenience or royal arrangement. Mark Phillips, born 22 September 1948, was just under two years older than Princess Anne and, to the delight of the Royal Family, had no skeletons in the cupboard, or rakish past that could be dragged out by the press. Mark had ridden his first pony at the age of three, the same age at which the Princess took to the saddle, and their lives were to follow a similar pattern. Mark was sent away to Stouts Hill prep school and the Marlborough College and soon proved his abilities as a sportsman, playing rugby, football and cricket for his school and breaking the school long jump record by reaching 14 feet 9 inches. But it was his abilities as a rider that shone through. He represented the Beaufort Hunt Pony Club team for five consecutive years and as a result was recommended for special training in three-day eventing. His father and grandfather had both served in the King's Dragoon Guards, his grandfather Brigadier John Tiarks being an ADC to King George VI, and Mark went straight to Sandhurst after leaving school and then joined the Queen's Dragoon Guards in July 1969.

It was the perfect background for a man who wished to marry the daughter of the Queen, and the fact that he was officially a 'commoner' seemed unimportant. Despite speculation as to the title he should be given Lieutenant Phillips refused to accept any kind of honour. Mark would never undertake official duties as a member of the Royal Family, he would receive no income from the Civil List, and there seemed no point in giving him a title merely for the sake of it. Older members of the Royal Family grumbled that when Princess Anne had children they too would be commoners, which seemed unthinkable for a royal princess, but Princess Anne thought it was what she wanted.

Untitled Mark Phillips may have been, but to Princess Anne he was her Prince Charming and someone for whom she had great respect. They both shared the admirable qualities of determination and dedication and Mark's easy-going attitude masks an incredible amount of stamina and drive. Unfortunately, members of the public never get to see the great sense of humour that Anne and Mark share, but they have been able to witness his skills on horseback which drew the couple together. Mark came fourth in the Burghley Horse Trials at the age of 18, and fourth at Badminton when 19, a remarkable achievement for one so young in competition with the best in the world. In 1971 and 1972 he went on to win at Badminton and in 1973 triumphed at Burghley in the Horse Trials, and he had been only weeks away from his twentieth birthday when he joined the British Olympics Team in Mexico. His calm exterior and placid temperament were the ideal combination for the Princess, and members of the Royal Family claimed that if the couple had been chosen by computer they could not have been better matched.

In recent years the couple have had to battle against malicious speculation that their marriage might be foundering, based purely on the assumption that because work keeps them apart there must be a breakdown in communications. Nothing could be further from the truth and the fact that they both work extremely hard has proved to be a satisfying bond that has united them even more. As Princess Anne is fêted as a celebrity, Mark is quite happy to stay silently in the background – he is not pushed there, it is through choice. Both believe in the work that they do, and just as the Princess works to justify her Civil List allowance in causes that she feels are worthwhile so Mark has to work to pay the mortgage. Being married to the Queen's only daughter has never spared him the worries of financial responsibility. Both Anne and Mark are independent, and he certainly made it clear from the very beginning that he was going to stand on his own two feet. Those that know the couple well say that Mark is Princess Anne's strength. Despite the tough and confident exterior she desperately needs him to lean on. That is the side that the public never see.

On the day that their engagement was announced Major and Mrs. Phillips met the Queen and the Duke of Edinburgh for the first time at a celebration lunch at Buckingham Palace, where the press were allowed to take photographs in the garden afterwards. Then for Mark it was back to join his regiment in Germany, whilst the working Princess flew to a riding school for the handicapped to watch disabled children riding ponies, which for them was as great a skill and achievement as winning a gold medal at the Olympics. By coincidence, the following week of official duties took the Princess to Germany, where she and Mark were able to snatch a weekend together in the fairytale setting of Langenburg Castle. Never the fairytale princess before, her romantic image was now being promoted around the world with the assistance of a glamorous set of pre-nuptial prints of the couple, and within weeks Princess Anne's face was adorning every possible item from tea-towels to T-shirts.

Although Princess Anne wanted a quiet wedding, royal weddings are not state occasions and members of the public have no real right to witness the ceremony, it was one battle that she was to lose. The last major royal wedding had been that of Princess Alexandra ten years before and nobody was going to let Princess Anne escape with a small private wedding, least of all the Queen. She, certainly, was not going to miss the chance of honouring her only daughter with a big celebration. The date was set for 14 November 1973 (which also happened to be the Prince of Wales' twenty-fifth birthday) and was to take place in Westminster Abbey. Preparations began in earnest and wedding gifts began pouring in several months in advance. Over 1500 guests were invited to the ceremony, there were seating plans to prepare, the reception to arrange and the honeymoon to plan, and most important of all the wedding dress to make. It was exactly like any other family wedding, except on a very grand scale, with hundreds of added hurdles to negotiate, such as security arrangements and protocol for the guests, coupled with the fact that 500 million viewers around the globe would be glued to their television sets.

Colour televisions were then a recent innovation and had just reached the price range of the average person. Princess Anne did more to boost the television industry than millions of pounds worth of advertising could ever have done. On the eve of the wedding Anne and Mark appeared in a specially recorded interview, shown by both the BBC and ITV. It was not something that Princess Anne relished doing, and the bland questions presented by Andrew Gardner and Alastair Burnet did not make riveting viewing. The responses from the couple were unenthusiastic. How does someone with their own housekeeper and lady-in-waiting respond to questions like 'Can you cook?' or 'Can you sew?' It was simply an embarrassing exercise for all concerned and achieved little.

The day of the wedding was cold and bright and saw over half-a-million people lining the route from Buckingham Palace to Westminster Abbey. Schoolchildren were given a day's holiday, and over 500 million viewers tuned in around the world to watch the day-long coverage of the occasion during which time commentators left almost no aspect of the couple's lives untouched. Mark Phillips and his best man, Captain Eric Grounds, arrived at the Abbey well in advance. By now the world had seen the diamond and sapphire engagement ring on Princess Anne's finger, but few had seen the Welsh gold wedding ring safely secreted in Captain Grounds' pocket, made from the same gold used for the Queen Mother, the Queen, and Princess Margaret's wedding rings. Later, in 1981, Princess Diana's wedding ring was also to be created out of that supply of gold.

At exactly 11.12 am the glass coach bearing Princess Anne and her father, the Duke of Edinburgh, left the Palace forecourt on its journey to Westminster Abbey and zoom lenses pried inside the carriage to reveal the long-awaited wedding dress. Nobody was disappointed. Princess Anne looked breathtaking in the gown of white silk created by Maureen Baker of Susan Small. With a dramatic high neckline and puffed Elizabethan-style sleeves, the dress had remained a closely guarded secret until this moment. The 15 girls who worked on the dress were each given one small piece to make and had practically no idea what the finished dress would look like when it was completed. The Queen was one of the few people privileged enough to see the creation when Princess Anne called her in at one of the final fittings. It was a dress that was particularly suited to Princess Anne, she had conceived the design herself and wanted to get away from the more traditional gowns

that were expected of her. This was her day and she was going to
enjoy it. When she joined Mark in his scarlet and gold tunic with
blue velvet collar and tight trousers, they really did make a fairytale
picture.

The wedding was Mark's first major public appearance and the
relaxed Princess guided him through the day, insisting that the
television cameras did not show the solemn moment when Mark
placed the wedding ring on her finger. After the short carriage drive
back to the Palace, through Parliament Square, down Whitehall
and under the arch at Horseguard's Parade and along The Mall,
the couple appeared with the Royal Family on the famous balcony
where Anne had first waved to the crowds below at her mother's
Coronation 20 years earlier.

Mark admitted later that he felt as if he was dreaming – a country
boy from Gloucestershire, married to a Princess, and now standing
on the balcony at Buckingham Palace with the Queen of England,
watched by millions of people around the world – his dazed parents
must have felt the same.

The couple spent their first night at Thatched House Lodge in
Richmond as the guests of Princess Alexandra, before flying the
following day to Barbados where the Queen had placed the Royal
Yacht *Britannia* at their disposal. Any criticisms of the extravagance
were immediately quashed when it was revealed that *Britannia* was
on her way to New Zealand anyway in preparation for the Queen's
next state visit and so Anne and Mark 'just tagged along'. There
was another reason for using the yacht as a base, for after a couple
of weeks holiday the Princess used the opportunity to pay official
visits to Antigua, Colombia, Equador, Jamaica and Montserrat.
The working Princess had no intention of wasting time and it was
an excellent chance not only to show off her new husband, but to
initiate Mark in the life that she led. Only through firsthand
experience did he realise exactly what hard work was involved in
the work of the royals, often waiting for Princess Anne to come to
bed because she was sitting up writing a speech for the following
day. The Princess has always written her own speeches from the
time of her first solo engagements. Few can appreciate the amount
of homework that she undertakes before any event so that she is
briefed about the people she is going to meet and the places she is
going to see, impressing people with the relevant searching questions that she asks.

After the honeymoon, in his new rank as Captain, Mark took up a position at Sandhurst as an intructor and he and Princess Anne took up residence at Oak Grove House on the Sandhurst Estate, for a rent of less than £500 a year. Having the Queen's daughter living in such a conspicuous position posed a few new security problems, but nobody seriously believed that anything could happen to the Princess, and apart from floodlighting the house and posting security guards outside the door very little was done. Nothing was to happen to Princess Anne at Sandhurst; it was in The Mall within sight of Buckingham Palace that she could easily have been assassinated, causing one of the biggest security shake-ups the police had known and a ripple of horror that travelled around the world.

On 20 March 1974, a cool Wednesday evening, Princess Anne and Captain Phillips were returning from a pleasant visit to the Riding for the Disabled Association. It was just after 7.30 pm and in the car with the Phillips were the Princess's chauffeur, Alexander Callendar, her lady-in-waiting, Rowena Brassey, and personal bodyguard, Inspector James Beaton. It was a quiet evening and the royal car, a maroon Austin Princess, swept sedately down The Mall. Within a few hundred yards of the Palace a white Ford Escort suddenly swerved in front of the royal limousine forcing it to stop. A gunman leapt out of the Escort and fired a shot into the royal car, then ran around to the Princess's side of the car and tried to drag her out, ripping the sleeve from her dress in the process.

What happened next was like a scene from an American thriller, no one would believe that this could happen within sight of Buckingham Palace. The bodyguard ran to protect the Princess and was shot from point blank range in the chest. Bravely pulling Princess Anne towards him, Mark Phillips shielded his wife with his own body and pulled the door shut. Inspector Beaton tried to fire at the attacker but his gun jammed, and the crazed gunman pointed the gun at Princess Anne and threatened to pull the trigger if Beaton did not throw down his gun. The Inspector did as he was asked and then put his hand over the barrel of the gun aimed at the Princess. The gunman fired. The bullet went through Beaton's hand and missed Princess Anne, and as he tried to hit the man he was shot again in the stomach and slumped to the ground in a pool of blood. No bodyguard could have done more to protect the Princess, but now he lay seriously wounded on the ground. Calmly, Princess Anne spoke to the gunman, attempting to gain his confidence, whilst Alexander Callendar, the chauffeur, quietly tried to get out of the car. Sensing a plot, the gunman fired the gun at Callendar hitting him in the chest. Only Princess Anne, Mark Phillips and Rowena Brassey remained unharmed.

Hearing the shots a young policeman, PC Hills, on patrol near Clarence House, ran out to see what was going on. Seeing the Princess in danger Hills radioed for help, then ran up and tackled the gunman. Another shot was fired and 22-year-old PC Michael Hills fell to the ground bleeding from the stomach. Three people lay wounded and the shooting was not yet over. The Princess's car had been followed by another car, which was forced to stop at the same time. The stunned driver, Brian McConnell, by coincidence a Fleet Street reporter, watched the scene before him in disbelief. By the time he got out of his car the attacker was panicking and before Mr. McConnell could do anything the gun was aimed at his chest and the trigger was pulled.

Within seconds The Mall was filled with police cars, and with no time to reload the gun the attacker, later identified as one Ian Ball, ran towards St. James's Park where he was immediately surrounded by police. His attempt to kidnap Princess Anne for a three million pound ransom had failed. It was barely 7.45 pm and four people lay shot, the most seriously wounded being Inspector James Beaton. Badly shaken but unharmed, Princess Anne and Captain Phillips were driven back to Buckingham Palace. Petals from the Princess's bouquet lay scattered amidst the bloodstains on The Mall as a grim reminder of the horrific attack.

Everyone present praised the bravery and courage of Princess Anne and Mark Phillips who miraculously escaped with barely a scratch. They had remained calm throughout the incident. Neither wanted any fuss, their only concern being for those who had been shot in order to protect them, and they waited anxiously for news of the wounded. Immediately Princess Anne rang the Queen, on a state visit to Indonesia, members of the Royal Family, and her closest friends to reassure them that she was safe. An hour later the BBC reported the news to the nation, and a debate in the House of Commons was halted to bring the news to shocked Members of Parliament.

Most people would have been shattered by the experience, even requiring sedation, but having regained her poise Princess Anne got into the driving seat of her Reliant Scimitar and drove herself home to Sandhurst. Yet one more example of the strength that Princess Anne has. She could easily have spent the night at Buckingham Palace but her strength of spirit would not allow her to be beaten. Nobody was going to weaken her confidence or destroy her freedom. On the drive home Princess Anne discovered that she had a larger police escort than usual but for once she wasn't complaining. Captain Phillips drove his own car home, not as a precaution but merely because it would be required the following day; the gallantry he displayed should never be forgotten.

Immediately, the Prime Minister, Harold Wilson, ordered an enquiry into the incident and the security of the Royal Family was seriously reviewed. The movements of each member of the Royal Family ceased to be common knowledge, cars were fitted with bullet-proof glass, and routes taken began to be frequently altered at the last minute to preclude any advanced planning. Now if the Queen goes to Westminster Abbey for a Commonwealth Observance Day service or rides to the Cenotaph on Remembrance Sunday she is taken by a different route each year. The down-to-earth Princess Anne admits realistically that if someone really wanted to kill her no amount of security would stop them unless she was to spend life in a bullet- and bomb-proof case, something she has no intention of doing. Although always conscious of the possibilities she is usually too involved in her work to contemplate the dangers and leaves the worrying to other people, confessing, however, that she is always subconsciously on the alert as a result of the kidnap attempt. When people comment on Princess Anne's dour expression it could just be a look of fear.

As soon as the injured men were sufficiently fit to receive visitors Princess Anne was one of the first at the hospital to give words of sympathy, support and gratitude. Without them she could have been taken prisoner, physically abused or even killed and she owed her safety to these men. When the men had recovered Princess Anne invited them and their wives along to Buckingham Palace so that the Queen could convey personally her appreciation. Inspector James Beaton was awarded the George Cross for gallantry, the highest honour that the Queen could bestow; PC Michael Hills received the George Medal, and the other men involved were honoured with the Queen's Gallantry Medal. A poor token, some may say, for being shot, but to the men and the Royal Family these pieces of metal meant far more than a mere gesture. Princess Anne was also honoured as a Dame Grand Cross of The Royal Victorian Order, and Captain Mark Phillips received the honour of being made a Commander of the Order, the first such gift he had ever received from the Queen. It was the end of a terrifying ordeal, and everyone involved was simply thankful to be alive.

The gunman, Ian Ball, appeared in court on 22 May 1974, where he was found to be mentally unstable and was ordered to be detained for an indefinite period. As a result of his actions life was never to be the same for the Royal Family, and Princess Anne was never again to appear in public without a string of plain-clothed security men, even when she is riding in private competitions they are there mingling with the crowds. Princess Anne jokes that she sees more of her detectives than she does of her husband, but deep down it is no joke. Even when she is out driving with her husband he is literally forced to take a back seat whilst an armed detective sits next to the Princess. To them it is a fact of life.

As life returned to normal Anne and Mark once more set their sights on the next Olympic Games, this time to be held in Montreal in 1976, and began competing in more events both at home and abroad. Having now brought Goodwill into peak condition, Princess Anne entered the European Championships of 1975 in West Germany and won herself a Silver Medal, a memorable moment for only one other woman in the history of three-day eventing had managed to reach such heights in the Championships on different horses. As a direct result Anne and Mark were shortlisted for the Olympic Games, although Mark was later relegated to reserve rider. Determined to visit Canada as part of the British team and not as a member of the Royal Family, the Princess wanted to be treated exactly the same as any other competitor within the limits of security. She and Mark flew with the rest of the team, not on the Queen's Flight but economy class, and stayed in the same lodgings with no added luxuries, actually seeming to enjoy standing in a queue with a tray rather than being waited-on at meals.

Disappointingly, Mark Phillips did not ride, and although the whole of the United Kingdom waited with baited breath it was not to be a triumphal event for Princess Anne. On the first day she was placed twenty-sixth in the dressage, and on the second, in the cross-country event, she fell at the nineteenth fence and suffered severe concussion. Mark Phillips and the Queen watched with horror, and viewers around the world could hardly believe it. Doctors afterwards claimed that she was medically unconscious, but Princess Anne climbed back on to Goodwill and completed the course. Stunned as she was the Princess knew that this was the Olympic Games, she was riding for Queen and country, and although there was little chance of a medal she had no intention of letting anybody down. The next day she used every ounce of stamina, realising that this was likely to be her only chance of riding in the Olympics, and came fourth in the final show-jumping stage. Just one position higher and she would have won a bronze medal. For both Anne and Mark it had been a very depressing experience, and despite previous triumphs this could have been seen as time to call it a day. Their goal had been to reach Olympic standard, they had been given the opportunity and failed. Anybody else might have given in, but then not everyone has the fighting spirit of these two.

In 1981 Captain Phillips won the Badminton Horse Trials for the fourth time, and in 1985, at an age when most jockeys have retired, Princess Anne attempted a new and exciting challenge and went flat-racing on the Derby course at Epsom. The race was intended to raise money for the Riding for the Disabled Association, and indeed almost £60,000 was collected, but when Princess Anne climbed into the saddle of her horse Against the Grain it became apparent that she had far more than fund-raising on her mind. For a first-time jockey she rode with all the grit and panache of a champion, and at 11–1 came in a very creditable fourth. Trainer David Nicholson said afterwards, 'She did everything right. I think she could have a lot of fun as a jockey and she can ride for me any time.' But Princess Anne was not so sure, 'I think I'll write that off to experience,' she said. 'The horse might have gone faster with someone else on board.' Yet the delight and pleasure she had gained were obvious in her face. It was another achievement that had nothing to do with being a princess. Already Anne was pencilling the next Badminton Horse Trials into her diary.

Since Goodwill retired in 1979 she has been searching for a horse good enough to take her back to the heights, and if one came along she would prove all the pundits wrong who claim that riders are past their peak at 30.

In the same year as the Montreal Olympics it was decided by the Princess that it was time to move, perhaps she and Mark had begun to think about a family. Anne knew that once she became pregnant it would put an end to any chance of taking part in the Olympics, but with that behind them, now was the time to settle down to a more private family life, and this could never be achieved at Sandhurst. So they began looking at properties. They had to be large enough, but not impractically large, and away from sightseers. In the grounds there had to be room for stables, and they preferred to be in the countryside so that they could ride whenever they wanted. For public duties it was also essential that the house was within easy reach of London. On the surface it would seem simple for a member of the Royal Family to find a house, but unlike ordinary married couples looking for something in their price range royalty tend to attact a lot of attention. If Princess Anne visited a house, so too did the press, revealing every detail from the dimensions of the bedrooms to the colour of the bathroom suite, and as his mother-in-law happened to be the richest woman in the world Mark Phillips suddenly found that properties were given an astronomically high price tag.

It was the late Lord 'Rab' Butler who came to the rescue, for his ancestral home in Gloucestershire was empty and up for sale. It was called Gatcombe Park. Gloucestershire was the ideal county for the Phillips at around a 1½ hour's drive from London, and close to Badminton, also not too far from Great Somerford, the home of Major and Mrs. Phillips. It was surrounded by 530 acres of land – 400 arable and 130 pasture – and although Mark had not really contemplated farming, it seemed an excellent way of earning money. Money was, of course, the problem. The estate cost around £450,000 and with Mark's annual income of £4,500 the couple didn't even have enough for a deposit, let alone almost half-a-million pounds for a house. As the not so subtle press were eager to reveal, the Queen came to her daughter's aid and helped the couple out, but did not, as people think, buy the property outright. Captain Phillips still has a very large mortgage to pay off. To give Mark a good start in farming, the Queen did buy the 600 acres adjoining Gatcombe from a 93-year-old local farmer, but it is her property and she leases it to her son-in-law. The Queen has never taken her money or position for granted and is an extremely astute businesswoman.

Uninhabited for over a decade, the damp crumbling house needed major structural repairs and complete redecoration, and there proved to be almost a year's work before the couple could move in. Money had to be found for repairs too, and Anne's Civil List income was all accounted for by official expenses. As Mark said, they were just like any other young couple trying to establish a home. Their home was on a much grander scale however! Today if you visit Gatcombe it is very much as one would expect from Princess Anne, practical and homely, with the atmosphere of a

large country house and certainly not a stately home. There are no
state rooms or priceless art objects; instead it is a real home with a
welcoming atmosphere of muddy boots, wet dogs, and endless
copies of *Horse and Hound*. Naturally there is a formal drawing room
for the couple to receive official guests, but it has an air of elegant
cosiness and is certainly never kept out-of-bounds to the children,
or the dogs.

Mark went to the Royal Agricultural College in Cirencester to
learn the practicalities of farming, but the major problem with
Gatcombe is that the land has no great depth of soil and in an area
known as the 'Cotswold Brash' is suitable only for corn and not
intensive crops. Today Mark has beef cattle and sheep, has built a
barn and outbuildings and invested in new machinery, such as a
combine harvester at which Princess Anne has to take her turn.
There are five permanent staff to be paid for their work on the farm,
and another five in the house – a butler, nanny, cook and two dailies
– and when the Princess remarked that corn in the garden was far
more practical than flowers, she meant it.

Having settled in to Gatcombe Park, in April 1977 Princess Anne
informed the Queen that she was to become a grandmother for the
first time. Despite the casual impression that she was in no real
hurry to have children, secretly she had fears that she might never
be able to have children due to the earlier gynaecological problems
she had had. Her fears were unfounded and on 15 November 1977,
the day after their fourth wedding anniversary, Princess Anne gave
birth to Peter Mark Andrew. The baby weighed 7 lb 9 oz, was then
fifth in line to the throne, and the first royal baby in more than five
centuries to be born a commoner. Princess Anne was rushed to
hospital by Captain Phillips in the early hours of the morning. This
was another 'first' for the Princess who, rather than have doctors
and equipment come all the way to Gatcombe, went herself to St.
Mary's Hospital in Paddington, becoming the first member of the
immediate Royal Family to give birth in a hospital. It was a
tradition that the Princess of Wales was later to follow when her
children were born. Master Peter Phillips made his entry into the
world just before 11.00 am, and at Buckingham Palace the new
grandmother was on her way to an investiture in the Throne Room
when the excited father, who had been present at the birth, rang to
tell his mother-in-law the news. Unaware of the family drama those
waiting to be invested sat nervously in the Throne Room wonder-
ing why the Queen, who is never late, did not appear. Could

something be wrong? People coughed and the small orchestra played on. Looking slightly flushed the Queen arrived at ten-past eleven, apologising for being late. 'I have just had a message from the hospital,' she announced proudly. 'My daughter has given birth to a son.' Loud cheers rang out through the Palace and the Queen went ahead with her duties, visibly thrilled by the news of her first grandson.

It was soon after the birth that Princess Anne was to drop a bombshell on the Queen by making her wishes known that she did not wish Peter to be titled. She had fought to stop Mark being created an earl and nothing was going to persuade her to change her mind about her children, even if they were in line for the throne. Princess Margaret's children, Viscount Linley and Lady Sarah Armstrong-Jones, both had titles because their 'commoner' father had been made an earl, and they were further away from the throne. Eventually the Royal Family simply had to accept Princess Anne's wishes and her arguments; not wishing Peter to escape his birthright, she wanted him to live as normal a life as possible without the handicap of being titled. If he does eventually go on to become a Counsellor of State it would not stop him signing official documents or statutes, even though the only previous commoner to sign state papers in British constitutional history was Oliver Cromwell.

Princess Anne was entering a period of battles, first with her family over her son's title, then the moment she left hospital to drive with her baby home to Gatcombe she caused a furore by sitting in the front passenger seat of the car without a seat belt. It was seven years before the law applying to seat belts changed, but the press quickly criticised the Princess for not sitting in the back of the car with her son. Not deliberately casting safety to the wind, Princess Anne simply got into the front seat out of sheer habit. Quickly she became a target of further criticism from the press and whatever she did was bad news. The greatest battles have been when the Princess is riding. She understands that people are interested in her, but with the pressures of eventing she can do without the irritation of photographers getting in the way, and she is always concerned that the horses might be disconcerted by the bright flashes and noise. When she shouted 'naff off' to a reporter it was a justifiable reaction, but it was to become part of her 'image' that she would never live down and the phrase became as hackneyed as her mother's 'My husband and I'. On the one occasion she fell into the

lake at Badminton hundreds of cameras flashed and that image of
her appeared in more newspapers and magazines than any other
photograph. Princess Anne had no objection to them taking the
photograph, quite aware of what a scoop it was, but she is irritated
by the fact that it appears with such monotonous regularity as to
give the misleading impression that she spends her life falling off
horses. In many ways Princess Anne has been far more co-
operative with the media than people give her credit for. The
smiling Queen Mother waves at the cameras, the Queen never
gives interviews, and most members of the Royal Family are seen
but seldom heard. Prince Charles is happy to give interviews and
talks about subjects close to his heart, such as the raising of the
Tudor battleship the *Mary Rose*, but Princess Anne is the one
member of the Family who has given interviews and answered
probing questions about herself. Her voice has been heard on
television more than the Queen's, she has made highly successful
appearances on chat shows with Michael Parkinson, in Australia in
1983, and Terry Wogan for the BBC in London in 1985, at which
time the press lauded her with such comments as 'she has the
timing and confidence of a professional performer . . . The Princess
revealed an engaging sense of humour and a razor sharp wit . . .
Much of the humour was used by the Princess to send up one
person – herself', and on numerous occasions the Princess has
allowed film crews and television cameras into Gatcombe to make
programmes. Even when a special programme was made about
Captain Phillips and his horses, Princess Anne joined in. In 1968
when a film was made about a year in the life of the Royal Family,
she co-operated to the extent of allowing cameras in on her French
lessons, which could have proved embarrassing.

By making herself so accessible there were obviously going to be
occasions when the Princess made herself a target for criticism. By
giving too much of herself, by being too obliging, she would inevitably find someone taking advantage of her. When she found her feet
carrying out royal duties, became fully in command of her working
life, Princess Anne learned to ignore the media and be totally
herself. She became the Royal they loved to hate. Twelve years
were to pass from the time of her first public engagement before she
was to become the Princess who could do no wrong.

Princess Anne's public image as created by the media has become a major topic for discussion. On one December day in 1984 it
was not so much what Princess Anne did as what she did *not* do that

gave the press a field day and in an attempt to create a real-life soap opera out of the Windsors, they invented a rift with the Princess of Wales. 'That was one of their better fairy stories,' she told Terry Wogan in a subsequent interview, after he had questioned her about the 'famous non-appearance' at Prince Harry's christening.

Sensationalists preferred to interpret the affair as a fit of pique because the Prince and Princess of Wales did not invite her to be a godmother to Prince Harry, and as a reaction to the so-called snub she stayed away. 'She was deeply hurt and disappointed,' mumbled one supposed intimate of the Royal Family, but really intimate friends let nothing slip to the press and only Princess Anne knew the truth. Knowing that *anything* she said would be misinterpreted, she felt as always that it was preferable to say nothing, but privately revealed that any royal rift between herself and the Princess of Wales was pure 'media mythology'. Long before Prince Harry was born Princess Anne and Captain Phillips had organised a social get-together and pheasant shoot at Gatcombe Park as a means of repaying all the hospitality they had received over the years. When the date for the christening was arranged, Princess Anne was not consulted and inevitably it coincided with her own 'event'. Had the Princess been invited to be godmother then presumably she would have attended, but undertaking no significant role other than boosting the already large ranks of Royals there seemed little reason for cancelling her plans. Buckingham Palace suggests that she may be a godparent to any subsequent daughter of the Prince and Princess of Wales. Much has been penned about the relationship of the two Princesses, and whilst both would admit that they are not bosom buddies, neither are they enemies. They simply have quite different interests and lifestyles. There are few bonds to draw them together. Diana, as the press would have us believe, adores clothes and shopping, for Anne clothes are practical and functional. Whereas Diana has a team of fashion experts behind her, Anne has often succeeded in capturing some of the limelight entirely alone. Barely out of her teens she became known as the 'Duchess of Luton' for the boost she had given to the hat industry (Luton being the hub of British millinery). When she swept into Grosvenor House for the 1985 BAFTA Awards in a '*Dynasty*-style' outfit with red streaks in her hair, she stole the show and won herself a standing ovation.

Princess Anne's love of horses is something that Diana does not share – having fallen off at a very early age destroyed her confidence. In January 1987 she was seen on a horse for the first time, under the Queen's careful guidance, but obviously very reluctantly. Equestrian conversations between Anne and Diana would therefore be limited. Although the void between them is vast, it is not unbreachable. Had Princess Anne been younger they may have been closer. Had the age-gap been greater perhaps Princess Anne could have adopted the role of a guiding 'aunt' and mentor, just as the late Princess Royal did to younger members of the Royal Family. Instead, they both continue to suffer the saga that script writers plot for them . . .

Chapter 5

*L*ove and marriage

Marriage to the working Princess has not been easy for Mark Phillips. After the initial excitement of his arrival into the Royal Family, interest quickly waned and he has never suffered the intense media exposure that the wives of Prince Charles and Prince Andrew have attracted, but he has constantly been plagued with adverse reports regarding his career, his character and the imminent collapse of his marriage. Speculation about the success of the partnership has dogged the couple, arising from the fact that their respective careers separate them for long periods.

In the New Year of 1987 a leading Sunday newspaper once again printed an 'exclusive' article proclaiming the 'Truth About Anne and Mark's Marriage'. A two-page feature declared that the marriage 'is a sham' and exists in name only. The entire article, like so many others in the past, was based purely on the fact that Mark accompanied Princess Anne only on nine of her engagements in 1986. Buckingham Palace point out that it is surprising that he undertook as many as nine, for he receives nothing from the Civil List and never officially undertakes royal duties. It was decided even before the marriage that he would not enter into the round of royal engagements and would continue with his own career. Mark Phillips has no desire to play second fiddle to his wife and tag along unnecessarily. They are two independent spirits. Occasionally he will attend a film premiere or sporting function, but only if it is of personal interest and the Princess needs an escort. To claim that the marriage is foundering because he does not join the Princess in her work is ludicrous.

Close friends credit Mark Phillips with taming the wildness of Princess Anne; his calming influence has done much to smooth down the abrasive side of her nature. Mark comes from a working family. His grandfather, William Garside Phillips, left school at the age of nine and worked a 13-hour day down the pits. After this marathon shift he would walk eight miles to night school and eight miles back again. Eventually he became mine manager, and later owner of the biggest mine in Warwickshire through nothing more than sheer hard work. Such grim determination is something that both Anne and Mark can identify with. He may not have been academically as clever as the Princess, he obtained one A-level in history, but he has a good business head, especially where matters of finance are concerned. After leaving Marlborough he entered the Army, first as a rifleman in the Greenjackets before moving on to Sandhurst and the Dragoon Guards. Being a competent horserider from the age of 18 months when his mother first put him on horseback ensured later equestrian success. Today he farms approximately 1130 acres of arable and pasture land, and when he can be spared from the farm he gives riding seminars, which can earn him £1500 a day. He also has a British Leyland sponsorship, and has recently been seen advertising tea on New Zealand television.

This enterprise certainly raised a few eyebrows in view of the fact that members of the Royal Family go to extreme lengths not to publicly endorse products and companies are not allowed to use them in any kind of promotion in this country. The ex-royal butler, Peter Russell, lost advertising contracts because his tenuous connection with royalty might lead to misinterpretation; when a leading children's wear company produced an advertisement in which the man bore too great a resemblance to Prince Charles they were forced to withdraw it, and when the author wanted to be photographed beside the waxwork of Princess Anne at Madame Tussauds in London, Buckingham Palace discouraged it in case it was ever used commercially, and Madame Tussauds panicked that the long history of royal patronage would be brought to a swift conclusion through one photograph of a royal likeness. How then can Mark Phillips, married to the Queen's only daughter, be allowed to advertise tea, even if it is on the other side of the globe? Ah, say Buckingham Palace, Mark Phillips is NOT a member of the Royal Family. He is merely on the periphery. So if he wished to enter commercials in this country there could be no justifiable criticism. At one photographic session before his marriage, Mark was photographed astride a large tank with its gun sticking out suggestively between his legs. Although circulated amongst newspaper editors, it has never been published. Should someone wish to do so, it could not be seen, in theory, to be denigrating the image of royalty.

Whilst Mark would no doubt prefer to shun any commercial project, he does have to earn a living. The running of Gatcombe Park, the funding of his equestrian pastime, the staff who work on the farm, all have to be paid for out of Mark's income, not from public funds. Princess Anne's Civil List income is spent entirely on her public engagements with the 78 different organisations that she supports.

In 1986 Mark Phillips' work and sport took him the length and breadth of Great Britain, covering approximately 30,000 miles, and more than double that distance overseas. He gave seminars around the world from the heat of Jamaica to the cold of Scotland. As an Olympic Gold Medalist and four times winner of the Badminton Horse Trials, he was keen to participate in the World Three-Day Event Championships in Australia, which take place only every four years, which meant a greater degree of physical preparation to make the 16,000-mile journey worthwhile. Training horses involves seven days a week exercise and practice to keep rider and horse fit and to a high competitive standard. He also took part in horse trials in America, where he has now become a big name. All this, on top of running the farm, resulted in few family holidays. The Phillips family manage a skiing holiday in January and then are seldom free to relax together until August.

Weekends are important for them, the Princess will only undertake a few Saturday engagements in any year, for it is the one time when they can all be together. Peter Phillips boards at Port Regis school in Dorset during the week, but is able to return home on Friday evenings. The youngest, Zara, still attends the local primary school at Minchinhampton near Gatcombe Park.

It was in the early Autumn of 1980 that Princess Anne found that she was pregnant for a second time, and it was an occasion when once again the press intervention marred an otherwise happy event. It was the year of Princess Margaret's fiftieth birthday and as a special family party had been organised at the Ritz in November, Princess Anne felt that this would be the best time to make the announcement. It is the natural desire of any daughter to tell her mother the news of the impending birth as soon as possible, but the

Princess felt that it would add to the sense of celebration to wait. The Queen must be informed before any public announcement, and so nobody but Anne and Mark knew. On 4 November Princess Anne told her mother at the private party. They returned to Buckingham Palace in the early hours of 5 November in jubilant spirits, the Queen obviously delighted that she was to be a grandmother for the second time. Yet within hours the delivery of the national newspapers to the Palace were to dampen spirits. The news of Princess Anne's pregnancy had already made the headlines. Once again the Royal Family had been betrayed by those in whom they trust and the news had been leaked to Fleet Street. Having learnt the pointlessness of fighting against the media, an immediate official announcement was made from Buckingham Palace that the Princess was expecting a baby the following spring, putting paid to any newspaper editor's idea that he had a scoop. It also precluded the need for the Palace Press Office to confirm or deny the story, but once again it made the Royal Family more cautious and colder towards the press. Anne and Mark regretted what was obviously too public an announcement. From now onwards any such private news would be kept for the security of the Palace walls.

The only problem created by the unexpected suddenness of the announcement was that Mark's parents, Major and Mrs. Phillips, were on holiday in Cornwall at their country retreat on the Lizard peninsula. They enjoy the remoteness of the area, but at that time had no telephone and Princess Anne was unable to contact them. Now Princess Anne desperately wanted to get in touch with them before a newspaper or radio report beat her to it. Princess Anne could think of only one solution. Within a short time the Cornish police visited the Phillips' cottage and Mrs. Anne Phillips ran to the nearest public callbox to telephone Gatcombe Park. Dialling the number, she breathlessly pushed in the coins and it was with enormous relief that she heard the Princess's voice: 'Nothing's wrong. I'm pregnant!'

In the same ward of St. Mary's Hospital, Paddington, in the Lindo Wing, where she had given birth to Peter, four years earlier, Princess Anne brought the Queen's first granddaughter into the world, on 15 May. Once again Mark sat with the Princess throughout the birth, setting an example that Prince Charles was to follow. The Queen drove from Windsor the following day to see the 8 lb 1 oz baby, again in line to the throne but born a commoner, and beamed at the waiting crowds around the hospital entrance.

When the Princess left four days later she sat in the back seat of the car to avoid any controversy.

When her son was born Princess Anne broke with royal tradition by naming him after Mark's father and not a member of the Royal Family. She was equally selective when choosing her daughter's names, settling on Zara Anne Elizabeth. The name Zara has no royal connections but is not unknown in royal circles since the daughter of one of the Princess's ladies-in-waiting was Zara Legge-Bourke. In the Gilbert and Sullivan opera 'Utopia Limited' there is a princess called Zara, and by a strange coincidence Prince Philip had a hand in sinking an Italian cruiser of the same name at the Battle of Cape Matapan on 28 March 1941. But Princess Anne insists that it was chosen simply because she and Mark liked it. Zara is in fact the Arabic word for 'morning star'. Although Zara has many of the tomboy characteristics that her mother possessed, Princess Anne has attempted to make childhood far more relaxed, without the protocol that she was herself subjected to. Her main concern has always been that both children are treated alike and that Zara never feels second to Peter because he is older. When either misbehaves, even if it is in public, they are reprimanded with equal severity. Princess Anne created controversy amongst modern mothers when she smacked both children at the Badminton Horse Trials when they were naughty, but as a traditionalist the Princess believes in old fashioned discipline. Seeing as many children as she does in her working life, perhaps the Princess realises exactly what the uncontrollable children have lacked.

As soon as her children reached the age of four they were both sent to the local primary school, and Princess Anne could frequently be seen dropping her son off in the morning along with the other mothers. Prince Charles did not attend day school until the age of eight, and she herself suffered the isolation of a private tutor and was determined that Peter and Zara would not. Realising the benefits of mixing with children of her own age at Benenden, Princess Anne wanted Peter to have the same advantages and experiences, and so in 1985 he began boarding at Port Regis co-educational prep school, which was chosen for its excellent facilities and reputation. Set in 150 acres of parkland it offers a privacy similar to Benenden's and provides excellent sporting opportunities, from canoeing to judo. Peter is very keen on sport, especially water sports as he proved on a private visit to the 1987 Boat Show at Olympia. Captain Phillips was particularly impressed by the modern academic equipment, including computers and an electronics workshop. Peter appears to be growing into a good-mannered and well-adjusted individual, suffering no obvious setbacks through royal connections. Possibly Zara will be considered for Benenden when the time arises. As plain 'Master' and 'Miss' the children are quickly accepted by their contemporaries, unlike Prince William whose character began to change in a marked fashion after a year at nursery school in Notting Hill Gate. From a smiling impish child it was noticed that he became sullen and withdrawn after starting school.

Princess Anne enjoys her role as a mother much more than she is given credit for, she is happy to mix with other local mothers and entertain Peter and Zara's friends at children's parties. Gatcombe Park offers plenty of space for the children to make as much noise as they like and the Princess has been known to participate in the games, producing an equal amount of noise. 'I don't see as much of my children as I would like, but we do things together as often as we can,' she confides. Any press photographer who follows certain equestrian events will have endless pictures of the Princess hand in hand with her children, either carrying them on her back, nursing sleepy heads, or pointing an admonishing finger. She closely guards their privacy and performs unexpected motherly tasks, such as sewing tiny pockets in the children's pillows to hold teeth that have fallen out for the 'tooth fairy'.

She firmly believes in not being swayed by public opinion as to how she brings up her children and when she took Peter to a pheasant shoot when he was six, she knew that it would cause an outcry with anti-blood sports campaigners. She is herself against blood sports, but shoots are very much a part of country life and she knew that it would be unrealistic to keep Peter shielded from the sport. Princess Anne walked him, with a toy gun in his hand, defiantly past photographers, and quipped: 'I shall be very disappointed if this isn't on the front pages tomorrow!' It was yet one more display of her openness. She could have played up to the image expected of her, but it is not in her make-up to lie and she would not ever avoid country pursuits purely because the press might misinterpret her actions. Princess Anne feels that she has to be objective and consider her children first, she must know from personal experience of aristocratic families who have tried to shelter their children from reality only to have them rebel and turn to drugs or alcohol. Princess Anne is anxious that this never happens to her children. She is open and forthright with them and hopes that when they reach an age when they have to make decisions for themselves they will feel able to turn to her for advice without feeling embarrassed or intimidated by her. If Peter and Zara go off the rails she knows that at the end of the day it will be her fault as parent.

As would be expected, Peter and Zara Phillips were introduced to the equestrian world at an early age. Peter has been in the saddle since he was three and Zara was given a pony of her own when she was two-and-a-half, a Christmas present in 1983. As they grow older the whole family will be able to enjoy riding together, and possibly the children will follow in their parents' footsteps, eventually even succeeding in the Olympic Games in the late 1990s to win the medals which escaped Anne and Mark in the 1970s. Princess Anne has always been extremely close to the Queen as an only daughter and it is known in royal circles that the Queen has a particular fondness for Anne's children. Although a grandmother can never prefer any of her grandchildren there is naturally a special bond with those that are born first. To Peter she is not the Queen but his 'granny' and he takes Her Majesty by the hand to show her his latest toys. They have been seen on their hands and knees together in the little Welsh cottage in the grounds of Windsor Castle that was given to the Queen and Princess Margaret as a playhouse when they were children.

Peter and Zara are very family orientated and are present at family functions even if Anne and Mark are absent, such as at Prince Harry's christening ('I think they made up for us in sheer decibels,' said Princess Anne afterwards). At horse trials the children can be seen hanging over the rails watching either one of their parents compete, and when Mark is working on the farm it is quite normal to see Peter, when not at school, running along behind in Wellington boots. Just as Princess Anne takes the wheel of a tractor or combine harvester when needed, it is certain that Peter will pull his weight on the farm when he gets older.

Chapter 6

*P*lanning the working life

A familiar part of life at Gatcombe Park for the children is the ever increasing number of souvenirs and mementoes that their mother has collected from around the world, now displayed on a special ledge around her sitting-room. Many are simple tributes hand-made by African children, and to Princess Anne they are worth far more than their weight in gold. Only friends and family ever get to see this very personal collection of curiosities, but for the Princess they represent a major and significant change in her life.

On New Year's Day 1970 she officially became President of the Save the Children Fund and although she worked tirelessly for the organisation it was not until both her children were born and her family life was complete that she really put her soul into the charity. In October 1982 she embarked on a gruelling tour of Africa for Save the Children and although she remained unchanged and hard-working as she had always been, it brought a new understanding of her by the world press. Suddenly the media looked at the Princess with newly opened eyes and instead of seeing the 'grumpy' or 'sour-faced' girl (an image that they had promoted) they saw a compassionate and caring woman of immense courage. The tour was exhausting but Princess Anne remained unflagging and gained national admiration. For the first time in a number of years Princess Anne was good news. Since 1982 the Princess has been to some of the poorest areas of the world to promote her cause and there is little that she will not undertake to raise money at every available opportunity. Even to the extent of getting her friends to help.

Princess Anne may have been criticised in the past for having any kind of association with guns, but she took the wind out of her critics' sails in the summer of 1984 by organising a shoot to raise money for the Save the Children Fund. Who could possibly object to her fund-raising attempts when the only pigeons being shot were clay? Past censurers were strangely mute. Princess Anne wished to raise enough money for two mini-buses to help not only children in this country but to aid the Afghani refugees in Pakistan, and for a private function she managed to gather together the greatest number of the 'royal circle' ever known at such an event with the assistance of her old friend, racing driver Jackie Stewart.

The two had struck up a great friendship in 1971 when Princess Anne won the European Three-Day Event Championship at Burghley and Jackie Stewart became World Champion Motor Racing Driver, and they were voted Sportsman and Sportswoman of the Year as a result. The friendship had grown stronger and so the fund raising became known as the 'Jackie Stewart Celebrity Challenge'. Taking part that blustery afternoon in North Wales were a very illustrious collection of VIPs including Prince Andrew, the Duke of Kent, King Constantine, Prince Albert of Monaco, Angus Ogilvy, the Earl of Lichfield, the Duke of Roxeburghe, Lord Tollemache, Lord Montagu of Beaulieu, and of course Captain Mark Phillips, whose loader was Princess Anne. Clay pigeon shooting takes a keen eye, a steady hand, and a skilful aim, qualities that Captain Phillips' team had in abundance, winning the day with 144 points. It is a sport that cannot be faked, skill alone is required to win. Well pleased with the fund-raising efforts, and having been sprayed with champagne by her playful husband, the Princess climbed into a helicopter with a very experienced pilot, her brother Prince Andrew, and set off to undertake another engagement.

Fund-raising events, like the clay pigeon shoot, are an important but light-hearted aspect of Princess Anne's working life. The *real* work is the five hundred or so official engagements that she carries out every year; functions where her sheer presence raises money, boosts moral and gives essential publicity to charities and causes. The knowledge, humour and interest that Princess Anne displays are a bonus to the prestige that the royal patronage offers. Most of the Princess's working diary is made up of visits to the organisations with which she is closely connected (see Appendix II). The Save the Children Fund and the Riding for the Disabled Association have perhaps received wider publicity than many of her other appointments, but the Princess attempts to give equal amounts of time to anything she patronises, be it the Missions to Seamen, the Spinal Injuries Association, the Jersey Wildlife Preservation Fund, or the Amateur Rowing Association. Each one will be a society or cause in which she has not only a special interest, but a detailed knowledge. Many are, for example, connected with equine sports, and these then lead on to more specialised involvement with medical associations that treat injuries that result from sport, or disabilities that can benefit from sport. The first close link with medicine came in 1970 when the Princess was appointed Commandant in Chief of the St. John Ambulance and Nursing Cadets.

Some members of the Royal Family undertake sporadic and informal visits to charities. The Princess of Wales, as Patron of Help the Aged, visited a number of day centres on the spur of the moment during the freezing winter of 1987, having deposited Prince William at a new school on the same morning. Her official engagement diary for that particular month had just four entries. Because of the great demand for Princess Anne, unannounced visits are rarer as her packed timetable has to be planned a long time in advance. For a member of the Royal Family to request a visit to an event is precluded by the fact that the mail bags are filled daily with invitations, and Princess Anne's is no exception. Although she may attend over 500 events in a year, these are a mere fraction of the offers she will have had.

Tentative planning of the engagement diary will begin at least six months in advance. 'Co-ordination' is the key word in any royal engagement, bringing together a well balanced timetable that will run like clockwork for any day. The handling of Princess Anne's engagements since 1982 has been in the hands of her Private Secretary, Lieutenant-Colonel Peter Gibbs, a former Coldstream Guards officer, who knows how to organise with the skill of a military manoeuvre. Apart from her ladies-in-waiting, personal friends as well as colleagues, he is the man who works most closely with the Princess and sees her almost every day, whatever the agenda. He works from an office on the second floor of Buckingham Palace, once Princess Anne's schoolroom, alongside two secretaries and a computer. Princess Anne was the first to install a computer at Buckingham Palace, now completely computerised, from the Royal Mews to the kitchens. The Queen has her own personal computer, a gift from Ronald Reagan, on which she monitors the progress of her racehorses, and develops a breeding programme.

The fact that private secretaries in the Royal Household are always from a military background is no coincidence when one considers the strategies involved in planning. Although invitations arrive on a daily basis, the programme of engagements is put together in two mammoth sessions held once every six months. This onerous area of administration was described by royal biographer Harold Nicolson as a nightmare, for although her Private Secretary officially organises the Princess's public life, what is ironically described as her 'private life' often requires an equal amount of administration. If the Princess is spending a weekend at Windsor, or staying with friends, she cannot simply depart without a certain amount of advanced planning. Not as much as the Queen, certainly, but the mantle of royalty can never be completely cast aside. Even in private Princess Anne requires constant security protection, communications have to be arranged for even the shortest visit so that the Princess can always be contacted should any emergency arise. As every detail of her life is monitored by the media, her Private Secretary must keep the Buckingham Palace Press Office constantly on the ball with proceedings, always ready with an answer and where possible keeping one step ahead of every newspaper editor. Is Princess Anne going to be divorced? Is she pregnant? Is it true that she has argued with the Duchess of York? These are the kind of questions that have to be fielded daily from newspaper and magazine reporters around the world.

On a day-to-day basis the Princess and her Private Secretary will go through the itinerary in the morning for that particular day, a copy of which Princess Anne keeps in her handbag on a small card for reference on the journey. Timetables for royal visits are photographically reproduced in miniature, containing not only the proceedings but the names and rank of each person she will meet during the day. As Princess Anne jokes, 'I seldom meet the same person twice,' so it is important to get it right. The lady-in-waiting for the day will also have a copy of this convenient pocket-sized timetable.

Having quickly settled the business in hand, her Private Secretary will present the Princess with items of correspondence for her perusal and approval. Princess Anne sees every letter that is personally addressed to her, but seldom is there time to read them all in detail. With her consent, her Private Secretary will already have categorised correspondence into various departments. Some, for example, might be questions that can be dealt with by the Press Office, others could be from children, which a lady-in-waiting will answer. Princess Anne's mailbag is constantly full of letters from children who are would-be horse riders or owners, others are from children that the Princess has visited in hospital or has encountered on a Save the Children Fund or Riding for the Disabled visit in this country. Occasionally letters will be sent direct to a particular charity to deal with, or a government department if they can deal with the matter more suitably. Off-loading correspondence enables the Princess to concentrate on the business of the day.

Applications come continually for grant of dedications of books or music (seldom accepted unless the Princess is closely connected with the individual or cause), requests for photographs or portrait sittings (not enjoyed by Princess Anne and rarely accepted). The Queen has sat for over 100 portraits, her daughter for less than ten in the last 20 years (see Appendix I); occasionally a decision has to be made as to whether a book or gift should be accepted (the Royal Family do not usually accept unsolicited presents). It is the daily invitations, however, that take up much of the time. Princess Anne does not plant trees or lay foundation stones, and if she is asked to open a building there must be a very good reason for her presence, other than good publicity for her would-be hosts. Commercial premises are not opened unless again there is a connection. Some questioned the re-opening performed by Princess Anne of Dillons Bookshop in London (see Chapter 8), but as they supply books to the University of London, it was in her role as Chancellor of the University that the Princess agreed to attend. Special thought has to be given as to where in the country the Princess should go, to avoid perhaps six visits to one particular county in a year, although just as the Queen undertakes a greater number of engagements in London, so for convenience Princess Anne is happy to accept invitations from Gloucestershire and the surrounding counties so that she can travel from Gatcombe Park.

At the six-monthly planning meetings the Princess, her Private Secretary and ladies-in-waiting will carefully consider future engagements. The Princess will sit with a large diary in front of her and listen to the suggested invitations that have arrived. She will note which are worthwhile causes to consider, which she has already visited in recent years, always something which will catch her interest that she will feel demands a little research into. The hardest part is fitting the jigsaw of dates together. If several invitations have come from one specific area or town often an attempt will be made to combine a number of visits into one particular day. All must be carefully considered so that royal visits do not clash and Princess Anne never arrives at a hospital only to discover that the Queen is at a reception half a mile away. Few of the Royals ever know what the rest of their family are doing, but they can be certain that not one of them will be on a public engagement in the vicinity.

Centenaries and anniversaries are always borne in mind when compiling the engagement diary as this gives a perfect reason for royal patronage. In 1986, for example (see Princess Anne's engagement diary – Appendix IV), it was the University of London's 150th anniversary, which provided an excellent opportunity to include their controversial Chancellor in as many activities as possible, from naming a locomotive at Euston Station in April to attending a Naval military display at Greenwich in October. It was also the tenth anniversary of the Missions to Seamen, the 750th anniversary of the town of Penryn's granting of a Royal Charter, the Diamond Jubilee of the Townswomen's Guild, the 40th anniversary of The British Residents' Association in Switzerland, the 25th anniversary of the Ryton Police Training Centre, the 40th anniversary of the opening of the Arundel Reserve in West Sussex, amongst others. These are key dates which must be pencilled in without leeway. Others include annual general meetings of the various charities of which she is Patron. Where possible, if a straightforward visit is requested, the flexible dates can be fitted in around the unchangeables. As a member of the British Royal Family there are also certain other dates which must be considered. Should the Princess attend the State Opening of Parliament in November? The Remembrance Day ceremony at the Cenotaph must be inked in. In 1986 it was the Queen's sixtieth birthday, and Princess Anne had to remain free for celebrations. Princess Anne is one member of the Family who will not attend a royal ceremony merely for royalty's sake. She will attend the State Opening of Parliament if she is otherwise free, but as she serves no useful purpose, if something more worthwhile comes along she will accept it. She tries always to attend the Cenotaph ceremony to honour the dead of the last two World Wars.

Each engagement is looked at from the point of location. For instance, when a number came from Nottingham it was possible to arrange six different engagements in the area in one single day. The Princess first opened the new extension at East Midlands Airport, went on to lunch at the Council House with local dignitaries, later unveiled statuary in the Old Market Square of Nottingham, visited

a Save the Children Fund shop, attended a buffet at the County
Hall and in the evening attended a Gala at the Theatre Royal,
before returning home to Gatcombe. As usual, each venue was
investigated long before Princess Anne even saw the invitation,
ensuring that the Princess did not find herself unintentionally
involved in any commercial or political scheme.

The final completed list, which is like a major jigsaw to compile,
provides a daunting insight into the number of official duties that
any member of the Royal Family undertakes. Only one or two a
month will be reported in the national press, yet in any given month
Princess Anne could have as many as 50 engagements. In one
afternoon she can unveil a plaque, make a speech which she will
have written herself, meet patients at a local hospital, tour an
exhibition, and encounter the inevitable handshakes and walkabouts. Even the simplest programme can involve hundreds of
miles of travel in one day, especially as the Princess likes to be able
to return home each night, no matter how late she finishes, often
driving herself home accompanied only by a detective.

For Princess Anne's Private Secretary, planning her official
duties and foreign tours means far more than filling in blank spaces
in an engagement diary. It frequently involves close liaison with
other members of the Princess's staff and organisers of each event.
Every detail of a royal visit must be planned down to the last
second, every step that the Princess will take will be measured and
counted, and if necessary male officials will don a skirt to establish
in advance that the Princess will be able to negotiate steps or a
gang-plank without difficulty or embarrassment. When Princess
Anne was to visit HMS *Eastbourne* 34-year-old Lieutenant-
Commander Stephen Emberton of Plymouth went through a special rehearsal in drag to ensure that the Princess 'would be able to
negotiate the narrow companion-ways, steep ladders and hatch-
ways in a tight-skirt'. Strangely, nobody ever considers that a
female might stand in for the rehearsal.

Lists of the people that the Princess will meet are compiled, and if
necessary vetted. Questionnaires invariably land on the Private
Secretary's desk from excited hosts, uncertain of the protocol involved in entertaining royalty. Should a cloakroom be set aside?
What kind of bouquet should be presented? Should the royal
standard be flown? Fully accustomed to such missives, the Private
Secretary has a set of stock answers. Yes, a cloakroom should be set
aside – it is unlikely to be used, but one must be made available.

The majority use an existing lavatory, often repaint the walls, put in an antique table or chair and a floral display, others even go to the extremes of changing the actual toilet seat so that the Princess will use something in pristine condition. It will be removed again after the visit. It is said that when Queen Mary used to visit the theatre a special commode was placed in an ante-room near the royal box for Her Majesty's use. On one occasion a cleaner at the theatre, desperate to relieve herself, made use of the commode that was untouched from a royal visit on the previous evening. Theatre staff finding that the convenience had been used, bottled the contents, believing it to be a royal sample!

Small bouquets of flowers that are in season are requested, along with an appeal for the flowers to be taped, not wired. The Queen once cut her hand on a sharply wired posy. The royal standard must only be flown if there is a vertical flagpole available. Food, if the Princess is dining, should be kept simple, nothing too rich, nothing cooked in wine, and hosts are reminded that Princess Anne does not drink alcohol. Buckingham Palace will not provide a list of the Princess's dislikes in food, but request a copy of the suggested menu and will make adjustments accordingly. Attending a recent luncheon for the Save the Children Fund in Bath it was pointed out, for example, that the Princess does not eat celery. Although the Princess does not smoke herself, a concession is made that people can have a cigarette or cigar after dinner without too much objection being raised. The fact that King George VI, her grandfather, died of lung cancer, and Princess Margaret has had lung problems, have probably been a major cause in the Princess's dislike of smoking.

Up to twelve weeks' preparation often goes into a two hour engagement, with draft after draft of the itinerary being drawn up. Who should the Princess meet first? If she visits a hospital, for example, who is the official host? The Health Minister, the Chairman of the Governors, or the Senior Surgeon? Understanding the protocol is an essential part of the Private Secretary's job. He must have a mind like a copy of Debrett's Peerage.

Princess Anne's involvement comes at the beginning and the end. She is there at the six monthly planning meeting to decide which engagements to undertake, and her word is final, at which point her staff will take over the arrangements until a few days before the actual visit when the Princess will do her homework (if necessary) on the project, the people and their achievements, and write a speech if required.

A characteristically informal portrait of Princess Anne painted by Michael Noakes which completely breaks with the tradition of formality in royal portraiture.

An equally informal portrait photograph of Captain Mark Phillips, taken three weeks before the wedding by Norman Parkinson.

Traditional royal glamour for an evening engagement. The Sound of Music
stage preview at the Apollo Victoria in London, 1982.

Above: *a serious moment in the working year at the combined Cavalry Old Comrades parade in Hyde Park, 1984.*

Below: *Princess Anne standing amongst the Children of Courage.*

The president of the Save the Children Fund tours Bangladesh in 1984.

Princess Anne fulfilling one of her many duties as Chancellor of the University of London.

Above: Princess Anne off duty with her children.

Below: Princess Anne and Captain Phillips combining business with pleasure on a visit to Dubai.

The Princess gained admiration from the world's media when she visited a leper colony in the Sudan.

Below: *in discussion about the problems of India.*

After the planning meeting the ladies-in-waiting will get together to work out a rota so that the Princess is attended on each occasion. The Queen's ladies-in-waiting work in strict rotation, with two weeks on duty and two weeks off. Princess Anne allows hers much greater flexibility. Around Princess Anne's own age, some, like her, have children at school and so prefer to have the holidays free. Others may enjoy foreign travel and be prepared to cover a foreign tour, while one may prefer if possible to deal with daytime engagements in London and the Home Counties. Unpaid, other than the reimbursment of expenses, the ladies manage to produce a schedule that keeps Princess Anne happy and fairly shares out the work. Although the Private Secretary and administrative staff are an essential part of Princess Anne's team, the ladies-in-waiting are indispensable. Everyone expects a princess to have a lady-in-waiting, it is probably one of the best known positions in the Royal Household, but they are taken for granted by the public and their role often remains a mystery. This is how they like it; discretion and confidence being the key to any royal employment. Ladies-in-waiting, for example, never upstage Princess Anne, they wear unobtrusive colours to remain low-key, and walk forever in the Princess's shadow to support, advise and smooth over any crisis. They can be seen relieving Princess Anne of coats, bouquets and small gifts pressed into her hand on walkabouts. Of ladies-in-waiting, Princess Anne says, 'they must be good at chatting to people and making them feel comfortable because that helps me really. It's no good at all if you get somebody turning up in the morning looking like death, and furious and ratty about life and uncommunicative and when they go out on a trip they're standing in a corner looking glum and bored. That's no help to anyone, least of all the people at the other end, never mind to me. So it is important that they should be capable of being interested and mixing with the people we meet.' As the Princess's engagement diary has filled, so the number of ladies-in-waiting has increased to seven.

Life for a lady-in-waiting, they insist, is never dull. The Princess has proved to be an amusing travel companion, with her deadpan sense of humour. 'Good God, his flies are undone!' exclaimed the Princess once, looking out of her aircraft window as the Andover of the Queen's Flight touched down in Africa, at the waiting Guard of Honour. Although the Princess kept a straight face at what was to be an 'eye to eye' greeting, her lady-in-waiting admitted that she had to bite her lip. The Save the Children Fund tours abroad can be gruelling, but they too have their lighter sides. The same lady-in-waiting, Sian Legge-Bourke, collects toilet rolls from each place they visit to ensure that she and the Princess have at least one luxury. 'I've nicked them from one embassy and two high commissions,' she says proudly.

From time to time a lady-in-waiting will be required to divert an otherwise embarrassing situation. They learn how to stop the over-zealous member of a reception committee who talks too long and hinders the Princess's progress; can calm the nerves of an anxious host by letting them know how smoothly the arrangements are going and how much the Princess is enjoying the visit; occasionally they can prevent a royal gaffe. Princess Anne has seldom unintentionally put her foot in it or made a public error, which the Queen surprisingly has. At a housing exhibition an enterprising exhibitor laid a piece of red carpet up to his show house, which the Queen and the Duke of Edinburgh unintentionally walked along and had an unscheduled tour. Her lady-in-waiting should perhaps have been more familiar with the royal route. The Queen's biggest *faux pas* probably came on a visit to an artificial insemination unit in 1983 when she pointed to something that she did not recognise and asked what it was. 'It's a cow's vagina, Ma'am,' replied the chairman. 'Ask a silly question,' grinned the Queen.

In May 1985, when Princess Alexandra was visiting St. Michael's Hospice at Bartestree, Herefordshire, she innocently asked a question about the establishment's finances and inquired of consultant Dr. Jeff Kramer, 'Are you well endowed?' Noticing his blushes and the suppressed giggles of the rest of the staff, the Princess's lady-in-waiting steered her swiftly but tactfully towards the ladies' room where they both collapsed with laughter. Another royal embarrassment had been got through.

While the ladies-in-waiting are sorting out their rota, the Private Secretary will begin planning a 'recce' of the venue. He and the Princess's detective will usually visit the area to check the minutiae involved in the planning. Arrangements will be made with the local police for the security of the royal visitor, something that has now become a priority. Although Princess Anne is herself too busy doing her job to be completely aware of the security around her, she is conscious that other people are constantly on the alert and from her own experience in The Mall is fully cognisant of the risks that any public figure takes. While visiting a shopping mall in Bracknell, Berkshire, the police received a telephone call claiming that 'something was going to happen'. Poised and calm, Princess Anne carried out the visit even though at one point a man carrying a gun was arrested only yards from where she was standing. The man was charged by the police and the Princess continued the engagement completely unruffled. 'Life must go on,' the Queen said, apparently unperturbed, after Marcus Sergeant fired blanks at her during the Trooping the Colour ceremony in 1981. But it highlighted the pressures that the Royal Family are forced to cope with and the risks that even the simplest everyday actions pose. If a 'walkabout' is ever part of Princess Anne's programme, every building along the route will be checked, and police marksmen will be in position on top of the highest.

Travel arrangements will be made for the Princess by her Private Secretary through the Crown Equerry at Buckingham Palace, where all the royal cars are kept at the back of the Mews behind the stables. Wherever the Princess travels officially one of the royal cars is always at hand, usually a maroon Rolls-Royce. There are twenty cars for the Family's use, especially adapted with bullet-proof glass in windows which are larger than usual, and raised seats so that the occupant can be seen. Inside each car is a radio, air-conditioning, spotlights, and a large clock. In March 1978 the Society of Motor Manufacturers and Traders presented the Queen with a £60,000 Phantom VI Rolls-Royce to mark her 25 years on the throne. It is 19 feet 10 inches long, weighs almost three tons, and seats seven people with ease. If Princess Anne travels with the Queen this car is put into use.

If Princess Anne is flying or travelling by train this can mean a car going in advance to be there for her arrival. A car even used to travel on board the Royal Yacht *Britannia*, but this practice has been stopped as the salt air of the sea corroded the bodywork. General day-to-day travel poses few problems for Princess Anne – on informal engagements she will frequently drive herself in a private car. It is when she travels further afield that greater co-ordination and planning are needed. The Royal Train is a popular mode of transport, enjoyed by Queen Victoria 135 years ago; it enables the Royal Family to travel at greater speed and comfort (they do not use normal British Rail timetables!) and causes fewer delays for motorists, who are stopped to allow royal cars to pass. There are three Royal Trains used by all members of the Royal Family, though priority obviously goes to the Queen. Each has bedrooms, bathrooms and a sitting-room, where the occupant can work on papers and write speeches, there are telephones with 28 lines, and accommodation for Household staff. For security reasons the Royal Train has been made completely bombproof, capable of withstanding a terrorist missile attack, and with an oxygen supply of its own which can be used independently in the event of a gas attack. Although the trains belong to British Rail, and are therefore paid for out of taxpayers' money, each member of the Royal Family using the train has to reimburse the expenses out of their Civil List income.

For longer journeys Princess Anne is flown by a craft from the Queen's Flight, which consists of three red Andovers and two Westland Wessex helicopters operating from RAF Benson, Oxfordshire. Ever concerned with safety, the Queen's Flight is maintained by over 100 men, 75 per cent of whom are technicians, ready to strip down the engines at a moment's notice. Just as every inch of the track is searched and every tunnel inspected before the Royal Train sets out, so the aircraft are subject to meticulous inspection. When a fault occurred during a flight made by the Queen Mother, the royal passenger had to land while an inspection was carried out. 'Wretched thing!' she exclaimed in her inimitable way, but even though the fault was very minor, no chances were to be taken. The Queen is known to dislike helicopters and to her relief has been advised against travelling in them because of the security risk they impose, not on account of terrorists but engine failure or adverse weather conditions. Likewise the Home Office insist, that no member of the Royal Family travels in a single-engined aircraft. The rule has been broken twice, once when the Queen flew to Northern Ireland by helicopter on her Silver Jubilee tour so that she could be flown away in seconds at any hint of danger, and again on a short trip to France in 1984 for the D-Day Anniversary celebrations. Princess Anne has no qualms about helicopters and those who live and work near Buckingham Palace can frequently see the Princess's helicopter taking off from the gardens at the back of the Palace for another engagement, or returning her late in the afternoon.

Before Princess Anne can use the Queen's Flight she, as does every member of the Royal Family, requires written permission from Her Majesty. Only the Duke of Edinburgh need not officially apply. When they are not being used for royal engagements, government ministers can hire the planes for their official duties. For longer, overseas tours the Princess often flies in a larger passenger jet belonging to British Airways, with added comforts not normally lavished on package tour travellers, although she has been known to travel economy class on an ordinary scheduled flight. In the adapted craft seats are removed to create a dining-room and a sitting-room; bedrooms and dressing rooms can be created if necessary. On a foreign visit, on the other hand, the Princess may use different airlines if her flight is ever paid for by the host country, and those may not always be up to the usual royal standard, as even the Queen has discovered. On one notorious visit to South America Her Majesty had to walk through the crew's cabin to reach the lavatory.

When travelling by air the Queen's Flight is given a 'purple' corridor to prevent any other plane crossing its path, although the Duke of Edinburgh caused a scare in November 1981 when, piloting an Andover, he flew out of royal airspace and missed a jumbo jet carrying 260 passengers by only ten seconds. Princess Anne causes fewer problems, preferring to be a passenger than a pilot. Members of the Royal Household who travel with the Princess suggest that she is much easier to travel with, taking less luggage than probably any other member of the Royal Family. The Queen can take 30 tons. Princess Anne's luggage is practical and uninspiring, certainly not a set of matching suitcases. She doesn't take dressy clothes. 'Anne's the only female royal who is able to undertake a foreign tour and leave her tiara in the wardrobe,' wrote the *Daily Mirror* in 1984 whilst following the African tour. The only distinguishing feature is that Princess Anne's luggage will always bear a green label. English may not be read by luggage handlers in foreign parts, but colours are universal and easily distinguishable.

Amongst clothes packed for a royal tour are usually a black dress, coat and hat suitable for mourning should anything untoward happen, not necessarily back home but in the host country. It was during Princess Anne's tour of Bangladesh and India in 1984 when the Indian Premier, Mrs. Indira Gandhi, was assassinated and keeping her luggage to a minimum, the Princess had to borrow suitable clothes from the British Embassy. If the Princess is on an official state visit, rather than a Save the Children Fund fact-finding mission, a suitable number of evening dresses will be added to the luggage. The official programme, the lengthy document printed as a timetable, will print the required dress for each engagement using the following code:

DJ	Dinner Jacket, Black Tie
LD	Long Dress
U	Uniform
LS	Lounge Suit
DD	Day Dress
TR	Territory Rig
CAS	Casual
T	Tiara
d	Decorations

There can obviously be a combination of symbols wherever necessary, for example, LD T d for an official state banquet. The symbols
are generally used as a source of reference by the staff and press
entourage rather than the Princess herself.

Deciding upon the *right* clothes is an essential part of any royal
visit. For Princess Anne clothes are not of very great interest and
her wardrobe is created to be practical, undatable (if possible) and
therefore long lasting. 'A good suit goes on for ever,' she says. 'If
made properly in the first place and has a sort of classic look about
it, you can go on wearing it *ad infinitum*. Those are the clothes I like.
There's an economic element in it. The economy is bred into me. I
was brought up by my parents and by my nanny to believe that
things were not be be wasted. All my childhood life, and that lesson
does last, there's no question about it. I expect my clothes to last a
long time.'

As she gets older she reveals that she finds clothes more fun. In
earlier years she had an insufficient interest to be the fashion leader
that the Princess of Wales has become, 'so whatever I wore was
obviously going to be bad news.' Although she is perhaps more
daring, certainly in evening wear, than she was a decade ago,
clothes must be 'functional'. Suits for daytime engagements are
particularly so. They look smart, dignified, and if a jacket is part of
the outfit it solves the otherwise clumsy problem of what to do with
a coat on arriving at a function. Either someone has to hold it
throughout (probably a lady-in-waiting) or else it would have to be
put away somewhere, where it would be a security risk, and cause no
doubt an embarrassing fumbling when it was time to put it on again.

Any critics of the royal wardrobe, and Princess Anne has been
criticised sometimes for looking like her mother, forget the limit-
ations that are imposed by the very nature of the work. Apart from
the obvious gangplanks and steps, the blustery wind can play

havoc with a flimsy skirt, so materials have to be relatively heavy in this country. In the hot climates that Princess Anne visits, cotton dresses are essential. To avoid having to duplicate a wardrobe for the sake of the weather, Princess Anne is happy to stick to cotton shirts and jeans, which are far more practical anyway for the foreign tours. Loyalty and trust, as we have seen, are essential to any royal appointment, so when members of the Royal Family find designers that they like, they tend to stick to them. Princess Anne is certainly no exception to this. For private life she will use off-the-peg clothes. Early in the Princess's working life she discovered Maureen Baker of Susan Small (who was later to make her wedding dress), who has now been creating much of the official wardrobe for 20 years. There is a good repartee between the ladies and Princess Anne knows that Miss Baker is able to make up an outfit that she has herself visualised. On her travels Princess Anne frequently buys cloth, perhaps handmade lengths in Africa and Hong Kong, and will bring it back to be made into dresses. In 1984 she was made Honorary President of the British Knitwear and Clothing Export Council, which has expanded her knowledge and interest in clothes, and she now takes a greater degree of interest in the actual manufacture of the garments. As President of the Council she visits a number of clothing factories throughout the year and seldom leaves without being presented with a very useful length of material. One of the perks of the job!

Along with the material, a designer will also receive a sketch in the Princess's own hand to provide the basic idea as to how she would like it made up. This will then be developed and modified until a mutually agreeable design can be reached. Apart from Maureen Baker, Princess Anne uses other designers such as Belville Sassoon, John Langberg of Christian Dior, Louis Feraud, Gina Fratini, and more recently Jacques Reiss, a London-based French designer, whose most memorable creation was the '*Dynasty*-style' creation worn for the British Academy Film and Television Awards in 1985, of which fashion editor Jean Dobson says, 'The main features were the huge romantic sleeves, heightening the effect of youth and slenderness. If it had been worn by Diana the collar would have been either demurely high or scooped low. But Anne's was cut like a shirt collar, the concession made by a sporty princess. What made the outfit and the evening such a coup for Anne was that, where the Princess of Wales is well-known to have the undivided attention of a team of fashion experts from Vogue magazine,

Princess Anne has succeeded in capturing the gloss of the catwalk entirely on her own.'

It may have been a triumph for the Princess, but credit must also be due to the designer, who has created a number of stunning outfits in the last two years, including the yellow lace creation that the Princess wore for the wedding of the Duke and Duchess of York. Fifty-one year old Jacques Reiss has one ambition, to get Princess Anne on the list of the Ten Best Dressed Women in the world, but he knows that the person he describes as a 'stubborn lady' has very little chance. 'Clothes are not her prime consideration. If she worked with me, I could do it in two seasons. But at the same time I respect her stand.' He knows that one day she will sparkle in his outfit, but hours later she will be seen wearing a khaki raincoat, headscarf and wellies. To enter the Best Dressed list you have to be consistent, and Princess Anne will never be a slave to fashion. Reiss first met Princess Anne in 1984 when he gave a charity fashion show in aid of The Home Farm Trust for Spastic Children. Princess Anne was the guest of honour as Patron. 'We had a talk before the show and I used all the chutzpah I have. There's one thing that I'd love to do and that is dress *YOU*,' he said to the Princess. He received the enigmatic smile. 'We'll see,' she told him.

Later in the evening he raised the subject again, but Princess Anne was not to be pushed. Some time later, when he had almost forgotten the conversation, he received an unexpected summons from the Princess's office. The first outfit he created was the BAFTA success. Now he makes day and evening wear for the Princess, who he describes as 'a dream to dress'. The main restriction any designer encounters is money. Being royal certainly does not mean *carte blanche* to buy just anything. As much of the wardrobe is paid for out of Princess Anne's private money, the budget must be adhered to. How much the Princess actually pays for an outfit is obviously a matter of some secrecy, but a general average from the charges designers would make for an average client results in approximately £400 for a day dress, £500 for a cocktail dress, and upwards of £1500 for an evening dress. The second restriction is often the battle between the Princess's ideas and the designers'. If Princess Anne doesn't like an idea, then that's the end of the matter. Maureen Baker has been along with a design that she feels is perfect, only to be told, 'I'm not wearing that!' Jacques Reiss knows that the Princess knows exactly what she requires, 'I get so far and then it's curtains.'

Any designer that the Princess employs must also be up with the lark. Dress fittings always take place at Buckingham Palace where her official wardrobe is kept, and usually at around 8.30 in the mornings before her first engagements of the day. The Princess will have been up at dawn, ridden for half-an-hour, and driven from Gatcombe Park to London arriving at around 7 o'clock. She will prepare herself for the day, apply her own make up and clothes for the first official meeting, and be studying papers and the day's agenda before the designer arrives. A dress can take up to four fittings and several may be tried on in one session. The Princess is down-to-earth in her approach and the raising of just one eyebrow can signify to the designer that something is not quite right.

Just as the Princess is loyal to dress designers, so she is faithful to her milliner, John Boyd, who has been making hats for her since she was 17. When Jacques Reiss suggested that he created a hat to match the outfit worn for Prince Andrew's wedding the Princess replied, 'Cobblers!' The Princess hates wearing hats and now wears them for only the most formal of occasions. John Boyd created the first of Princess Anne's wide-brimmed hats, with which she did set a trend in 1969. He also makes hats for Margaret Thatcher and the Princess of Wales. In February 1986, one of John Boyd's hats made the front pages of the tabloids when the Princess wore a beige velvet cap with a large daisy appliqued to the back. It was the big talking point of her visit to the British Equestrian Trade Association exhibition at Sandown Park in Surrey. John Boyd will create around 30 new hat designs each season, and then makes each design in different colours in his Walton Street shop in London, but if any particular design is chosen by the Princess it is withdrawn from public sale.

Shoes cause greater problems because Princess Anne spends so much of her working life on her feet. This means that shoes must be comfortable. This immediately rules out anything fashionable because by the time they have been completely broken in they would be out of date. They cannot have too much of a heel because this can be tiring on the ankles and toes. So the Princess prefers to have a few well-worn comfortable pairs in basic colours that can be co-ordinated with any outfit, much to the despair of dress designers who would like their outfit to be total. A matching pair of shoes would not only be prohibitive in cost, the Princess hates 'spending money on shoes', but would be crippling on the feet. The Queen is often criticised for her flat shoes, and on a visit to Australia the press wrote 'Has The Queen Only Got One Pair Of Shoes?', but when standing or walking for any length of time comfort always takes precedence over fashion.

Princess Anne's crowning glory must be her hair, it is she says a lifetime's work taming it because it is thick and wiry but it was considered to be the best head of hair in the Royal Family, until the Duchess of York's long Titian locks became a rival. Looking at photographs of Princess Anne's hairstyles over the last 20 years displays instantly the versatility that her hair offers, and she generally washes and styles it herself, except for important public functions. Notably the famous BAFTA Awards, where, to compliment Jacques Reiss's evening dress, hairdresser Michael Rasser of Michaeljohn put dramatic pink streaks in her hair. He described the look as 'our private little joke', but it is not something that is likely to be repeated in the future. 'I said: "Let's go a bit nutty" and she agreed, much to my surprise. It is a fun fashion thing, a one-off.' Friends say that Princess Anne became adept at doing her own hair through necessity. When younger she used to share the Court hairdresser with the Queen, which she found frustrating. Her Majesty always took priority and Princess Anne had to wait. As she had been forced to manage her own hair at Benenden, it came as little hardship. Any suggestion that it would be easier to manage in a shorter style is instantly frowned upon. 'Short hair is boring,' she insists. Michael Rasser first styled Princess Anne's hair in 1971 for her twenty-first birthday portraits and has continued to condition and style her hair for important functions since. For practical reasons her hair is kept up during the day in the now familiar fashion.

Deciding what to wear, and how her hair should be styled, depends very much on the type of function that the Princess is attending and often will not be decided until the very last minute. The variety of Princess Anne's public engagements is vast. If it is a visit to one of her charities or medical appointments it can mean being dressed crisply and practically; if it is an invitation from the Services it can mean donning the relevant uniform; for a film premiere it is necessary to provide glamour; if anything connected with the equestrian world something functional is called for. In any one day the Princess can change up to five times depending upon her programme of engagements, ranging from riding hat and jodhpurs for the early morning ride, jeans and sweater for the drive to London, formal suit and hat for the day's visits, with a possible change into a uniform or overalls if it is a factory visit. A further change may be required if she is attending an evening reception, which will be replaced by something more casual at the end of the day for the drive back home. As Buckingham Palace houses her office, it is used as the working base, the home of the wardrobe and the point at which ladies-in-waiting, the private secretary, private detective and the Princess will meet up for the day's itinerary. Princess Anne can frequently be seen in the courtyard of Buckingham Palace with an armful of clothes that she has brought back from Gatcombe to add to the official wardrobe. She uses the appropriately named 'Luggage Entrance' in the courtyard as it is closest to her office on the top floor of Buckingham Palace, above the famous balcony.

Princess Anne may wear many 'hats', both literal and metaphorical, in any one working year, but one appointment has by far eclipsed all others. It is a cause for which she has been lauded, valuable work that she has highlighted, the role for which she has gained the greatest recognition and respect. Since 1982 her patronage of the Save the Children Fund has changed the headlines from 'Princess Sourpuss' to 'The Caring Princess'.

Chapter 7

Working abroad

On 31 October 1986, the Save the Children Fund made the decision not to feed any more people in the Sudan. Wanting to help a nation devastated by famine and lacking the necessary funds to do so causes an agonising situation. Having the finance, being able to provide grain and transport, and knowing when to *stop* giving aid is an equally agonising decision, but there comes a point when, for its own sake, a country must be allowed to stand on its own two feet however much it would like to cling on to the support.

In 1984, after four disastrous harvests, one and a half million people in Western Sudan faced starvation as food supplies ran out. Early in 1985 the Save the Children Fund set up a distribution network in Darfur, the westernmost province, an area twice the size of Britain with only one tarmac road, and began the near impossible task of large-scale food distribution and medical work. The famine was not through total lack of rain, the rains had come on time but by the hand of fate stopped a month too soon. The promise of crops ended as the under-developed plants withered and died. As Princess Anne had said, 'At the end of the day the real answer is in the hands of the Bon Dieu.'

The relief operation was the SCF's largest, using a transport fleet of 137 trucks and 23 Land Rovers. Their object was to provide a distribution of grain to the villages. In conjunction with Oxfam an appeal was made to British and United States governments that four million people would starve if something was not done quickly to feed them. Not only did the Sudan have its own famine, but refugees from neighbouring countries continued to pour in, swelling the numbers. By early 1986 the Save the Children Fund teams had managed to control the problems of severe malnutrition, overcrowding and disease. Gradually people returned to their own country, reducing the numbers, hopefully to plant their own crops. SCF staff set up a camp at Umbala near the Western border to accommodate some 20,000 refugees from neighbouring Chad, and training programmes began.

There is an old saying which goes, 'Give a man a fish and you feed him for a day; teach a man to fish and you feed him for a lifetime.' A large-scale health programme involving immunisation, and education in basic hygiene can go part of the way to aiding survival, even though the fundamental causes of the disaster remain.

The Save the Children Fund is Britain's largest international children's charity, founded in 1919 by a teacher called Eglantyne Jebb. She died on 6 May 1978, at nearly 80 years old, but the principles which she envisaged are still strongly adhered to. In 1923 she drafted the 'Rights of the Child', which still form the basis for the fund's work:

1   The Child must be protected beyond and above all considerations of race, nationality or creed.

2   The Child must be cared for with due respect for the family as an entity.

3   The Child must be given the means requisite for its normal development, materially, morally and spiritually.

4   The Child that is hungry must be fed, the child that is sick must be nursed, the child that is mentally or physically handicapped must be helped, the maladjusted child must be re-educated, the orphan and the waif must be sheltered and succoured.

5   The Child must be the first to receive relief in time of distress.

6   The Child must enjoy the full benefits provided by social welfare and social security schemes, must receive a training which will enable it, at the right time, to earn a livelihood, and must be protected against every form of exploitation.

7 The Child must be brought up in the consciousness that its
   talents must be devoted to the service of its fellow men.

These are the overriding principles which govern every aspect of
the Fund's work, and 'The Rights of the Child' are frequently
referred to in any speech given by Princess Anne as the President.

It was in 1970 that the Princess agreed to take on the role of
President. Although the Fund was founded by a woman, the Princess is the only female to hold this office out of the six presidents
since 1919. Save the Children has to raise £75,000 *a day* to maintain
its commitment to children in need in the 50 countries where
mother and child health services, nutrition schemes, immunisation
campaigns and emergency relief are carried out. Princess Anne's
presidency creates invaluable publicity for fund-raising events, her
visits abroad to the various projects are great morale boosters for
fieldworkers, and her attendance at numerous events throughout
the year provide the essential funds. Her visits abroad have taken
her to Nepal, East Africa, the Middle East, Pakistan, West Africa,
Morocco, India, Bangladesh, Mozambique and the Sudan. Less
publicised are her visits to projects in the United Kingdom, from
the launching of an Asian Health Campaign in 1984 to visiting
gypsy families in Hammersmith.

The Save the Children Fund headquarters is housed in Camber-
well, London, at Mary Datchelor House. Once a school, the building, naturally opened by the Princess, still has the air of an educational establishment about it, with its plain corridors, with offices
(once classrooms) off them. To enter, the door has to be opened for
you by the receptionist, for security reasons, and it is seldom the
kind of charity worker you would expect to encounter at the reception desk. A burly, bearded man who would look at home on a
rugby pitch, or behind the wheel of Land Rover in Africa, answers
the telephone which rings ceaselessly, and deals with the constant
stream of visitors. The only tranquil part of the building is the
library, which again has the air of a school library, which as well as
having books and files on every aspect of the Fund's work has a
comprehensive collection of press cuttings on Princess Anne's activities as President, in this country and overseas, plus tapes of radio
interviews given by the Princess and video recordings of coverage of
her visits to both overseas and UK projects.

Here there is a department for every aspect of the Fund's work,
from finance to publicity. Whatever their function, every single

department has nothing but praise and admiration for the work that Princess Anne undertakes. She provides the inspiration that is essential to the Fund's work. Talk to any field worker, or 'inhabitant' of Mary Datchelor House and you find total dedication to their work and to their President, yet few are in awe of the Princess and treat her rather as a charity worker than as a member of the Royal Family.

This becomes apparent at the Save the Children Fund Annual General Meeting which the Princess chairs. At the Royal Albert Hall (which must almost seem like a second home to Princess Anne from the number of engagements that she attends there in any one year – see Appendix IV) on 21 October 1986, some 6000 branch members from all over the British Isles, having come as far afield as the Hebrides and Northern Ireland, gathered for the 67th AGM. It was the first time a Save the Children Fund AGM had been held at the Albert Hall since the very first in 1919. Then, on 19 May, Eglantyne Jebb spoke to 8,000 supporters. Twenty-five year-old Elizabeth Woodburn had been present at that meeting and made no concession to age in supporting the Fund 67 years on, aged ninety-two.

The day-long meeting was staged with the panache of a political party conference, with a large video screen dominating the stage so that everyone could see the speakers in close-up, and with an equally worthy slogan for the day of 'MAKING A GROWING IMPACT', which was to be the text of several speeches. Here the Princess is treated as any chairman might be. It is the Save the Children Fund's day and she attends as President, not as a royal guest. There are no fanfares, no words of introduction, no visible security, and no obvious lady-in-waiting in attendance. At exactly 10.30 am the Princess appeared from behind the screen in a business-like fashion, and opened the meeting. 'I can hear a little rustling so I assume someone's out there . . .' she began, blinded by the powerful lights and unable to see further than the inevitable press contingency who had been suitably cordoned off at the front of the stage.

In her five-minute opening address Princess Anne confided, 'I had a seriously bad day yesterday, a typical Monday morning when nothing went right. I went racing at Chepstow in the afternoon, that wasn't good either . . . but at the end the sponsors gave a me a cheque for the Save the Children Fund, which improved things enormously.' There is little that she is not prepared to do, within reason, if it will raise money for the Fund and it was with obvious pride that she revealed that the total income for 1986 had been £43.3 million. Donations had actually been down by £6 million for the year, following a decline in the momentum that the previous year's Band Aid/Live Aid appeals had set up, actually causing an increase in monetary gifts to all charities through their conscience-pricking approach, but the overall income had been increased. This was aided by an increased government grant from £2.8 million to £5.4 million for the Save the Children Fund in Africa. Legacies were up by 14 per cent, and obviously interest was made on money waiting to be spent. The full total reflects financial income only; from foreign governments come gifts in kind of grain, lorries and equipment. Of the money received the Fund set aside 15 per cent for overheads and administration, leaving 85 pence in every pound for the children. In reality, explained Treasurer Richard Brandt, 90 pence in the pound is used to save the children.

Princess Anne may have joked that Monday 20 October had been a bad day, but it had been a sad day with the death of President Machel of Mozambique, whom she had visited only months earlier. In a country severely disrupted by conflict, the Fund had worked with Mozambique's Ministry of Health on an expanded programme of immunisation, assistance with health education, nutrition, assistance of disabled children and support of social welfare. The Princess expressed concern that without President Machel's co-operation the Fund's work could be severely hampered in the future.

In the afternoon Princess Anne gave her annual report and spoke of her recent visit to Tanzania, Zambia, the Sudan and Zanzibar on a fact-finding mission. 'I go with an open mind,' she said, as she has done so many times before. Health, hygiene and nutrition were the three main areas that needed to be continually worked at in all countries she explained. 'There is no room for complacency. The need is always there.' Surprisingly the need exists in Britain, with some three million children growing up below the poverty line. In our enlightened age the gap between the rich and the poor is widening and the role of the Save the Children Fund in the United Kingdom is to deal with the poorest members of the community and attempt to change the environment in which they live, which is the root of the problem in many cases.

Speakers throughout the day praised Princess Anne's contribution to the Fund's work. Nicholas Hinton, the Director General, outlined how the Princess has the ability and the position to *demand* for rights, she sees that where necessary red tape is cut to provide a better future for the children. Coming to the end of his five-year term of office, retiring Chairman Giles Witherington praised the 'tireless contribution of the Fund's President. During the past year Her Royal Highness's involvement has become yet more varied. The Princess has chaired two of the seminars in the significant series run by Save the Children on *Prospects for Africa*. She had addressed a capacity audience at a Chatham House Conference, and has spoken to a yet larger Institute of Directors meeting at the Albert Hall. These engagements have been in addition to visits to many SCF projects in the UK, many fund-raising events and a major African tour.'

It was four o'clock when the meeting ended light-heartedly with a game of *Any Questions* chaired by television personality David Jacobs – but nevertheless raising relevant topics for conversation and discussion. Princess Anne had been at the Albert Hall for six-and-a-half hours, her involvement had been total throughout. Outside the rain fell gently. Only the most observant of passers-by noticed that soon after 4.15 pm police outriders formed a subtle break in the Kensington traffic and the Princess's car slid discreetly back to Buckingham Palace, where she changed from her crisp white dress into evening attire, and made final adjustments to a speech, before attending a Farmers' Club dinner in the evening. Earlier in the day Giles Witherington had quoted the late Sir Noël Coward, 'Work is much more fun than fun'. Princess Anne smiled in agreement.

Princess Anne agreed to accept the Presidency of the Save the Children Fund very early in her working life after the retirement of Viscount Boyd of Merton in 1970. It was a personal choice, and one that she considered very carefully before accepting. 'I think what really decided me to accept the Presidency . . . was that I'd had quite a few invitations to become patron of various institutions, and I think "Patron" is a frightfully vague office and that the office of "President" gives the idea of doing something more definite. I don't think children really came into my original thoughts about it, not necessarily because I like children – if you've got two small brothers that isn't the first thing that enters your head, but I think it is a tremendous work to do because they are a very important age-group and they need a lot more help than possibly later. If they can get a good start, it is very encouraging for them. I hope I have accepted it for the right reasons.' This statement was made soon after accepting the position and it is interesting that the decision was not made initially because it was a children's charity. Some would have found it hard to refuse *because* it was for children, but Princess Anne looked at them more as the next generation. The children of today are the adults of tomorrow. To improve the quality of human life and promote our survival it is essential to concentrate on the young. 'What you are really after,' she says, 'is to give them a chance of survival.'

Although the majority of Princess Anne's engagements for the Fund are in the United Kingdom, it is on foreign tours that she gets involved with the Fund's most important work and witnesses at first hand how the money she helps raise is used. Amongst the heart-breaking sights that she is faced with Princess Anne gains comfort from seeing children who are alive only as a result of the Fund. Many are underfed and unbelievably tiny, but they have a future that would otherwise be denied them. Many recall how the Queen fought back the tears at seeing Jamail in a nutrition unit in Dhaka, a pathetic wasted baby, reaching out to touch her hand. The photograph, syndicated around the world, plucked at a million heartstrings and money flooded in. On her tour a year later, Princess Anne saw Jamail, having won his battle against tuberculosis and playing happily in the sunshine. Without the Fund he would have been another mortality statistic. Jamail's mother took hold of Princess Anne's hand and squeezed it. No words were necessary.

Few meetings are as happy. For every baby that Princess Anne sees alive perhaps a 100 more will die. In Bangladesh she looked down on a tiny baby wrapped in bandages, with a drip from his arm. 'How old is he?' she asked, and appeared shocked when she heard that he was four months old. The baby was tiny for four-months she said, but Princess Anne had not caught what the doctor had said. The baby was 24 months. 'Two years old?' she gasped almost in disbelief, and looked back at the lifeless bundle, too weak even to cry. The bravest amongst them struggled not weep.

The Save the Children Fund have projects underway in Africa, Asia and the Americas, more specifically in Ethiopia, Gambia, Kenya, Lesotho, Malawi, Mali, Morocco, Mozambique, Somalia, Sudan, Swaziland, Tanzania, Uganda, Zimbabwe, Bangladesh, Hong Kong, India, Kampuchea, Laos, Lebanon, Nepal, Pakistan, Philippines, Sri Lanka, Thailand, Vietnam, Colombia, Fiji, Honduras, Papua New Guinea, and Peru, all of which the Princess has visited as President (see Appendix III) but it was not until her visit to Nepal in 1981 and Africa in 1982 that people really began to sit up and take notice.

In Nepal the Princess spent ten days visiting the SCF's four projects in the foothills and valleys of the Himalayas, which provide basic health care for mothers and children. Around 300 children attend the clinics daily, trekking long distances to do so. Training programmes have expanded to include local people from the nearby villages. Formerly faith healers, they were the people that villagers first turned to. To educate the faith healers about modern practices breaks down the barriers and encourages better hygiene and medical practices. To visit one clinic, Princess Anne had a strenuous four-hour walk through the mountains, proving her stamina – physical and psychological. 'She is always incredibly well-briefed,' says ex-Director-General John Cumber, 'and talks about Third World problems, both practically and philosophically.'

When the Princess set off for a tour of Africa in 1982 it was to be a major turning point, not only for the Save the Children Fund, but for her private life also. In July of that year she visited Canada alone. The press, anxious for a story, latched on to the fact that she had travelled without her husband. Speculation of an imminent divorce filled the papers, and so great was the strain that Captain Phillips felt compelled to issue a statement to explain his absence. 'I am a full-time farmer and am too busy on the farm. I have to make the business pay like anybody else.' The Palace Press Office constantly told reporters, not for the first time, that Mark Phillips receives nothing from the Civil List and does not officially undertake royal duties. At the end of July Captain Phillips said, 'This week has been one of the worst I have experienced.' Further sensations occurred with reports that he was having an affair with TV personality Angela Rippon, the two having collaborated on a book about horses. The Princess's character was blackened when she visited Blandford in September and allegedly ignored children waiting in the rain to see her. Truth or media myth? Whatever the image, all was to change in October with the gruelling tour of eight countries in three weeks, covering 14,000 miles, working from 7.30 in the morning, often until midnight. The press who accompanied her could have nothing but admiration at the end of it. From Swaziland, through Zimbabwe, Malawi, Kenya, Somalia, Djibouti, North Yemen, to Beirut, the Princess was not always happy with the media, but this time it did little to destroy their admiration. Visiting the Victoria Falls she found herself surrounded by photographers, which she suffered in silence before snapping 'Can I go and look at the Falls now, please?' Yet by the end of the tour she did comment on the changing attitude towards herself. 'I noticed that I'd undergone a miracle cure.'

'Her commitment to her job sometimes comes as a surprise to people,' said John Cumber. 'Unless they've met her, our people don't know what to expect, and tend to pitch the explanations of their work at the sort of level any layman could understand. But she knows her stuff all right and they find that they have to pitch it at a much higher level.' A local aide said that Princess Anne insisted on hearing every aspect of the field work 'warts and all'. When presented with a calabash pipe by the native people she took a puff, although it was later rumoured to be filled with a brand of marajuana. In Swaziland she was nicknamed 'Child of the King' and in Somalia mothers held up their sick babies to be blessed by the sight of a princess. A Save the Children Fund official said, 'We are not counting the press cuttings, we're weighing them!'

In Swaziland she toured an immunisation centre where polio and typhoid are being fought. 'They are in the middle of nowhere, no doctor, two nurses and a handyman who is a well-meaning dogsbody,' she said later. She visited Project Zondle which enables 14,000 people in one area to receive a hot meal daily. In Zimbabwe she saw children so crippled that they pull themselves along by their fingers, dragging their bodies behind them. In Malawi there was a rabies epidemic, in Somalia she saw a camp with 40,000 refugees. It was a long and punishing schedule.

PRINCESS ANNE'S ITINERARY

Sunday 24 October	Arrives Swaziland
Monday 25 October	Visits: Emkhuzweni Health Centre and District Cold Store Immunisation teams at Nkomazi Primary School
Tuesday 26 October	Visits: Swazi SCF Kitchen, Mbabane Save the Children Fund Offices

Wednesday 27 October	Visits: King Subhuza Clinic and Cold Store Leaves Swaziland Arrives Zimbabwe
Thursday 28 October	Visits: Jairos Jiri Centre for the Physically Handicapped
Friday 29 October	Visits: Bindura Training Centre
Saturday 30 October	Visits: (Binga) Kariyangwe Training Centre (Primary Health Care) Mobile Maternity Child Health Care Clinic Site at Lubu
Sunday 31 October	Rest Day
Monday 1 November	Leaves Zimbabwe Arrives Malawi Visits: Save the Children Headquarters – Malawi Against Polio Section
Tuesday 2 November	No SCF
Wednesday 3 November	Visits: Save the Children Cold Store Mitundi Nutrition Centre SCF Village Rural Site (Immunisation)
Thursday 4 November	Leaves Malawi Arrives Kenya
Friday 5 November	Visits: Starehe Boys' Centre and School
Saturday 6 November	No SCF
Sunday 7 November	Leaves Kenya Arrives Somalia
Monday 8 November	Visits: SCF HQ Boroma
Tuesday 9 November	Visits: Boroma Refugee Camp Leaves Somalia Arrives Djibouti

Wednesday 10 November	Leaves Djibouti Arrives North Yemen
Thursday 11 November	Visits: Rawdah Clinic (Primary Health Care)
Friday 12 November	Leaves North Yemen Arrives Beirut Visits Bourj-el-Barajneh Clinic Leaves Beirut Arrives London

Half-way through the tour she received a communiqué from the Foreign Office in London urging her to cancel the remainder of the tour. War between Ethiopia and Somalia flared up once again, but the Princess refused to cancel any of the itinerary (reputedly saying, 'Damn them, I'm going!') and undertook a five-hour drive over bumpy dirt tracks to fulfil her intended mission. By now she had the media's total admiration. Apparently unperturbed by the war zone, she did admit to being frightened by one of the drivers. Totally against the government's wishes she visited the Boroma refugee camp, just five miles from the Ethiopian border. Despite the dust, heat, mosquitos and general discomfort she was spared nothing.

A later stopover in Johannesburg was almost cancelled when the South African media attempted to involve the Princess in propaganda, announcing her arrival as full acceptance of the apartheid system. Before she landed in Zimbabwe test pilots were arrested at gunpoint on a charge of spying. The one aspect of the tour which won universal admiration was Princess Anne's decision to spend a day in Beirut the day after 62 people had been killed by a bomb which had destroyed the Israeli military headquarters in Tyre, and despite the civil war which had killed hundreds of civilians. She toured the Lebanese capital for ten hours, passing through some of the worst hit areas, visiting refugee camps and medical centres, and had an audience with President Gemayel.

The courage that Princess Anne displayed in the face of obvious danger can be seen as a landmark in her relationship with the press and the resulting reports that were to change her image. 'She is a royal rose,' wrote one journalist. 'What a difference a smile makes,' declared the *Daily Express*, choosing to print a picture of happiness in place of their usual grim choice. Commenting on her often serious expression, the Princess says: 'I have to keep an intelligent interest in what is going on, and it is difficult, I always think, to take an intelligent interest *and* wear a grin.'

On her return she had lost several pounds in weight through picking at her food and drinking Coca Cola, but looked healthier and the press quickly noted that it would be 'a treat for Mark'. Whether or not he approved of the weight loss, it was a positive comment on their marriage for the first time in months.

Of the tour Princess Anne said of her role, 'As President, quite apart from the fact that it helps to see what they are doing and how the thing is really working, one of the few things I suppose I can achieve is publicity, and that's not blatant in the sense that I'm going around banging the drum, but if it has that effect so much the better because that is something that I can do reasonably quietly and still bring people's attention to what is going on.'

The following year, 1983, at the beginning of May, she visited Pakistan on the way back from Japan and Hong Kong, and this time the media men who had joined the earlier tours in the hope of finding something sensational, but not necessarily benevolent, to write were eager to attend. Since covering the visit, television journalist Trevor McDonald has become a keen supporter of the Save the Children Fund and happily took part in the *Any Questions* quiz at the 1986 AGM. Whether or not his admiration increased his patriotism we do not know, but he was later to make a television programme about the Queen and the Commonwealth, for which Her Majesty provided much of the commentary – a rare television coup considering that the Queen never grants an interview with journalists.

Just prior to Princess Anne's visit seven Fund workers had been kidnapped in Ethiopia by the Tigrai People's Liberation Front, and so security for the royal visitor to Pakistan was more than usually tight. The Fund has been providing medical supervision in Pakistan since 1980 and community health workers are recruited from refugees to provide help for 2½ million people. Local women are trained as midwives and birth attendants, so that out of over 7000 people concerned with health and community care, less than 30 are from the Save the Children Fund. This is the Fund's aim, to achieve a longer lasting effect they need not only to give what help they can themselves, but to train the local people so that care will continue indefinitely.

This tour had been different for Princess Anne in that she was accompanied by Captain Phillips. Would this have been so had there not been adverse press reports about their relationship? 1983 was to be an eventful year for them both and they were to be seen together publicly more than in previous years. Princess Anne was seen playing bingo, and she and Captain Phillips visited the Moulin Rouge in Paris where topless dancers performed, even though modestly attempting to cover themselves with ostrich feathers. In the equestrian field Princess Anne was unable to compete at Badminton, after selling her favourite horse, Stevie B. Captain Phillips competed on Classic Lines in an attempt to win Badminton for the fifth time but was thrown during the cross-country. It was not to be a successful year for them. Captain Phillips sustained two injuries, to his shoulder and leg, from falls. Every horse in the Gatcombe Park stables contracted influenza. In April when Captain Phillips was competing at Hagley one of the riders, 17-year-old Rebecca Weston, was killed in a fall, and three weeks later a girl was murdered during the Amberley Horse Trials at Cirencester.

1984 was to be far more successful for Princess Anne when she visited Gambia and the Upper Volta (now Burkina Faso) in West Africa, the poorest regions in the world and said to be the toughest tour ever to have been undertaken by any member of the Royal Family. Before she could depart, the Princess subjected herself to a course of nine potentially dangerous injections – inoculations for meningitis, rabies and hepatitis. The Hepatitis B vaccine is thought by some doctors to be more harmful than the disease itself, but there were no obvious side effects. Having spent five days in the cold of Sarajevo at the Yugoslavian-based Winter Olympics watching speed-skating, the British bobsleigh team, ice hockey and ice dancing, she travelled 9000 miles to the dusty heat of Africa to visit areas that had not seen a drop of rain for over a decade. 8500 miles of the journey consisted of a series of short flights in an Andover of the Queen's Flight, followed by a 500-mile drive along almost non-existent roads, to embark on her most ambitious mission. In ten days she was to see some of the most unimaginable sights, ten spaces in her engagement diary that were to leave a lasting impression:

Wednesday 15 February

Princess Anne made a brief visit to Morocco where she toured a Save the Children Fund School near Rabat, a residential primary school for handicapped children. The 124 pupils are taught to make the most of the abilities they have rather than concentrating on their disabilities. The school is funded to a large extent by the Inner Wheel of Great Britain and Ireland. Orthopaedic equipment, such as calipers are made at an SCF workshop in Casablanca to increase efficiency and ensure that children receive the correct medical help, rather than waiting for the Moroccan government to produce the goods.

After leaving the school, Princess Anne was driven to nearby Rabat to visit the Moroccan Royal Family at the Royal Palace before attending the British Ambassador's dinner in the evening. This first day was little more than a public relations exercise, for visiting the Moroccan Royals ensured goodwill and continued support. Without their co-operation 'you would not stay in the place too long'. About to visit the local people who have nothing, it must be galling for the Princess to dine in palatial splendour out of little more than respect for the country's hosts, when in one small area alone that she was to visit in Africa approximately 4000 people out of a population of 40,000 die each season from malaria.

Thursday 16 February

Leaving Rabat, Princess Anne flew to the Gambia where health care is a vital part of the Fund's work. Primarily the problems are economic, resulting from poor harvests. Bad nutrition, and a poor economy, lead inevitably to ill health, but these were to be comparatively luxurious surroundings compared to the days that lay ahead. In a green and orange dress, complete with hat, the Princess went straight to the British High Commissioner's residence for an informal reception to meet members of the British community. This gave the Princess an opportunity to discuss the country's problems and the work of the Fund. A restful day, it gave her the opportunity to prepare herself mentally.

Friday 17 November

Having risen early the Princess visited the British-backed Medical Research Council laboratories at Fajars, also visiting the outpatients clinic, at 9.00 am. To honour their royal visitor the people of Banjul presented Princess Anne with the keys to the city. She visited the President of Gambia, Sir Dawda Jawara (and was presented with three kaftans by the President's first wife), before touring the Port of Banjul, and a peanut oil mill. In the evening she changed from an orange flowered dress into a yellow chiffon evening gown to attend a Presidential reception for Independence Day meet Government dignitaries, and the President's second wife. The women present were strangely fascinated by Princess Anne's long white gloves and so began an unexpected new fashion amongst the wealthy.

Saturday 18 February

Gambia's Independence Day. Princess Anne attended a parade in MacCarthy Square, Banjul. She boarded a 700-ton river cruiser the M.V. *Lady Chilel Jawara* named after President Jawara's first wife, where she remained overnight travelling up the Gambia river.

Sunday 19 February

Dressed for action, Princess Anne disembarked at Carrols Wharf wearing a headscarf, cotton shirt, fawn skirt and ankle socks, to begin an 'up country' drive. Already conditions were becoming primitive, with straw huts and fishing as the main 'industry'. She travelled by Range Rover to Buduk to tour a sub-dispensary and health workers' compound. From now onwards it was mud huts and bamboo fences, occasionally a wooden building had a corrugated tin roof. At a school in Buduk the only bell originally came from a bicycle. At Ker Jibel she visited a village well, often the source of health problems, then on to Kuntaur Health Centre and a school at Galleh Manda. The most touching call of the day was to the Allatentu leprosy camp. Here she shook withered stumps that had once been arms and met men and women who could only crawl around on their knees. Some had no arms or feet and were blind. 'Glory to God that you have come to see us,' said 85-year-old Mr. N'Dao, 'You are a wonderful person.'

Princess Anne ate with Save the Children Fund staff at Bansang before being briefed, at her request, on Primary Health Care and their work at Bansang. Finally she was driven to a field station at Basse Santa Su to be briefed on a schistosomiasis research project. It had been an arduous day. On one gruelling five hour journey Princess Anne had helped pull on a rope to bring their car ferry across a river.

Monday 20 February

Having spent the night at Basse Sante Su, a shanty town where many of its inhabitants sleep in the streets, the Princess toured a health centre, then a hospital at Bansang. Here she was told that the overworked staff, who work alongside SCF volunteers, have to perform up to 300 operations a day. On to Kerewan-Samba-Sirra, a village of mud huts, where she met and talked to a health worker. A further village, Madina Umfally, and more discussions on health. After a visit to a health centre at Kudang, the Princess was driven on a rough road for four hours back to Banjul and the luxury of a restaurant meal with the crew of the Queen's Flight, with whom she was to travel the next day.

Tuesday 21 February

In an Andover of the Queen's Flight, Princess Anne was flown to Ouagadougou Airport, the capital of Burkina Faso, and landed unintentionally beside Colonel Gadaffi's own private jet. She was met by Comrade President Sankhara who had come to power in a coup six months earlier. Trained by Gadaffi, Sankhara had a gun in his belt throughout their half hour meeting, for which Princess Anne was required to put her oral French lessons into practice. During the day she visited the US Ambassador in Burkina Faso, the Minister of Health, was briefed by SCF workers on their projects, attended a reception for members of the British community at the Hotel Silmande in Ouagadougou, and later attended a dinner given by the British Ambassador.

Wednesday 22 February

Princess Anne was flown to the heart of Burkina Faso to the desert town of Gorom Gorom where she met thousands of children who faced death within weeks. She saw children who 'look very tired, they have rather old faces' which she described as one of the worst sights on her tour. Here life is in the hands of the weather. If the rains do not come the people starve. Cattle and camels, skeletal in shape, wander slowly around, whilst vultures hover simply waiting for them to die. At the hospital in Gorom Gorom the Princess saw children with spindly legs and pot bellies through lack of food. Those too weak to move lay on rush mats, covered with flies. She brushed the swarming insects from one child's brow, but it was a futile task. 'You *have* to stay remote,' she said, 'or you'd just crack up.'

At Gorom Gorom the roads ended and the Princess continued her journey for nearly three hours bumping across the desert terrain to Dori Hospital, visiting Jonja village on the way. At Dori three children had died prior to her arrival. More were expected to die. All had begged for food until they had starved. Here the full scale of the situation was brought home to all who looked on helplessly. Faith seemed the only answer and even that was in short supply. At one oasis in the desert there was fruit and coconuts, but this was no diet for the famine stricken. Grain was all they could digest. If Princess Anne is ever questioned on the Common Market surplus, the butter mountains, and obscene excess, she points out that the starving do not eat that kind of diet. She ended the day by visiting the Save the Children Fund Nutrition Centre and later had supper with the United States SCF Director to discuss the scenes that she had witnessed.

Thursday 23 February

Unable to sleep, Princess Anne got up at 6.15 am. An hour later her party began the three-hour drive to visit the Save the Children Fund team at Sebba, described as the most desolate village on the tour. There the Princess looked at the school and the Health Clinic. Less than two hours later she began a five-hour drive to reach a deserted airstrip from where she flew back to Ouagadougou to visit the US Ambassador.

Friday 24 February

A light day after the rigours of Thursday. She attended a farewell reception at the United States Embassy before taking a 6½ hour flight from Ouagadougou to Banjul. At midnight she caught a British Caledonian Airways scheduled flight arriving at Gatwick Airport at 7.00 am, British time. She had been flying for almost 20 hours but she drove herself home to Gatcombe Park, refusing to be chauffeur driven.

On her return 40 Members of Parliament tabled a Commons motion to pay tribute to Princess Anne's courage; the Save the Children Fund were overwhelmed by her stamina, calls were sounded suggesting that she should be given the title of Princess Royal, the press called her a 'latter day Florence Nightingale' and proudly announced that her image had been 'de-naffed'. For the Princess it had all been part of the job, but it was an area of the work that has held a great fascination. She feels that she is doing something worthwhile, and the people that she meets often have no idea who she is. A royal Princess means nothing to them, all that matters is that this white lady with her hair tied back is obviously concerned and offers something that is in short supply – hope. To many she seems like a saint, but the realistic Princess knows that she merely represents the hard work that the Fund volunteers carry out, knowing that however hard she works herself, the work will always be inadequate. There is always more to do.

If Princess Anne had not visited any of the country's poorest areas again, after her African tour nobody would have condemned her. To be confronted by death and disease is not easy for anyone, but scarcely had she returned than it was announced that she would visit India and Bangladesh in the autumn. What spurs the Princess on is that projects she saw beginning are now achieving their aims; each time she returns she witnesses the progress made and knows that the work is not in vain. Although the greatest credit must go to Fund workers, the results are due to people from all walks of life. In Bangladesh Princess Anne was to see British Airways pilots knee deep in human excreta digging a latrine, and stewardesses painting the walls of an orphanage that is maintained only by donations. British Airways alone have raised over £500,000; Townswomen's Guilds in Britain have been raising £750,000 so that another nutrition unit can be established. It takes time, money, hard work.

The benefits that Princess Anne can bring to the Fund are often unexpected. Her visits are a morale booster, certainly, but journalist Stephen Lynas who accompanied Princess Anne on the 1984 tour reported that negotiations were going on in Bangladesh for a new nutrition unit. The price was £200,000 and no amount of discussion by the Fund workers could reduce the figure. The day after Princess Anne had visited the site, the government reduce the figure to £40,000.

In October 1984 the Princess visited three projects in Bangladesh, and met living examples of the Fund's success, and even though admissions to the health unit had risen by 30 per cent they could still claim a 95 per cent success rate. She saw flood recovery programmes, which are ironically necessary. In some areas she visits there has been no rain for ten years and the people starve, in others, as in Bangladesh, the monsoons come and rural areas in the north suffer as the Jamuna river breaks its banks destroying crops. Too much water can be as devastating as too little.

Princess Anne had undertaken a dangerous drive through the Himalayan foothills to a school for Tibetan refugees when rumours began to circulate of a tragedy in Delhi. The Princess still had 11 more full days of the tour left and was anxious to visit every possible venue on the agenda. She was appearing more relaxed than on any other tour, having seen noticeable improvements since her previous visit. She rode camels, ate hot curries, chatted to a witch doctor, and watched, with delight, previously sick children dancing in her honour. There was still so much more to do. Talking animatedly to the Tibetans, a member of her party whispered that Mrs. Gandhi had been assassinated. A momentary look of shock appeared in her eyes, then she smiled and returned to her conversation betraying no hint of the imminent repercussions that were bound to result when news of the murder became common knowledge.

She had flown to India to see the promotion and strengthening of human life, and within 48 hours she was to be standing beside the corpse of Indira Gandhi, whose life had been brought to an untimely end by a hail of 37 bullets. It was also a swift conclusion to what had looked to be Princess Anne's most successful and positive tour. Within hours of the funeral she boarded an Andover of the Queen's Flight and was flown to safety.

Standing next to the British Prime Minister, Mrs. Margaret Thatcher, at what was for them a strange and awesome funeral as Mrs. Gandhi's son Rajiv lit his mother's funeral pyre and later raked through her ashes, Princess Anne must have contemplated the vulnerability of key figures. The contrasts of a life being brought to a deliberate end whilst she had been attempting to save the lives of the poverty-stricken children must have been only too apparent. She must have been conscious too of the babies she had seen dying unnoticed, unmourned, and yet here the death of one woman rocked the world and caused riots. If people could become as emotional and frantic about the starving perhaps more would be done to help.

Disappointed at the curtailment of her tour, Princess Anne remained undaunted and in good spirits, and just over a month later she embarked on a tour of the Middle East after a promise of £20,000 for Save the Children was made. The offer was not without conditions and Princess Anne immediately rose to the challenge and took Mark with her to make sure that they fulfilled the necessary requirements. The offer of £20,000 was really a bait to get the Princess back in an arena on horseback, and although she was out of practice in competitive riding she had no intention of turning down any kind of help for the cause so close to her heart. It seemed almost a means of paying off the debt she owed the Fund by failing to complete the Indian tour, even though it was through no fault of her own. A show was organised at which Anne and Mark were to be the star attraction, but it was to be no ordinary event for the Arabs are noted for their steeds and their horsemanship.

Anne and Mark had been apart for some time owing to their various duties and even when they visited Los Angeles for the 1984 Olympic Games they had to stay in separate hotels, leading to rumours once again that their marriage was on the rocks. When Anne returned from India, Mark was fulfilling commitments in Australia and New Zealand and so the invitation to visit Dubai and Abu Dhabi provided an excellent opportunity to spend some time together, which gave a welcome slap in the face to those speculating about their relationship. The couple spent the first two days alone enjoying one another's company, not for the benefit of the media but simply because they had spent so much time apart that they wanted to be together. They had been offered separate accommodation, separate because the royal princess was invited to stay at a sultan's palace, but Princess Anne shunned luxurious splendour and instead joined Mark in an hotel.

This was to be no ordinary equestrian event and for the second richest country in the world the £20,000 offered to the Save the Children Fund was a mere drop in the ocean. Although Anne and Mark had to work very hard against a number of top international riders, their task was made all the more enjoyable by the sheer luxury lavished upon them. Five British horses were sent to the Gulf by ship at a cost of £50,000 and a £130,000 six-doored golden Rolls-Royce was put at their disposal. As Princess Anne sat down at the breathtaking banquets held in her honour, far more exotic than any state dinner at Windsor apart from the absence of alcohol, it must surely have crossed her mind that it would have been far more beneficial to raise the donation to £200,000 and cut out all the theatricality. But the extravaganza was all that the Arab sheiks were interested in. They had tempted the Queen's only daughter to their country and they were going to make the most of the sport. The equestrian event began with spectacular parades, parachute jumping, and carefully selected 'British' brass bands to give that 'royal' touch, but for Princess Anne the main concern was doing well in the dressage display. She need not have worried, for with Mark's encouragement and very protective attitude towards his wife, Anne disappointed no one and with an almost faultless per-

formance under the blazing Dubai sun she won a silver cup. Both
husband and wife beamed with pleasure and relief as they were
congratulated by the President of the United Arab Emirates, Sheik
Zayed.

Princess Anne's visit to Dubai coincided with 'British Week' and
the working Princess quickly organised herself a programme of
visits to occupy her time. Despite the splendour of the gilded
palaces this was not going to be a holiday by any means and she was
soon visiting all the local industrial plants which are manned by
British engineers and workmen. Mark accompanied her wherever
she went and to both it must have been reminiscent of their honeymoon, when Mark was first introduced to the royal way of life. Both
were already well sun-tanned (Anne from the Indian sun and Mark
from his earlier visit to Australia) and made a very handsome
couple, although Arab law dictated that the Princess always wore
long-sleeved high-necked dresses and white gloves whilst in this
male-dominated community Mark was allowed to sunbathe and
wear short-sleeved shirts without question or offence. When the
Queen visited the Gulf States in 1979 she wore long dresses
throughout the tour (royal watchers noted that they were
shortened and used again on her return to Britain) a concession
that Princess Anne did not make, wearing her dresses at mid-calf
length.

As Anne and Mark toured the Gulf States moving from Dubai on
to Sharjah and then to Abu Dhabi, the Princess visited as many
schools and children's charities as possible, genuinely interested in
their work and progress, her quick brain making comparisons with
other similar organisations that she had visited around the world.
Of all the splendours that she saw, there is one moment that has left
a stronger image in her mind than any other, more impressive than
any show of wealth. At the Aseef School for Physically and Mentally Handicapped Children a bouquet was presented. There is nothing extraordinary to the Princess about receiving flowers, but this
one was presented to her by a tragically crippled 12-year-old girl
who could only walk with the aid of a metal frame. Knowing that
Anne was a royal princess the little child was determined to curtsy:
despite the pain and severe disabilities she insisted that the metal
frame be taken away and bringing a lump to Princess Anne's
throat, the girl curtsyed. A simple act which took courage and
determination. Princess Anne had provided the necessary inspiration to make the apparently impossible happen. If money and

research can help these children then Princess Anne will go to the ends of the earth to get it.

After an exhausting tour, Anne and Mark returned home to the cold British winter and the chill of the journalists' words when they missed Prince Harry's christening. Few people in Britain were aware that Princess Anne had been abroad; the world knew that she did not attend the baptism. This is something that she has learnt to contend with, but it seldom gets any easier. That Christmas gifts appeared in royal stockings from the Arab souks and bazaars, local craftwork given with all the warmth of the Arab sun.

In February she returned to India to fulfil her promise to relief workers that she would return. In Calcutta she witnessed poverty that brought Kipling's image of the 'city of dreadful night' to reality. She was taken to one of India's poorest states, Orissa, to see the work of the relief agencies. At a family planning clinic she watched a sterilisation operation without flinching. It is said that the work of the Save the Children Fund achieves results slowly, almost unnoticeably, never overnight, but they are long-term results and far reaching; Princess Anne, in her own way, achieves instantaneous results. On this brief visit to India an anonymous donor gave a cheque for £50,000, money that would not have come in had she not been present. With extra funds, the SCF have been able to establish a variety of projects in India, irrigation and water schemes, low level village agricultural development aid and agricultural improvements, set up hostels for remote and migratory tribal children, establish children's crèches, mother and child clinics, Balwadis (kindergartens), train health staff, develop the handicapped children's project, offer postgraduate training for development workers, as well as providing feeding schemes and disaster relief. With a little extra money and a great deal of inspiration, much can be achieved.

In India and Bangladesh Princess Anne has seen the problem facing slum dwellers, where villages become overcrowded by migrating destitute families. If poor dwellings are overcrowded and without water or adequate latrines, disease takes hold. An 'outreach' programme has meant that the Save the Children Fund can now provide health care for over 1000 slum-dwelling families. There are three clinics with visiting health workers in one area of south-west Bangladesh where simple distribution of vitamin A tablets has prevented nutritional blindness, 88 per cent of mothers have received anti-tetanus vaccines, and over 80 per cent of the children have now been immunised. Children in various communities have been encouraged where possible to tend their own small vegetable plots. Here new vegetables can be introduced, which not only provides instructional help to the next generation in the planting of crops, but gives added nutrition in the diet.

At the end of 1985, the year in which the plight of Africa and especially Ethiopia had been constantly highlighted in the media, Princess Anne went back to Africa, to Tanzania, Mozambique, Zambia, and the Sudan. Her tour receiving less publicity than the Band Aid appeal, *The Times* wrote on the eve of it: 'Princess Anne will carry on long after Geldof has returned to his full-time rockery'.

This time Princess Anne was to spend almost a month visiting the four countries, the climax of which was to be a week-long trip to the famine stricken Sudan.

Sunday 17 November	Left London for Tanzania
Monday 18 November	Arrived at Dar-es-Salaam
Tuesday 19 November	Flew to Mbeya to visit hospitals
Wednesday 20 November	Visited the rehabilitation centre Flew to Songea
Thursday 21 November	Flew to Zanzibar, visited the hospital
Friday 22 November	Visited the Ngorongoro crater
Saturday 23 November	Flew to Mozambique
Sunday 24 November	Flew to Inhambane to visit SCF projects
Monday 25 November	Visited health centres in Maputo
Tuesday 26 November	Visited Quelimane. Flew to Zambia
Wednesday 27 November	Visited a Cheshire Home and hospital in Lusaka
Thursday 28 November	Flew to Mwinilunga to visit a hospital
Friday 29 November	Flew to Chipata to visit a hospital
Saturday 30 November	Visited a copper mine and flew back to Lusaka
Sunday 1 December	Flew back to Dar-es-Salaam
Monday 2 December	Flew to the Sudan
Tuesday 3 December	Visited a hospital in Khartoum

Wednesday 4 December	Flew to Niyala, visited the SCF workshop
Thursday 5 December	Flew and drove to Umbala refugee camp
Friday 6 December	Drove to Zalingei before returning to Khartoum
Saturday 7 December	Flew to relief camps in Gedaref
Sunday 8 December	Returned to Khartoum
Monday 9 December	Visited the War Cemetery before flying home.

On each of the long days the Princess not only fulfilled a number of engagements, but flew great distances, something that she describes as an occupational hazard of the job. She has landed on the most barren airfields in the Third World, where even her pilots admit to being nervous at landing. There have been occasions when the Princess has expressed personal disappointment at being denied a visit through hazardous flying conditions. On the tour of India in 1984 she had hoped to visit Ladakh in the north of the country where the Save the Children Fund have a project, but the Andover of the Queen's Flight could not safely complete the flight over the mountains and lives would have been put in jeopardy. This is about to change in 1987 with the addition of two new aircraft to the Queen's Flight. The BAe 146, at £16 million each, has longer range, can travel twice as fast as the Andover, can take twice as many passengers, twice the amount of luggage and can fly over 1500 miles at a stretch, giving the Princess greater scope and perhaps fulfilling ambitions. Studying the new craft she said, 'As a professional passenger ... I have a vested interest in very safely and well-built aircraft. I am sure that these will certainly be that.'

This ambitious tour combined tragedy with optimism. At Umbala refugee camp in Darfur, 600 miles from Khartoum, 25,000 people were suffering from what has been described as 'the worst famine of all time'. At the camp were 7000 people suffering from severe malnutrition. Four people died on the day that Princess Anne visited, which was said to be 'fairly average'. For a long time the Princess had wanted to see at first hand how the famine could be coped with. She had just one week in which to see as much as possible. Some seven million pounds had already been ploughed into the country where the lives of over 100 million people were threatened.

Dressed in jeans and a T-shirt, cotton headscarf to protect her hair and a bush hat to keep off the sun, Princess Anne never flagged in the 90pF heat. Everywhere that she went the dusty hands of half-naked children were pushed into hers. 'Amira, Amira' (Princess, Princess) they would cry, aware only that she was special. 'Salaam', she said to each one on this unusual royal walkabout. Year after year the rains had failed to come. Through lack of grain people survived through eating poisonous berries, soaked in water to remove their potent properties. Some were so desperate that they even broke open termite nests to reach any grain that the insects might have secreted inside. The Save the Children Fund sent out two emergency teams; three airlifts of relief supplies were lifted out at Christmas 1984, and more followed. A feeding centre was set up in the Sudan three days later, feeding 1500 children a day, which gradually increased to 50,000. The fact that half-a-dozen people were dying daily during Princess Anne's visit was nothing compared to the 100 people that made up the statistics of the daily deaths when the camp first opened. Although grain distribution was widespread, so was the hunger. Just before Princess Anne arrived at Umbala a train of wheat was ambushed at the tiny railway of Nyala by over 200 women who had to be fought off.

At Umbala, Princess Anne spent the night in the staff compound. She slept in a small mud hut with an iron bedstead and a mosquito net. The time spent in it was short for she sat up half the night discussing the problems of the Third World with relief workers and was up early for the next stage of her tour, confident that the worst of the crisis was over, and could be kept under control just as long as the Fund could continue to obtain money.

Disease is as much a problem as malnutrition. Lack of medical supplies can often be the greatest worry. At one hospital an 11-year-old girl was admitted after being bitten by a snake, and her chances of survival were slim unless she could receive blood. Princess Anne's was not compatible, and one by one the team of press reporters were tested in a mud hut. The BBC's correspondent, Mike Wooldridge, fortunately was compatible and donated four pints. The girl survived. This was a rare case. Usually the children are suffering from diphtheria, cholera, meningitis, whooping cough, anaemia, kidney and liver diseases, always made worse by lack of nutrition. One nurse told of how she takes a photograph of each child that is admitted to the hospital to send back home to her friends and family in the hope that they will be able to send money. It is heartbreaking to find that often the child will be dead before the photographs are even developed.

For Princess Anne it was initially difficult to come to terms with the death and disease that surrounded her, but she has learned from relief workers that it is possible not to give in to despair. When actually confronted by the situation she finds it much easier to cope, '. . . it is much more difficult to gauge it when you are sitting in your comfortable home, in front of a television set or listening to the radio, and you're surrounded by hot and cold running water, and electric light and all the things that we take for granted. In many of these places the people are happy with what they have. To some extent, it is their normal way of life . . . but obviously there are moments when their conditions get worse, but again, it's not as if it were something out of the blue or completely new to them. Many of them have experienced it before. So it's easier to look at what you're seeing from a practical point of view, in terms of how you're going to constructively help those who are suffering, and what you can do to stop it happening quite so badly again . . . when you're there and actually seeing children who are severely malnourished, possibly on the point of dying, it's never a sight that anybody really wants to see, but I think you are in the business of actually trying to help.' Although she may see thousands of sick and dying children, it is perhaps easier for her than relief workers who work in the camps all the time. Princess Anne never gets personally acquainted with an individual, cannot become emotionally involved in the case, and must find it easier to switch off than a nurse who has looked after a child for weeks only to look on helplessly and watch it die.

The disaster in the Sudan is now over. Until the *next* time if sufficient money is not found. Ironically there is a grain surplus in the Sudan, whilst many are still hungry. Money is required to buy the grain from the relevant parties and distribute it to where it is needed. That is something that cannot be done instantly or easily. However well meaning the Save the Children Fund may be, they cannot simply march into a country and attempt to put it to rights. They always have to begin on a relatively small scale and extend them into long-term projects, which often means convincing the local people that they *do* actually need help, that help *can* be made available, and that with a little guidance the people can actually help themselves. In the Sudan the Princess ate goat meat and was surprised to discover that courgettes were available, introduced by expatriate workers, 'they do grow very well and people are getting a much better variety in their diet because of that.' There is no special menu, she eats the same diet as the other Save the Children workers, she showers under a converted oil drum, and throughout the week in the Sudan she rose at five every morning. For most of the day she was plagued by flies, and at night a scorpion almost landed on her bed in the night, but she laughs off any suggestion that it has been an uncomfortable time. 'I've been sitting down for most of it,' she laughed, modestly referring to the amount of travelling she had undertaken in 23 days.

Not all of Princess Anne's overseas visits are for the Save the Children Fund, and not all are hazard-free. She has been close to the war zone in Ethiopia, has risked disease in Africa, but it was on a simple three-day visit to Brazil to attend a gala performance of the Sadlers Wells ballet in Rio de Janeiro that Princess Anne, in March 1986, came close to a repeat performance of the 1974 plot to kidnap her in The Mall. A drug-trafficking gang mounted a plot to kidnap her and hold her hostage in exchange for their jailed leader, Jose Carlos dos Reis. Reis is serving a 30-year jail sentence and has an army of followers living in the Rio de Janeiro slums that scar the city and were part of the Princess's schedule. Known as 'Escadinha' (Portuguese for 'Little Ladder') he has attempted to escape from jail many times, the most spectacular of which was when a helicopter attempted to airlift him out of the maximum security prison yard, resulting in a shoot-out with the police.

Police were tipped off that drug gangsters plotted to kidnap Princess Anne and immediately tightened the security around her. Her schedules and routes were suddenly changed and, much to her annoyance, she spent the remainder of her visit surrounded by bodyguards armed with machine guns. Mrs. Caroline Ure, wife of the British Ambassador, John Ure, bravely acted as decoy. She travelled in Princess Anne's official car amid the motorcade because of her resemblance to the Princess, being the same age, build and colouring, while Princess Anne travelled anonymously behind in an unmarked Jaguar. 'The police advised us that the Princess would be most at risk during the drive to the airport,' said Mr. Ure. 'This gang has committed some very large-scale crimes and the threat was very real indeed. It had to be taken seriously.' Fifty armed police protected both Mrs. Ure and Princess Anne and the flight was delayed by 45 minutes, annoying for the passengers on this commercial flight, in an attempt to fool the gang. When Princess Anne was told of the threat, Mr. Ure remarked that she 'didn't even bat an eyelid. She was cool, calm and just concerned with getting on with her visit. She's very courageous and that shone through.' Typically the Princess insisted that a news blackout was maintained until she was back in London and until she could personally break the news to the Queen on her return, rather than cause any unnecessary worry at home.

In a television interview with the Archbishop of Canterbury's special envoy, Terry Waite, himself no stranger to the subject, Princess Anne openly discussed kidnapping and the possibilities of assassination: 'If someone decides it is worth their while either kidnapping or just killing you, I don't think there is anything constructive either we or anyone else can do about it.' Asked if she was worried about terrorism, she replied: 'When things are going well people tend to forget about it, and that makes it more dramatic when it happens again. Most people would consider us very fortunate because we are unlikely to face mugging or robbery. It is a very much more personal fear.' Smilingly she dismissed the seriousness of the attempt to kidnap her in The Mall in 1974, feeling that she stood a marginally better chance because the man was on his own, not part of an international gang, but she is still conscious of the fact that one bullet could end her life and that needs only one madman on the trigger. In any other walk of life the chances of being shot are around a million to one, but for Princess Anne her life is endangered through nothing more than being born royal.

In the interview, recorded at Buckingham Palace, the Princess discussed her role as President of the Save the Children Fund and her work as a Third World campaigner. She admitted that she had not originally had any great ambitions in this, or any other direction, but that her work in the Third World gives her great satisfaction because 'you can produce a startlingly quick improvement.' In the two decades that she has been President the work of the Fund has been remarkable, due in the main to a growing awareness by the Western World of Third World problems in general. It is a war against hunger and disease caused by political factors or natural disasters. In panic, starving people journey to areas where they hope to find food; hunger makes them highly susceptible to disease, and interacting with one another the problems cause a vicious circle of starvation and disease that is difficult to combat. It is a war that Princess Anne knows can never be completely won because of nature's destructive intervention but it is a battle that the Princess will continue to fight as the colonel of the Fund's battalion.

Chapter 8

_A_ day in the life of Princess Anne

Another afternoon. Another engagement. At Dillons bookstore in Bloomsbury an air of controlled excitement pervaded as the time of Princess Anne's arrival drew near. As Chancellor of London University, the Princess had agreed to re-open the bookshop that supplied educational texts to the students, after a £1.5 million rebuilding and refurbishing programme. An acknowledged leader in academic and general bookselling, Dillons aim to become the best bookshop in Europe. Anyone who questioned the fact that a member of the Royal Family was giving prestige to a commercial enterprise was hastily quashed.

Dillons bookshop, opened by Una Dillon, have been supplying books to London University for over half a century. Miss Dillon opened the shop in 1936 on a borrowed capital of £800. When her original shop in Store Street, London, was destroyed by a bomb during the Second World War she moved premises to a spot in Gower Street where the shop is today. As neighbouring shops became vacant they were purchased so that Dillons could expand and it now occupies all of a striking neo-Gothic building designed by Charles Fitzroy Doll in 1908. By 1969 the turnover was over a million pounds a year; today it is over ten million.

After Una Dillon's retirement in 1967 (she was later awarded a CBE for services to the book trade) the shop was taken over by Pentos, formed by Mr. Terry Maher, who own over 80 specialist book, art, and stationery shops under many well-known high street names. As the jewel in their retail crown, it was a coup for Mr. Maher, and indeed Miss Dillon, that Princess Anne accepted the invitation to perform the re-opening ceremony of this sizeable bookshop, comprehensive in its stock and well catalogued and indexed. A leading contender to rob Foyles of its title as the best bookshop in London. 'We were surprised when Princess Anne agreed,' said one of the organisers, 'and even more surprised when they said that she would stay for one-and-a-half hours. We thought we'd only get a few minutes.'

An hour before the Princess was due to arrive invited guests began to gather for a champagne reception. Chairman Terry Maher fidgeted nervously with his papers, grinning broadly to give the appearance of confidence. He pulled the cord unveiling and veiling the plaque three times to satisfy himself that there would be no embarrassment when Princess Anne pulled the cord. In the entrance to the bookshop this plaque was intended to be a proud lasting reminder.

A young girl, Verity, who was to present a bouquet to the Princess, jumped up and down anxiously.

'This may be the first time for you, but Princess Anne has received umpteen bouquets. She'll make it easy for you,' Verity was briefed. As the minutes ticked by there were to be tears from the worried Verity before the appointed moment came. She was overcome with the enormity of the task of handing over a small bouquet of mixed flowers, an 'honour' which sends hundreds of children either rushing to their mother's skirts or brings out their most extrovert qualities at countless royal gatherings.

A royal-blue carpet leading from the edge of the pavement into the main entrance of the shop was unrolled, rolled-up, unrolled, swept, turned round, and re-rolled before the baffled crowds who had gathered on the streets outside, many aware that 'something' must be happening. Few knew what. 'Typically British,' laughed a woman, 'start a queue and people soon tag on, even if they don't know what they're queuing for!'

Two Japanese tourists raised their Nikons, and a young American attempted to join the small party of press photographers, hoping not to be noticed. 'Back behind the rope,' said a sharp-eyed policeman, pushing not only the American but some of the waiting journalists also, smartly behind the rope well away from the blue carpet.

'Here she is!' came a shout as a huge yellow delivery van parked inadvertently at the foot of the now unrolled and spotless carpet. Officials, who had momentarily panicked that the Princess was early, smiled with relief, barely in the mood for jokers at this late stage.

Inside the shop the reception committee drained their champagne glasses before moving into line. Some worthy of a handshake, some less so.

'He went to two meetings to decide whether or not the shop should still be called Dillons bookshop and not Boots the Chemist or something,' said a girl, pointing to a portly gentleman who had taken up a prominent position. 'They're the ones who've done the hard work,' and she indicated some of the staff standing high up on the staircase, straining to catch a glimpse of the monarch's only daughter. For many it was the nearest they would ever be to royalty, and an occasion that would be talked about for years to come. 'As soon as the Princess has unveiled the plaque, back to your departments everyone,' came the orders. The Press Officer tried, meanwhile, to calm Verity's nerves. Una Dillon, now in her eighties, and her sister, Carmen, who had travelled from Hove for the event, were given seats close to where the Princess would stand. Both too frail to remain standing for too long. To many Una Dillon was a legendary figure, the Queen of the bookshop.

Terry Maher adjusted the buttons on his double-breasted suit, clutched the notes for his speech, and looked calmer than he had done all afternoon at the moment he had been given the signal that the royal visitor was on her way.

At approximately 3.15 pm, Princess Anne had left Buckingham Palace for the short drive to Bloomsbury. Along the carefully timed route, policemen were stationed at the main road junctions to temporarily stop the traffic so as not to impede the royal progress. Each has a small radio to receive advanced warning of the imminent approach. With Princess Anne are a lady-in-waiting, and a personal detective. Princess Anne, as always, sat calmly on the offside of the car behind the driver, which allows the Princess to gather her handbag while the door is opened, the lady-in-waiting gets out and finally the Princess steps out with much greater dignity than if she sat on the nearside.

At precisely 3.30 pm the Princess's maroon Rolls-Royce pulled up gently beside the blue carpet, preceded by police outriders on motorcycles. Princess Anne stepped out, relaxed and alert, in a navy checked wool suit, serviceable, smart, classic and slightly ageing; it had first been worn on 10 September 1984, at the opening of a new kidney unit at the Royal Devon and Exeter Hospital, two years earlier. The small crowd outside waved and cheered enthusiastically, many realising for the first time why there had been so much excitement. Once inside, Verity curtsyed, handed over the bouquet and within seconds her moment of glory, the days of anguish, were over.

Slowly Princess Anne walked down the waiting line of the reception party, asking pertinent, well-informed questions, oblivious of the cajoling photographers, clicking grotesquely with their intrusive lenses trained on her every move. As the Princess approached, sweaty palms were wiped in anticipation of shaking the navy-gloved hand. Each was greeted with a warm smile and with practiced professionalism. Princess Anne often brought instant relaxation by including two people in one conversation. She listens intently out of a genuine interest for what people have to say. Questions are not cursory, asked out of politeness. They are based on her own knowledge. In the case of Dillons she asked intelligent questions about the redesigning of the shop, the work involved, the upheaval and difficulties that obviously resulted out of continued trading throughout the transformation. Behind the scenes some staff also had their own discussions, revealing details that would never have been conveyed to the Princess.

After ten minutes Princess Anne arrived at the foot of the plaque. In front of her sat the formidable figures of Una and Carmen Dillon. Terry Maher gave a short speech, welcoming the Princess and the Dillon sisters. Here, as throughout the afternoon, one almost felt that there was greater reverence and respect for this doyen of the book trade than for Her Royal Highness – it was, after all, Una Dillon's day. With no business experience and hard work alone, on borrowed capital, she had created a multi-million pound empire. Knowing this, Princess Anne summed up the situation in a few words. If the new-look shop had the approval of Terry Maher and Una Dillon, who was she not to give it her blessing. She deftly pulled on the cord and unveiled the plaque. The staff scattered discreetly and Princess Anne began her lengthy tour of the store. Champagne flowed for the 60 invited guests remaining, smoked salmon, pâté, cream cakes and other such delicacies were offered in abundance.

From department to department the Princess undertook a long but leisurely walk around the store, asking questions of the hundreds of staff, whilst downstairs publishers, book distributors, and authors gorged themselves. A display of a recently-published biography of Princess Anne was hastily removed at the orders of Buckingham Palace for fear of causing the Princess any possible embarrassment, and to avoid the inevitability of a photographer taking a picture of the Princess beside the books just in case it could be turned into a publicity stunt.

It was almost five o'clock by the time Princess Anne returned to her starting point beside the plaque for the return journey. Ten minutes before the Princess appeared a car arrived to take the Dillon sisters to the Hotel Russell where a dinner was to be held to honour the occasion. Una Dillon rose from her seat and walked down the blue carpet outside to her car, still clutching a glass of champagne, which was prised from her hand at the last moment. A noticeable feeling of relaxation and jollity filled the foyer as the Dillon car departed. Princess Anne was still in the building, but the merriment continued. Eventually the Princess appeared with the entourage she had gathered along the route and continued to chat animatedly, almost reluctant to leave. Her departure was unhurried, even at the car she joked and continued chatting, obviously in high spirits, and had not touched one drop of the alcohol which had flowed throughout the afternoon in plentiful supply.

Arriving back at Buckingham Palace at 5.15, there was time to wash, repair the make-up, alter her hairstyle and change into evening dress. It was time to change 'hats'. From being Chancellor of London University she was back to one of her most familiar roles as President of the Save the Children Fund to attend the film premiere of *Eleni* at the Cannon Cinema at the Haymarket in London. *Eleni* is the true story of an American journalist's attempt to discover the truth about his mother's death during the Greek Civil War. Attending a film premiere, for many, is a place to 'see and be seen' and for a royal premiere high ticket prices are an enjoyable way of raising money for charity. The premiere of *Eleni* in one evening raised more than £20,000 for Save the Children and the Anglo-Hellenic League.

At 7.00 pm, only 40 minutes away from Princess Anne's arrival, the small foyer of the cinema was filled to capacity. Men walked stiffly and unnaturally in dinner jackets. Women flamboyantly pulled off enormous fur coats (despite the fact that it was September) to reveal their latest Jasper Canran, Gina Fratini or Bruce Oldfield gown, whilst ushers attempted to seat everyone before the Princess's arrival. Many left their entrance until the last moment. By the time the maroon Rolls-Royce came to a halt, this time at the foot of a red carpet, the foyer contained less than twenty-five people – the official line-up, Chris Thornton (Press Officer for Save the Children) and a number of photographers wearing a blue cardboard disc bearing the magic words 'Royal Rota' which enable, them to stay close to the Princess. Each had been issued with a final programme to match names to the faces that appeared in the resulting photographs. Similar lists are issued to all concerned with any royal visit, a miniature version of which is in Princess Anne's handbag:

Final Royal programme for the attendance of Her Royal Highness The Princess Anne, Mrs. Mark Phillips, GCVO, as President of Save The Children, at the film premiere of 'Eleni' at the Cannon Cinema, Haymarket, London SW1

7.40 pm   *Her Royal Highness arrives and is attended by:*

> Mr. J. Morley,
> General Manager, Cannon Cinema.
>
> Mr. W. Yates,
> Chairman Premiere Committee.

> *who escorts Her Royal Highness and presents:*

> Mrs. Yates.
>
> Sir Michael Stewart,
> Past Chairman Anglo-Hellenic League.
>
> Lady Richards,
> Save the Children Council Member and Co-Vice
>   Chairman Anglo-Hellenic League.
>
> Mrs. K. Lentakis,
> Co-Vice Chairman Anglo-Hellenic League.
>
> Mr. Jenkins,
> Managing Director, Cannon UK.
>
> Mr. Michael Gifford,
> Managing Director and Chief Executive, The Rank
>   Organisation.
>
> Mr. James Daly,
> Managing Director, Rank Film and Television
>   Services.
>
> Mr. F. Turner,
> Rank Film Distributors.

Mr. David van Houten,
Worldwide Advertising and Publicity, CBS
  Productions.

Mr. W. Self,
Independent Producer, CBS Productions Division.

Mr. G. Phillips,
Managing Director, CBS Broadcast International,
  Europe.

who presents:

Mr. N. Wooll,
Producer, 'Eleni'.

Mr. P. Yates,
Director, 'Eleni'.

Members of the cast:
Miss Dimitra Arliss
Mr. Oliver Cotton

A bouquet will be presented by:

Katy Phillips (aged 2t)

Mr. Yates escorts Her Royal Highness into the auditorium.

Having changed into a flowing red silk evening dress, the
Princess looked cool and relaxed, her hair swept up with a spark-
ling diamond clasp in the back. Two-and-a-half-year-old Katy
Phillips presented the Princess with an all white bouquet, containing roses, carnations and freesias. Katy was chosen because her
father, Gregory Phillips, is managing director of CBS Broadcast
International and had worked on the film. Along with representa-
tives of the Rank Organisation and the Cannon Group, The Princess was introduced to the director, Peter Yates, and last of all two
stars of the film, Oliver Cotton and Dimitra Arliss.

As always, Princess Anne's questions were direct.

'How did the script come about?' she asked.

'It's based on the book,' she was told.

That was insufficient for a probing Princess who is used to more
specific answers.

'What do you mean it's based on the book? Does it follow the
book exactly, has it been adapted loosely from the book, is it . . .'

If the probing Princess asks a question you have to think very carefully about your answer. A relief worker that she met from the American branch of the Save the Children Fund makes a comment typical of many that she meets: 'I thought it would be just another public relations exercise,' he said after meeting Princess Anne in Burkina Faso. 'Instead, I was grilled in minute detail by somebody who knew exactly what she was talking about.' Questions came thick and fast, the Princess eager for 'more and more detail'.

As Princess Anne moved down the line of people, the one who she had just spoken to discreetly left the foyer and went to find their seat so that the line gradually diminished. 'Princess Anne! Princess Anne!' shouted photographers, less than two feet away from the Princess, hoping that she would turn so that they could obtain an individual picture suitable for syndication. Chris Thornton physically kept the eager photographers at bay. Princess Anne continued with her conversation, an expert in the art of ignoring photographers if they interfere too closely in her work. Even the most hardened photographer knows never to shout, 'Look this way, love,' as happened in Australia, when the Princess snapped, 'I am *not* your love!'

It was after ten o'clock before the Princess departed, shaking hands along the way once again, and midnight before she eventually returned home to Gatcombe Park (after a quick change at Buckingham Palace on the way) at the end of another long day.

Chapter 9

Working in Britain

A large part of Princess Anne's working life is involved with raising or receiving money on behalf of charity, for which she is prepared in her own words 'to attempt anything legal'.

However long her working day might be, it is never short of variety. One day it can be an audience at Buckingham Palace or acting formally as a Counsellor of State, standing in for the Queen whenever she is out of the country. This is one of the Princess's little known roles which enables her to sign official documents and hold investitures. In 1980 Princess Anne represented the Queen in Fiji and was able to bestow knighthoods. Another day she can be in overalls visiting a container terminal, as in September 1986 when she climbed a 115-foot ship-to-shore gantry to get a bird's eye view of the port. 'The Princess really enjoyed herself,' said George Blackhall, managing director of what is now the United Kingdom's largest container port, 'and was thrilled to see the harbour from such a great height. She was not scared at all and showed a lot of interest in the crane as well as in all the other equipment and machinery at the docks.'

Always ready for a new experience, when visiting Silverstone she did 25 laps in a Formula One racing car. At a police training centre in Sheffield she agreed to try out a breathalyser, even though she is practically teetotal. The experiment was to demonstrate what can happen if a breath test is wrongly carried out. She took a sip of sherry, which she said was more than she had ever had in her life, and immediately blew into an intoximeter sending the reading soaring. To the policemen's amusement she pretended to be drunk and slumped sideways in her chair. The initial high reading did not count and when taken three minutes later proved to be negative. In practice the police must wait twenty minutes after a driver's last drink to allow the concentration of alcohol in the mouth to evaporate before taking the test.

Whatever the situation Princess Anne has the ability to remain open and uninhibited. When visiting the Charnos factory in Ilkeston, Derbyshire (famed for their 'sexy underwear') to receive a cheque for £100,000 from factory workers, for improved hospital facilities, she was presented with a silk negligé and matching nightie. She remained unabashed. When presenting the Pye Television Personalities of the Year Award at the Hilton Hotel in London, she made no pretence that she recognised the recipients. The winners of the annual award, Leslie Grantham and Anita Dobson (Den and Angie Watts from the BBC Television soap opera *EastEnders*) admitted their surprise when the Princess asked of the pair, 'Who are you?' There is obviously one Princess who has little time for television serials which require regular viewing and is not one of the 23 million viewers that the programme regularly attracts. The Princess of Wales has acknowledged that she is a fan, but Anne was in the dark.

What could have been one of the most challenging attempts to boost donations was to go before a trade union conference of the Inland Revenue to drum up money for children in northern India. To many it would seem a ludicrous exercise, but if Princess Anne could get money from the taxman it would be possible to get it from anyone! Naturally there was some opposition and many delegates threatened to walk out if the Princess addressed the conference, but undaunted by the Militant Tendency supporters she went ahead and only nine out of 700 delegates walked out. The Save the Children Fund ended up £1000 richer. It was only the second time that a member of the Royal Family has faced a trade union, Prince Charles having once addressed the steelmen's union.

In the light of this success she spoke to over 3000 businessmen at the Institute of Directors' Convention at the Royal Albert Hall and appealed for private firms to pump more effort and cash into Britain's problems. She talked of the hardships of inner city life – social isolation, high unemployment, poor housing and lack of community services. She raised the subject of the 'no hope' generation. 'The effects of gangs of so-called friends, lack of communication with parents – nothing original in that – and very few job prospects all add to the problems that all young people suffer from, however well off,' she said. 'Pinching cars and motorbikes for excitement, money for things they want, or just the goods themselves, often clothes and shoes, there isn't any one answer to that, but the answers have to come from greater community imvolvement . . . Helping in the community isn't about being less competitive, but being more aware that all business is related to the lives of your consumers and we are all consumers.'

The greatest surprise of the morning came when Princess Anne revealed that one-third of the Save the Children Fund's budget is spent tackling problems at home in the United Kingdom. It was early in 1986 and those who listened confessed that until that time they had associated the Fund's work exclusively with Third World countries, never thinking that charity begins at home. By the end of 1986 the Princess had begun to educate the public as a whole, through personal interviews with journalists and co-operation in a television programme which was shown on New Year's Day 1987. This was part of her campaign to emphasise that Save the Children is for *all* children, not just the famine-stricken on the other side of the world. With increasing social problems, unemployment and the resulting lowering of living standards there are problems on our own doorstep.

From 1983 until the time of her speech, Princess Anne had visited 18 separate projects in the United Kingdom.

Since that time the number of her projects has increased. On a fact-finding mission she visited inner city areas in London, Birmingham, Liverpool, Glasgow and Belfast, the visits at her own request and often unannounced. When she toured the Glasgow slums she was visibly shocked by what she saw. Unlike any other royal visit to Scotland no special concessions were made, there was no attempt to disguise the squalor. The sight of endless windows boarded up, walls covered with graffiti concerned the Princess and she was even more horrified when she was told what percentage of the population of Glasgow are unemployed. 'Nobody knows about these problems except at a local level,' she said of the work she undertook in the UK.

In all geographical areas, not just the inner cities, children are growing up in difficult and isolated surroundings. High unemployment and lack of community services leads to children growing up under severely restricted circumstances. Although love may exist within the family, pressures cause friction and children grow up

UK PROJECTS VISITED BY HRH, THE PRINCESS ANNE, SINCE 1983

Date	Name of Project	Project Service	Location
28.11.83	Pilton Adventure playground indoor centre	Young people's centre	Edinburgh and Glasgow
	Harmeny School	Emotionally disturbed children	
	Knightsbridge open air adventure playground	Playgroup	
24.9.84	Gainsborough Project	Travellers/liaison with local community	Gainsborough, Lincolnshire
13.6.85	Overstream House	Child care, family centre	Cambridge
3.10.85	The Sunshine Playgroup	Playgroups for 3m5 year olds	Deptford, SE8
	Pepys Playgroup		Deptford, SE8
	The Rainbow Centre		Southwark, SE1
4.11.85	St. Aiden's Playgroup	2tm5 year olds	
	Harley Playgroup	2tm5 year olds	Birmingham
	Summerfield Community Centre	Children and family centre	
15.2.86	Ladymuir Youth Project	Youth and community centre	
	Darnley Street Family Centre	Wide range of activities for children and parents, including toy library	Glasgow
17.2.86	Patmore Project	Activities for parents and children	Wandsworth, SW8
	St. Peter's Children's Centre	Child care for parents and playgroup	Battersea, SW11
21.2.86	Milestones Centre	Intermediate treatment for young offenders	Sunderland
20.3.86	Westway Gypsy Project	Pre-school/liaison	London, W10
	African Family Advisory Service	Advice for African parents and foster parents of African children	SCF Southern Regional Office, W12

uncertain about relationships. The Save the Children Fund in the United Kingdom say that their main role 'continues to be supporting parents in their all important task of childrearing, the emphasis is on helping families to help themselves through increasing their confidence, knowledge and skills so as to enable parents to take more responsibility for their children's lives'.

A high percentage of the Fund's work is involved with the difficulties of ethnic minorities who have to encounter racial prejudice at work, in schools and even from neighbours. Prejudice begins at an early age and children can be deeply affected by the way they look and talk if they *seem* different to the majority. A number of projects have been set up in an attempt to overcome social difficulties – the Hopscotch Centre works with Bengali families, there is a Vietnamese Children's home, a Community project at Howgill in Cumbria, and The Building Blocks Project in South London which works to change attitudes and improve the quality of life for disadvantaged children from a variety of cultures. Many of the projects use very basic ideas, such as encouraging children to paint and learn about colour, which can then lead gradually into a discussion about skin colour and eventually alter their whole perception.

Save the Children has projects for adults too and the Hopscotch Centre helps Asian women who perhaps have difficulties with the language, the currency, or who may feel isolated if their husbands are away at work, and can need help bringing up their children. The Vietnamese Children's Home is the only one of its kind in Europe. Staffed largely by Vietnamese people it enables children to keep in touch with their cultural roots, at the same time adapting to life in the United Kingdom.

Save the Children has over 300 different projects in the UK, a large number of which Princess Anne takes a personal interest in.

PROJECTS

Support For Families

Family Centres	19	Holiday Playschemes	25
Community Playgroups	80	Mother and toddler groups	22
After School Clubs	30	Toy Libraries	16
Youth Projects	15	Centres for Childminders	4

Support For Families *cont.*

Playbuses	3
Single Parent Groups	7
Home Visiting Schemes	15
Counselling Services	17
Short-term residential care centres	3
Ethnic minority schemes	24
Clubs for the handicapped	5
Literacy Schemes	5
Adventure playgrounds	3

Intermediate Treatment

IT Centres	4
Training and consultancy centres	3
Projects that include IT	3

Work with Traveller Families

Pre-school/liaison projects	7
Mobile education project	1

Care and Education

Vietnamese Children's Centre	1
Residential Schools	2

Promoting Health

Health education campaign	1
Child health project	1
Hospital play schemes	15

Many are projects that the majority of the population might not know existed or indeed realise the necessity for. One such is the literacy scheme – teaching children *and adults* to read. Illiteracy is far more widespread than one would expect and a contributory factor to unemployment. In the Brighton and Hove area shocking new evidence has revealed that some 30,000 people would have difficulty reading this sentence. Figures released by Granada Television's *World in Action* programme showed that 13 per cent of Britain's population have acute literacy problems, ranging from a total inability to read to being unable to spell even the simplest words. The manager of one job centre believes that the problem is national and growing, 'We notice that more and more people of all ages need help to fill out the forms properly. With reading, writing and spelling problems people are debarring themselves from finding work.' The problem can be self-defeating. Without literacy skills the work is unavailable; without work there is no money for adult literacy classes.

The most controversial project in which Princess Anne has become involved is that of travelling families. In September 1986 she caused a stir by visiting three 'gypsy' sites in Buckinghamshire. She had been President of Save the Children for 16 years and no other visit on their behalf caused such an outcry as that of a member of the Royal Family consorting with the country's 'unwanted people'. On a fact-finding mission she went to look at the health of travellers, the conditions in which they live, and in particular the children. Some newspapers accused her of obtaining 'cheap publicity', residents who have traveller caravan sites on their doorstep said, 'Royalty have no idea what it's like to live alongside gypsies day to day', others suggested that if Princess Anne was so concerned she should give over a few acres of Gatcombe Park land to ease the problem. Wherever the travellers settle thousands of people campaign to have them removed. There are no objections to 'pikers', 'didikois', 'romanies', call them what you will, as a whole, but the mountain of rubbish that inevitably results from their lifestyle always causes offence. In 'royal' Dummer, the former home of the Duchess of York, everyone, including the Duchess's father, Major Ronald Fergusson, has signed a petition to prevent a proposed local traveller camp.

The blame lands fairly and squarely on the shoulders of many local councils for failing to offer suitable sites and for providing inadequate services and facilities. Travellers in Iver told Princess Anne of the appalling conditions on the site first given to them 22 years ago. 'Bucks County Council provided the site, but expected 30 families to use a communal toilet, and gave us no drainage,' said traveller George Davis. 'I tell you, the canal at the side of us has got everything in except water.' Susan Smith, a mother bringing up four children, told Princess Anne, 'Every time anyone had a bath the council expected us to empty it bucket by bucket into a cesspit a long way away. In the end we dug our own soakaway into the canal.' The Caravan Sites Act requires local authorities to provide permanent traveller sites, but many councils have failed to do so and some 50,000 travelling people have nowhere to stop *legally*. Wherever they set up camp they are immediately evicted.

Princess Anne decided to see the problem for herself. 'We hope her visit will lead to a better understanding of the needs of travellers,' said a Save the Children Fund spokesman. 'They have a right to good health, welfare and education and our role is to help them gain equal access to the services available to others.' Dressed in a high-necked brown wool coat and long boots, Princess Anne walked through the mud, rats and rubbish to see what travelling life entailed. In one day she toured three sites, one at White Hill near Amersham, and two in Iver, at all three she was told, 'This is not a place to bring up kids.' No one, not even the royal visitor, stood on ceremony. She chatted to nearly everyone as people crowded around her to put their own point of view. She talked to one man who had a Jack Russell terrier around his neck like a fur collar, she had tea with another on the site of an old chemical dump, and saw a playbus provided by the Save the Children Fund for pre-school children. 'She's a wonderfully human princess who has a deep understanding of our problems,' came the unanimous agreement at the end of the visit.

On the return home she talked about her views. She was worried that travellers bring up children in the worst possible conditions, injurious to their health and harmful to their education. The fact that many of the conditions are of the travellers' own making does not concern her – she is not there to moralise but to help. The lifestyle of the travellers is something she will not be drawn on. She is concerned only with the children and the work of the Fund, and can offer clear-headed, practical advice. It could have been the other way round, she suggests, travellers could represent the majority and anyone who lives in a house would be seen as 'a bit of an oddball'. There is no clear answer to the problem; living conditions could be improved with local government help, children's health can be better cared for with Save the Children Fund education in self-help, but for as long as travellers exist the problem will always be there. Public attitudes could change.

In Belfast Princess Anne visited another Save the Children project which is close to her heart, a day centre with a playgroup for young children. In their formative years the Princess is convinced that interaction with other children is essential to development, and helps them later to settle quickly into an educational school environment. As an advocate of the playgroup system, she sent both her children to the local village school in Minchinhampton. In a city torn apart by hostility, the Eliza Street Family Day Centre in Belfast is almost a refuge where children and mothers alike can seek salvation. Catholic and Protestant children play contentedly together unaware of the violence and hatred outside. No threat of terrorism has ever deterred the Princess from visiting Northern Ireland. When most of the Royal Family attended a VE-day service of thanksgiving in Westminster Abbey on the fortieth anniversary of peace in Europe in 1985, Princess Anne attended a similar service at St. Anne's Protestant Cathedral in the centre of Belfast. A huge security operation, which included undercover men of the SAS, was put into force and there was spontaneous applause from the appreciative crowds outside the cathedral when she left. Almost as if to cock a snook at the terrorists she went on a walkabout wherever possible and chatted freely with the people. 'If someone really decides that they want to kill you, there's very little you can do about it anyway,' she says, and is prepared to take the risk.

Not all of Princess Anne's work involves visiting war-torn or famine-stricken areas, or dealing with the problems of society, but, given the choice, she prefers a challenge and a worthwhile cause to a state banquet. Once a year she has the opportunity to turn a formal society event into a very special thank-you party for some of the hundreds of charity workers that she meets in a year. The occasion is one of the most fascinating royal rituals – the Buckingham Palace garden party. Few people are ever invested with a Knighthood, created Peer of the Realm, receive Royal Maundy money or find their name in the New Year's Honours List, but 95 per cent of the 35,000 guests invited annually to the afternoon garden parties are untitled and come from all walks of life, their only bond being some kind of public service. A number will have received unexpected invitations on Princess Anne's recommendation. Queen Victoria initiated the Palace garden parties so that she could meet more of the aristocracy. Today they are more democratic, although with approximately 8000 people present at each event the number who actually meet members of the Royal Family are limited, and the Queen still has her own tea tent set apart from the lower echelons.

The invitation card itself is uninspiring and plain, but the honour is great. Invitations are sent not from Buckingham Palace, but from the Lord Chamberlain's Office, who take on 'permanent temps' for eight months of the year to deal with the task. The recipient gets an admission card and details of parking on the day.

Guests begin arriving from 3 pm onwards, driving grandly down The Mall in their moment of glory, clutching the much vaunted invitation. Each car has a special sticker with a black X placed in the windscreen to enable it to park, although guests are advised to use public transport if possible. After being searched (cameras are always confiscated) guests are taken through the Bow Room to the crowded lawn at the back of the Palace, where the better advised among them make straight for the tea tent for sandwiches, cakes, scones and Indian tea supplied by J. Lyon and Co., not the Palace kitchens, knowing that anyone hoping to see the Royal Family must eat first and queue later.

The Yeomen of the Guard line the edge of the garden, and the guards bands play selections from light opera in which the inevitable melodies of Sir Arthur Sullivan predominate, as guests form up leaving a mere corridor of lawn for the royal party to traverse from the terrace to the tea tent. At 4 pm the National Anthem is played and the Queen appears with as many members of her family as she can recruit for the afternoon. Attendance is not obligatory and Princess Margaret tends to avoid them like the plague, but Princess Anne is one of the stalwarts. Dressed in a crisp day dress, usually with a wide brimmed hat, it is a social event that provides an opportunity for her to express her gratitude personally. She is always accompanied by either her Private Secretary, an equerry or lady-in-waiting. People will be selected apparently at random, but some at special request will have been strategically placed in a prominent position. An usher will ascertain individual names, business and reason for being present, before the Princess approaches so that she can be introduced on arrival.

'This is Mrs. ——, Ma'am, former President of the —— now engaged in voluntary work with the physically handicapped.'

Having been given a starting point for conversation, the Princess will often display a surprising knowledge of the individual's background and highlight their common interest, be it charity or business. For several minutes she will give that one person her complete attention, leaving a lasting impression that the pleasure has been all hers. 'Whether or not she enjoys these functions, we shall never know,' said one party-goer, 'but she certainly has the knack of making you feel as if you're the most important person present.' It is only a short distance from the terrace to the royal tea tent, but it always takes the Princess over 50 minutes to reach it, one year it took almost 1½ hours to cover the 200 yards.

Having reached the refreshment tent she drinks tea, eats little and is constantly engaged in conversation. Noticeably there is always more laughter surrounding Princess Anne and her father than anywhere else on the 40-acre lawn. The return to the Palace is again relaxed, unhurried. Figures from the equestrian world appear with uncanny frequency on the Princess's side of the route, possibly by design rather than coincidence, but it ensures that she is never lost for words. Garden parties are a successful royal public relations exercise that provide a worthy once-in-a-lifetime experience for thousands of deserving people. The Queen hosts a similar garden party at Holyroodhouse in late June or early July for her subjects north of the border, and Princess Anne organises her Scottish engagements so that she too can attend.

There is often a lot of laughter in the functions that Princess Anne attends, and rarely more so than when she attends an appointment with one of the Services. She holds 26 official titles within the Services (see Appendix II), is Colonel-in-Chief to 11 regiments, and holds other positions ranging from Chief Commandant to Air Commodore. As always, these are roles that she has not accepted lightly nor is she merely a figurehead at the top of official notepaper. Every year she will visit each regiment at least once, will take part in military exercises, and is kept fully informed of all operations. Before she visits any unit to look at equipment or discover more about their work the men and women are advised never to be too technical or try to blind her with science. It comes as something of a shock when the visiting Colonel-in-Chief arrives and actually begins asking highly technical questions, not through being well briefed beforehand but from a genuine interest. Although Princess Anne rejected any suggestion of a university education for herself, she was a little envious of her brothers in their opportunities within the Services. Like her father, the Princess is a great lover of boats and the sea and had she not suffered from sea-sickness she may well have undertaken a period of training in the Navy. One of the earliest Service appointments that the Princess agreed to take on was that of Chief Commandant of the Women's Royal Naval Service (WRNS); she is also Patron of the Association of Wrens, President of the Royal Naval Service Benevolent Trust, a Life Member of the Royal Naval Equestrian Association, and President of the Royal School of Daughters of Officers of the Royal Navy and Royal Marines. Positions that she has held since 1974. Ten years later she agreed to become President of the Missions to Seamen, an organisation that provides hostels and places of refuge for a million and a half seamen in over 300 ports around the world. Not only has she visited branches around the coast of Britain, but in areas ranging from Singapore to Australia, Dubai to Dar-es-Salaam. A voluntary organisation, the Mission provides food, warmth, shelter and companionship for all who work on the sea, be it in the fishing industry or sea rescue.

Many of her posts have been inherited from past royal princesses. Princess Marina, the former Duchess of Kent, had been Chief Commandant of the Women's Royal Naval Service until her death in 1968, and Princess Anne's predecessor as Colonel-in-Chief of the Royal Corps of Signals was the formidable but well-loved Princess Mary, Countess of Harewood, better known as the Princess Royal. Princess Mary was also Colonel-in-Chief of the Royal Scots, another position that Princess Anne now fills. When she became Colonel-in-Chief in 1983 the regiment presented her with the same diamond brooch that her aunt, the Princess Royal, had worn since the First World War. When Princess Mary died in 1965 Princess Anne was too young to take over her roles, and had she been offered them they would have been firmly declined. Not until she felt able to take an active and committed part would Princess Anne accept any part in the Services. So keen were the Royal Corps of Signals to have her as their Colonel-in-Chief that they waited 12 years for her to accept. On 11 June 1977, she was finally appointed.

The late Princess Alice, Countess of Athlone (Queen Victoria's last surviving grandchild) was Commandant-in-Chief of the Women's Transport Service for almost half a century. When she died in January 1981, a month short of her ninety-eighth birthday, there seemed no more fitting person to step into her shoes than Princess Anne. As a relatively recent appointment, the new Commandant has taken an extra interest in the Corps and has a more modern and active approach than obviously Princess Alice could ever have had in her advanced years. This comes as a pleasure to the women, who accept her as a young career woman. The Princess respects their traditions and encourages their ideas.

Whatever the Service, Princess Anne has a lively rapport with 'her' men and women, and she does look upon them with a deep sense of responsibility. If she, for example, visits the 14th/20th King's Hussars in Germany she remembers faces from previous visits, eats in the officers' mess with absolutely no adjustment to the menu, puts on uniform and is prepared to trample through the mud, handle weaponry (in 1985 she fired the gun of a Chieftain tank, using live ammunition and scored direct hits), examine engines and machinery, and makes no concession to the weather or her appearance other than the addition of a Dior headscarf to her green denim uniform. She has the men's total admiration. Princess Anne also derives great enjoyment from mixing with the wives and children of serving officers, perhaps because she can identify closely, being married to a former Army captain herself. She knows what the hours of separation can mean, and through her own travels understands the situation of being posted to work in a strange country. On a more personal level through Prince Andrew's involvement in the Falklands War she knows only too well the fear of having someone close to you in danger. In the conflict nearly 1000 servicemen lost their lives, many more were seriously wounded. For Princess Anne the Falklands War was an anxious time on a variety of levels. From a working point of view her support was needed from the Services of which she is head. Men she had met were killed. Widows needed to be comforted. Morale had to be boosted. In all aspects of her work during those tragic months the campaign overshadowed everything.

From a personal standpoint she had a brother, the one to whom it is said she is closest in spirit, who was in obvious danger. Although she spoke to him on the telephone it was to be over five months before she would see him. Even closer to home the Princess had to support her mother. The Queen suffered enormous stress, as any mother would throughout the time of uncertainty, coupled with the added burden of monarchy during a time of war. 1982 was the year in which the Queen visibly aged. On 16 June, celebrated as VF-Day in Britain, her relieved face appeared on the cover of every national newspaper in the country. Three weeks later Michael Fagan broke into her bedroom at Buckingham Palace; one week later the Queen went into hospital for the first time in her life to have a wisdom tooth removed. Barely recovered from the operation, news was released that her personal bodyguard, Commander Michael Trestrail, had resigned after a homosexual prostitute had attempted to blackmail him, and the following day IRA bomb explosions in Hyde Park and Regent's Park in London killed 11 of the Queen's men of the Household Cavalry. Seven horses were killed and over 50 people injured in the blasts. It was one of the most distressing years of the Queen's reign and throughout it all her daughter proved the greatest support.

A connection with one or more of the Services appears almost compulsory for members of the Royal Family, but some of Princess Anne's appointments have been more controversial. Notably her election as Chancellor of London University in 1981. The Queen Mother had been enrolled as Chancellor of the largest university in Britain with over 40,000 students in 1955. The Chancellorship is for life if the occupant so wishes, but on reaching the age of 80 the Queen Mother felt that it was time to step down and retire gracefully in favour of a younger and more active person. Presenting degrees to 1500 students a year can in itself be a tiring procedure, especially combined with keeping abreast of the academic advances and the institutions within the University.

The Queen Mother was the first woman to hold the position of Chancellor, not only of London, but of any university. The University felt that they wanted to retain a royal female and it was agreed that Princess Anne should be approached and, in consultation with her grandmother, she agreed to accept. Naturally there was criticism. Many grumbled that the Princess had not herself been to university and had no higher qualifications than A-levels, but then neither had the Queen Mother and she had been deemed an acceptable Chancellor for nearly three decades. To avoid any future resentment it was decided that her appointment should be put to the vote. Two more candidates were put up to oppose the Princess. The imprisoned Nelson Mandela, and retired trade union leader Jack Jones became her opponents. Both received a great deal of publicity and apparent support from the students, but on the day of the election on 17 February 1981, Princess Anne was the outright winner. Out of a possible 42,212 votes she received 23,951 – 13,444 more votes than the runner up, Jack Jones. In a fairly fought election nobody could now doubt her popularity, but she still had to prove her suitability.

She gained immediate respect at the time of her installation in October 1981, by refusing an honorary degree. Having originally declined a course of study for a degree after leaving Benenden it would, she felt, have been hypocritical to accept one now. Almost a decade now since her appointment, Princess Anne still considers everyone to be very tolerant of her non-academic background. Although her role is largely ceremonial, attending three degree ceremonies at the Royal Albert Hall annually, various dinners, and functions for retiring dignitaries, she enjoys taking an active part in the Students' Union and discovering more about the various faculties. She has even managed to win over militant students at social functions, impressed by her energy, obvious intelligence, and what they call her 'ordinariness'.

As Chancellor, Princess Anne is particularly supportive of student sporting activities, and it is as a sportswoman that she was asked to become President of the British Olympic Association. Although the Olympic Games are held only every four years, there is an enormous amount of work involved in the intervening years, raising sponsorship money and training athletes. When approached by an organisation the Princess usually takes time to weigh up the situation and consider what benefits she can bring before accepting the challenge, but as a former Olympic competitor herself she did not hesitate in saying yes to the Olympic Committee. Both she and Captain Phillips know what it is like to train for four years and then for one reason or another be unable to take part either through injury, ill health, politics, or simply not making the grade. The career of many athletes is short-lived and to work towards the Olympics and fail can mean the swift end of all hopes. In another four years it could be too late. No sooner had Princess Anne attended the 1984 Olympics in Los Angeles then she and the International Committee began preparations for the 1988 Games in Seoul, South Korea. Prior to the 1984 Olympic Games the Princess paid a four-day visit to the United States, travelling over 14,000 miles to attend 24 fund-raising engagements, and netted £35,000 in donations in the process. 'We knew that Princess Anne would be good for us,' said one member of the British Olympic Association, 'but even we didn't reckon on the stamina of that girl. If there were an Olympic marathon for fund-raising, she'd win hands down, there's no doubt about it.'

As with most of her work, it is a labour of love. She meets every member of the British team because she wants to, there is no question of duty. At the 1984 Winter Olympics in Sarajevo, Yugoslavia, and the main Los Angeles Olympics she watched as many events as was humanly possible, and if she could fit in a sporting fixture with an official engagement, so much the better. In February 1987, with a planned tour of the United Arab Emirates, Qatar, Kuwait and Jordan already in her diary she decided to leave early and paid an unofficial visit to Western Australia for the closing stages of the America's Cup.

Perhaps the strangest entries, and least known to the general public, in Princess Anne's working diary are those which involve livery companies (see Appendix II). The entry for the morning of Thursday 29 January 1987, read: 'As Master of the Worshipful Company of Carmen, attend a Court Meeting of the Company at Carpenter's Hall, Throgmorton Avenue, London, EC2.' For the unitiated these peculiar sounding sects sound somewhat clandestine and sinister, yet they are steeped in history and are of highly reputable origin. Princess Anne is a Freeman, Yeoman, Warden or Master of a number of Livery Companies in the City of London. Every year she will visit each Company with which she is involved at least once. In past centuries every type of industry or trade had its own association, in the same way that some professions have their own union today. There are today 98 livery companies, the oldest being the Saddlers, with Anglo-Saxon origins, and the Weavers, who trace their origins back to the reign of Henry II. In many cases livery companies have strict control over their particular trade, craft or skill, so that apprentices for any of the professions reach a standard approved by the City of London Guilds. This has the effect of keeping control over training, thus preventing any unqualified person setting up a particular type of business without qualification; this in turn protects employers, who know immediately if a job applicant has a sufficient standard of work, and protects customers, who know that the business is good if the relevant certificates have been awarded.

Livery companies have less jurisdiction than in the past when they had their own courts with the power to punish unscrupulous traders and flog obdurate apprentices. Today the liverymen still have considerable powers in the City of London under the Lord Mayor, who is 'King' of the City with only the monarch ranking above him. There are a dozen main companies known as 'The Great Twelve', whose order of precedence has remained unchanged for 500 years:

1 The Mercers (woollen, cotten and linen merchants)
2 The Grocers
3 The Drapers
4 The Fishmongers
5 The Goldsmiths
6 The Merchant Taylors*
7 The Skinners*
8 The Haberdashers
9 The Salters
10 The Ironmongers
11 The Vintners (wine merchants)
12 The Clothworkers
* Alternate order of precedence annually, one year in sixth position, the next in seventh.

Livery companies also include: Apothecaries, Gunmakers, Goldsmiths, Blacksmiths, Dyers, Spectacle Makers, Gardeners, Fruiterers, Glovers, Tallow Chandlers, Barbers, Leathersellers,

Carpenters, Pewterers, Stationers and Farriers. Most major companies and warrant holders providing a service for the Royal Family will be affiliated to the relevant livery company. The Spectacle Makers, for example, grant diplomas in Optical Dispensing; the Apothecaries grant diplomas in Surgery, Medicine, Midwifery, Venereology, Pathology and so on. Those who handle perishable goods, such as the Grocers, Fishmongers and Butchers, undertake quality control checks on produce to maintain standards. For major ceremonial occasions the livery companies may supervise or supply essential items, such as at the Queen's Coronation in 1953. The Glovers provided the Coronation Glove which Her Majesty wore on her right hand, the hand that receives the Coronation ring. The Girdlers produced the golden girdle and stole with which the Queen was adorned as part of the ceremony; Tallow Chandlers gave the candles and the Gardeners the Coronation bouquet.

Princess Anne is connected, not surprisingly, with some of the equestrian and agricultural companies. She supports them because of the money they raise each year for charity and education, and attends dinners and meetings in their very grand guild halls. Once all livery companies had a hall, but the Great Fire of London in 1666, and two World Wars put an end to many. Of the 98 companies only 35 now have a hall, but many that do still exist retain their former splendour, like the Goldsmiths' Hall – which introduced the word 'hallmark' into our language, the Goldsmiths being responsible for the mark that tells us the quality, date and maker of solid gold objects. Livery companies today work tirelessly for charity, often unacknowledged, and over the centuries have founded many schools and institutions. The purpose of the Guild Halls was to provide a meeting place for members, who had formerly met in churches. The religious influence is still apparent in each company for every craft adopted a patron saint from the church where they originally met.

A major function of the livery companies is that they elect the Lord Mayor and Sheriffs of London. Each livery company has a number of positions which are elected annually. Heading each company is a Master (a position that Princess Anne now holds in the Worshipful Company of Carmen), four Wardens, a Clerk and a Beadle, the latter carries a mace in any procession or ceremonial event concerning his company. Elections and ceremonial rituals take place on the relevant saint's day of the company.

One particular ritual can be seen at any livery dinner, when a loving cup is passed around to each member. One person holds the cup while a second drinks and a third stands guard. This odd custom is said to be in memory of King Edward the Martyr, assassinated in AD 978 when, at the institution of his half-brother Ethelred, the King was stabbed whilst drinking from a loving cup which occupies both hands. Someone now always stands guard as a symbolic form of protection; when Princess Anne drinks from the cup her protection is anything but symbolic. The very existence of livery companies provides an assurance that the craftsmen who serve the Royal Family are of the highest standard of workmanship and skill. Princess Anne can certainly rest safe in the knowledge that everything from her horses' saddles to horseshoes will be of the finest quality.

Princess Anne's working activities whether at home or abroad are diverse. Her days are unpredictable; her tasks multifarious. Yet, what benefit does her work actually bring? She provides no visible service, indeed if she visits a factory, shop or business the working output of others will actually diminish during the time of her visit and the hours of preparation required employ many man hours that could probably usefully be engaged elsewhere. If the Princess decided to retire from public life there would be no visible, practical loss; there would be no specific vacancy that it would be necessary to fill with urgency. In reality a role has been created *because* she is a Princess, *because* she decided after leaving school to undertake royal duties. It is hard to define Princess Anne's job, difficult to pinpoint a validity. There may not be a specific hard and fast function, but her achievements in two decades of royal service have been remarkable, the least of which is the vast amount of money that she has raised for valuable causes often through her sheer presence. After attending a charity show in aid of handicapped adults the organiser said: 'To put it bluntly, we got front page coverage with a picture of the Princess in the *Sunday Telegraph* magazine, and with her London Paladium show attendance, we trebled the money we had made with any other single event.' If *one* person benefits, if one single child lives who would otherwise have died, through Princess Anne's involvement she feels that her work is worthwhile. In the end it comes down to far more than hard cash. She also provides the motivation, inspiration, and realisation for thousands. Something no amount of money can ever buy.

Chapter 10

*T*oday and the future

She has been voted Woman of the Year by the BBC, Sportswoman of the Year by the Sportswriters' Guild of Great Britain, has been interviewed on chat shows by Michael Parkinson in Australia and Terry Wogan in London, even breakfast television with David Frost. She became the first member of the Royal Family to undertake a live radio phone-in and appear in a television game show, and in 1987 she won the Variety Club's International Humanitarian Award for her work as President of the Save the Children Fund. 'We believe she has done more for children than anyone else in the world,' said a Variety Club spokesman.

Much has been made of Prince Edward's entry into the TV world, under the gentle guidance of favoured royal director Bryan Forbes, but Princess Anne is unquestionably the communicator in the Royal Family, the most experienced handler of the media and a positive success in every radio and television appearance that she makes. Always asked *what* she would do if the Royal Family were abolished, or if she had not been born royal, the Princess falls back on stock answers connected with farming and horses, but it would not be immodest for her to suggest that she could easily have been a television presenter or interviewer. Having appeared in public from a few weeks old, the Princess is used to handling people and making speeches and displays no obvious nerves. Her television appearances have been relaxed, her enjoyment unequivocal. Her only reservation is the royal mask which she never once allows to slip. She offers complete friendliness until someone attempts to get too close, any bordering on the over-familiar brings on the ice. In

January 1987 she made an unannounced visit to the BBC's Manchester studios to take part in the panel game *A Question of Sport*, joining the team of former England soccer captain Emlyn Hughes as a 'visiting player' for the 200th edition of the programme. She was in a buoyant mood, correctly answering ten questions (although there seemed a greater number of equestrian questions than usual), but her exuberant team captain found it extremely difficult to keep his hands to himself. Princess Anne tolerated the proddings, pattings and arm flinging of Emlyn Hughes. Jokingly she threatened to hit him with her handbag several times, but when Hughes attempted to become a little too friendly, the royal mask came firmly into place. The Princess sat visibly on the edge of her seat in an attempt to stay out of arm's reach. After the show she went with her team members to the hospitality room for tea and sandwiches, but the conversation revolved strictly around sport and her own riding career. With practiced art she appeared to give so much of herself, but revealed nothing.

Princess Anne's appearances before the camera have been many. Informally she appeared in the now classic television film *Royal Family*, the first major attempt to show the human side of royalty and break down the barriers of remoteness. Between 8 June 1968, and 18 May 1969, a film crew under the direction of the late Richard Cawston (who for many years directed the Queen's Christmas broadcast) spent 75 days filming members of the Royal Family in almost 200 locations. The resulting 43 hours of film were edited down to 1 hour 50 minutes and watched by 25 million people on its first showing. It was a major breakthrough in television history, shedding a new light on royalty in a decade when their popularity had been on the wane, their relevance questioned? Putting them under the spotlight in a year which was climaxed by the Investure of the Prince of Wales resulted in a new wave of patriotism. Royalty enjoyed a new popularity that had not been known since the Coronation. Elderly peers frowned on the display of human weaknesses shown by the monarch, but the majority appreciated this unique and privileged glimpse of the Queen as a wife and mother.

Princess Anne was shown in a variety of situations – at a family luncheon; grilling steaks and sausages at a family barbeque on the Balmoral estate; in glittering evening gown and tiara at a diplomatic reception at Buckingham Palace for ambassadors and high commissioners; chatting with the British Olympic team at a buffet luncheon; on a stud farm looking at racehorses; decorating the Christmas tree at Windsor Castle; training labrador puppies on the Sandringham Estate; taking French lessons after leaving Benenden; meeting Richard Nixon, then President of the United States; and being slung across on a rope from the Royal Yacht *Britannia* to an escorting frigate. Never had the general public seen the Princess in such detail. Until now she had been hidden behind the walls of Benenden, and had not yet blossomed into womanhood. A leading women's magazine said of her, 'Poor Princess Anne. She's eighteen and nobody thinks she's a pretty girl. If I were her mother, the first thing I'd do is slim her down; she has to stop looking like her mother. The frumpy fur stoles, the middle-aged evening gowns. The over-done hair. The under-done hair. The sloppy grooming. It's about time Anne was allowed to blossom on her own.' Within a year of the *Royal Family* film, the *Daily Mirror* was writing, 'Princess Anne is growing up the wittiest, gayest, and most natural of Royal Princesses', and she was embarking on a new televison project. This time a royal safari for the popular children's television programme *Blue Peter*. With televison presenter Valerie Singleton she flew to Kenya for eight days to visit game parks, but more importantly it was her television debut as President of the Save the Children Fund. It is with her in this role that many other television programmes have followed, including *Saving the Children* which concentrated on her tour of the Gambia and Burkina Faso. As a seasoned performer now, when documentaries are made about her working life it comes across that although she is conscious of the cameras, the work takes priority. The film crew are secondary and very much part of the scenery. Those who work with her in this capacity for the first time admit to some trepidation in the wake of Princess Anne's reputation, but they find her professional in her approach and unexpectedly co-operative, even to the extent of discussing camera angles and the best shots. In a number of documentaries about her charity work she has been happy to provide the commentary. If the correct balance is achieved, as she wishes, the end result is not her own blossoming as a television star, but a far greater public awareness of the causes close to her heart.

In these circumstances Princess Anne endears herself to the public and media men alike. She comes across as human, intelligent and witty. As we have seen, clashes with the media occur in those grey areas that Princess Anne regards as private and the press men see as interesting news. Competitive horse-riding is the main area in question. When Princess Anne rides it is as a sportswoman, not as a member of the Royal Family. Unfortunately it takes place in public and so coverage by the press is unavoidable however irritating it may be to her. To the media royalty are only off duty when they are out of sight. If they step out in public, be it to visit a restaurant, theatre, or take part in sport, they are considered fair game for the cameraman. When the cameras pry into her children's lives, Princess Anne gets particularly annoyed. Interest in them is obvious because they are the Queen's grandchildren and that, she says, 'will be with them for the rest of their lives', but as far as possible she has attempted to shield them from the public gaze. As they get older, pressure from the press begins to mount. On 19 January 1987, Zara Phillips arrived with her nanny, Sarah Minty at Beaudesert Park prep school, two miles from Gatcombe Park. It was her first day at the new school following the closure of nearby Blue Boys school that she had previously attended, and the newsmen were out in force to take what turned out to be very uninspiring pictures. Princess Anne was not pleased. As Peter and Zara reach their teenage years speculation will begin as to possible future marriage partners, intended careers, and nothing will dim the spotlight. Princess Anne had to suffer, and for her children there will be no escape.

Where journalists have consistently aggravated Princess Anne is through their invention of stories to sell newspapers, and fabricated anecdotes that can never be verified. With constant speculation about her supposedly foundering marriage, it was inevitable that eventually a newspaper would begin to explore the area of possible extra-marital affairs. Wearing a slightly more risqué gown than usual, the Princess was photographed apparently gazing into the eyes of actor Anthony Andrews at the fiftieth birthday celebrations of the Piccadilly store Simpsons. Some newspapers failed to mention that Andrews' wife, Georgina Simpson, is a director of the shop and it is she who has been a close friend of the Princess and Captain Phillips for a number of years. This Golden Jubilee celebration at Simpsons was Princess Anne's fourth engagement of the day and proceeds and donations went to the Save the Children Fund.

The most dramatic revelation had arisen a year earlier when, in 1985, a national Sunday newspaper serialised an exclusive story from one of Princess Anne's former bodyguards, Sergeant Peter Cross, which implied a closer 'friendship' between the Princess and the detective than would normally be expected. Members of the

Royal Family quite naturally build up a close bond with personal detectives. They spend a great deal of time in each other's company travelling to and from engagements and spend much of the working day together, in close proximity for obvious security reasons. A detective is always in residence when the Princess is at Gatcombe Park, and although she can horseride on her own estate without too much risk, protection is needed at even the most private of sporting events. Policemen become part of the Royal Family's working team, the Princess calls hers by their Christian names, and it is quite natural to see the detective at horse trials giving Peter or Zara a piggy back, or carrying the Princess's harness or saddle. Sergeant Cross apparently misunderstood the Princess's familiarity and read more into her friendliness than she had ever anticipated. He was immediately removed from Royal Protection and transferred to uniformed duties, with a reduction in salary. It was not long before this reduction was boosted with a £200,000 fee for the sale of his 'exclusive' story to the *News of the World* about his relationship with Princess Anne. There was a public outcry as a result, in defence of the Princess, and Members of Parliament called for stricter controls on the Official Secrets Act. Members of the Royal Household today must sign the Act, which makes it illegal to reveal anything that they have seen while in Royal service. In 1950 ex-governess Marion Crawford published an account of her years with the young Princess Elizabeth and Princess Margaret, called *The Little Princesses*. Although it revealed nothing too shocking, the Royal Family felt betrayed by their former employee. Following the success of her book, in 1955 Marion Crawford turned her hand to writing magazine articles, penning an account of The Trooping of the Colour ceremony and the Ascot races that year. Her blow-by-blow account was published in June, revealing all that had taken place – yet both events were actually cancelled because of a rail strike after the magazine went to press, bringing 'Crawfie's' new career to a swift conclusion. Today to prevent any other ex-employee revealing all to the press, before joining the Household every member of staff is forced to sign the Official Secrets Act. On rare occasions now when former staff sell their story to the newspapers, an injunction is brought out to prevent publication. In America an ex-valet of Prince Charles, the late Stephen Barry, made in the region of a million dollars out of his best-selling autobiography, and although it was harmless and fully supportive of the Prince of Wales, it was not allowed to be published in Britain because of the Act. The police, however, even those in the Royal Protection Squad are not yet required to sign the Official Secrets Act, which is how Cross was able to get away with his so-called revelations. Fortunately both the Princess and her husband have the ability to laugh at the fabrications involving them.

In February 1986 a German magazine shocked Princess Anne by publishing an 'exclusive' anouncement that she was expecting her third child. They obviously knew something that she didn't! The Buckingham Palace Press Office is completely non-plussed by any 'exclusive' in a foreign publication. They once started to collect cuttings of the ludicrously fabricated stories, such as the Queen's imminent abdication, Her Majesty's and Princess Anne's divorce, and various reports ranging from family feuds to abortions. Eventually the files became too large and the task impossible to keep abreast of. It was expected that this story would disappear into obscurity like the others, but a few days later the *Sunday People* printed their own front page exclusive, headlined ANNE'S BABY SECRET She Has Seen Her Doctor And Told The Queen. 'Princess Anne is to be a mum again,' wrote journalist John Jordan, 'Doctors have confirmed that her third child is due in late summer.' The article went on to state as fact where the baby was conceived, while Anne and Mark were on an Alpine skiing holiday that was described as a second honeymoon.

The stories emerged from little more than the fact that the Princess returned from the holiday looking radiant and happy. Nothing more than one would expect after a family sojourn away from her punishing work schedule. When asked outright if she was pregnant, when attending the annual dinner of Bristol Chamber of Commerce and Industry to thank them for presenting a Land Rover to the Save the Children Fund for use in deprived countries, Princess Anne simply smiled. Immediately the ink in columnists' pens began boiling; their fertile minds worked overtime. If the Princess were not pregnant she would not have smiled. Buckingham Palace refused to issue a denial, adding fuel to the already well-lit flames. The general public wanted the Princess to have a child, it would seem a happy conclusion to the less happy rumours about the state of her marriage. On Princess Anne's instructions the Palace Press Officer refused to comment, determined not to be pushed into making a statement one way or the other on a speculative and untrue story. Even if the Palace had commented it would not have been believed, denials being forever suspect since they made the error of covering up Princess Anne's romance with Mark Phillips only hours before their engagement was announced.

Eventually Princess Anne quashed the rumours in March by announcing that she would ride as an amateur jockey in the forth-coming flat race season, effectively putting an end to any possible speculation. Royal or not, no right-minded doctor would allow a five- or six-month pregnant woman to race.

With this infuriating episode behind her, the Princess launched an attack on the news media using a dinner hosted by the board of directors of the Associated Press as the perfect opportunity. 'This year,' she said, 'I suffered severe aggravation from the amount of unadulterated trivia, rubbish and gratuitous trouble-making that appeared in all sections of the so-called media in response to a perfectly normal family occasion (referring to stories published before the wedding of Prince Andrew to Sarah Ferguson) . . . I would like to be able to read a newspaper, magazine or watch the news on television without having to make constant translations and adjustments for exaggerations and sometimes lies.' At the end of the 15-minute speech, which she had, as usual, written herself, she was applauded warmly by the 160 guests who included leading British newspaper publishers, editors and broadcast executives, many of whom were guilty parties in the scandalmongering. Com-bining her attack with jokes, Princess Anne raised the subject of ancient practices that required slanderers to pay fines or have their tongues cut out, 'Well you know where I stand!' she said. It was a brave and successful attempt to hit back at the media, and no doubt removed many deep-seated grievances from the royal target's sys-tem. 'Nobody could accuse her of lack of guts,' said the Associated Press chairman, Frank Batten.

Although journalists are not a favoured breed amongst royalty, Princess Anne has given more interviews to writers and offered a greater degree of co-operation than any other member of the Fami-ly. Obtaining an interview with a member of the Royal Family is one of the most difficult assignments that a journalist will ever have. In an interview with journalist and writer Douglas Keay in 1970 the Duke of Edinburgh pointed out that anything the Queen said in an interview would be laid open to misinterpretation and would therefore do more harm than good. The television coup of the century, the Queen being interviewed by Terry Wogan (who has declared himself second only to the Royal Family in fame) will unfortunately never happen.

To obtain an interview with Princess Anne is a greater possibility, but still extremely difficult and it has often taken journalists over a year to achieve. The great majority are disappointed; their subject matter must be immediate. To plan an interview six or eight months in advance would lack the essential news impact for many newspaper editors. To begin the procedure a journalist must in the first instance write to the Queen's Press Secretary, not directly to Princess Anne's office. A telephone call to the Press Office is insufficient; the Press Secretary must have written details of the writer's name, publication and subject matter. It is insufficient to request simply an interview, there must be a concrete reason for doing so. If the Princess has been overseas on a Save the Children mission, if she has launched an appeal for the Riding for the Disabled Association, if she has a cause (such as the travellers) that she wishes to highlight, a journalist may possibly get her to talk formally about these areas of her work.

Forty-nine times out of 50 the request for an interview will be politely but firmly refused, always ending with the phrase 'I'm sorry to have to give you this disappointing reply'. In these cases Princess Anne will not even be aware that a request has been made. If, however, the Press Secretary feels that the journalist's project is worthy of consideration he will pass the letter over to Princess Anne's Private Secretary. As Princess Anne's closest working contact, the Private Secretary will have some idea as to the reaction he will receive on raising the matter with her. Often he knows that it will be a waste of time even suggesting the interview and so he personally will contact the journalist and decline. If he feels that there is a distinct possibility that an interview might be granted, he will add the request to the agenda for Princess Anne's next six-monthly planning meeting. If the journalist makes his approach at the end of July, for example, it could be that he will have to wait until December before the next planning meeting. Another six month delay.

At the meeting the request will be put before the Princess. Here the worthiness of the subject is paramount. The schedule is full of charitable causes; if the journalist wishes to cover old ground then the Princess will consider an interview a waste of her time. 'It's been done before,' she will say wearily, and the proposal will be relegated to the rejection pile. The lucky and rare individual who captures the Princess's attention will receive an approving nod and a provisional date will be pencilled in at a time convenient to the

Princess, not the journalist. The date can be anything up to a year in advance, and the Private Secretary will send a letter of agreement detailing time and venue and will request that the journalist submit a list of proposed questions. As only 15 or 20 minutes will be granted the questions must be relevant and concise. Depending upon the journalist's style of questioning, the list will be returned intact or with a number of deletions. The questions will have been discussed with Princess Anne beforehand.

For the journalist there is little more to do than complete the necessary wait. The day before the interview Princess Anne will study the questions again and formulate some answers. It will almost certainly be an area of her work that she knows well and will require little preparation. Occasionally she will check facts and figures for accuracy. On the appointed day the interviewer will arrive at Buckingham Palace, where interviews are generally held in the second floor office. Occasionally for convenience of the Princess and the journalist, or after a special request, the talk will be held in the sitting room at Gatcombe Park, a room filled with souvenirs that have been acquired on world travels.

At Buckingham Palace, after giving your name to the policeman on the right-hand gate of the Palace (used by royalty and visitors alike on a general day-to-day basis), if you have been granted an interview you go to the Privy Purse Door, up the crimson carpet steps, which can be seen from The Mall, to the door itself, opened for you by a scarlet-clad footman who again takes your name before ushering you into a nearby waiting-room containing impressive gilded chairs and two paintings by the Victorian artist W. P. Frith. Here you will be left to wait. In keeping with the calm air that pervades Palace life, all is leisurely and unhurried. Eventually a footman will collect you and lead you to an equally slow lift to begin your journey to Princess Anne's office. As you approach, the door (already ajar, as are many office doors within the Palace m telephone conversations can clearly be heard ringing down the crimson carpeted corridors of this museum-like building) will be opened by the Private Secretary or, more usually, Princess Anne.

At the initial introduction she will be brisk and business-like; the handshake firm, the eyes of cold grey blue will almost penetrate into your inner being as she evaluates you as a person. You have yet to prove your credibility. She has no patience with time-wasters and the ill-prepared; she does not suffer fools gladly and you must be equally firm and confident.

If you succeed, the eyes warm to you, the frostiness melts. Princess Anne will put you immediately at ease. If you fail, if you take her for granted, abuse the privilege of the meeting, display disrespect, you will get short shrift. Journalists who win her over can get an hour of relaxed conversation, the less careful get ten minutes of concise to-the-point answers.

The office, once the nursery, overlooking The Mall, is elegant, chintzy, but decidedly practical. Antique furniture is intermingled with modern teak. There are framed family photographs standing on top of a large television set, and a modern wooden sculpture. The high-ceilinged room has animal paintings. On top of a loud-speaker stands a toy plastic 'gonk', and as with practically every room in the Palace there are floral arrangements, the Queen spending over £250,000 annually on flowers. The room looks comfortable and lived in. Adjacent is Princess Anne's business office where a secretary works and her computer is housed.

Interviewing Princess Anne can be an extremely enjoyable experience. She has a very dry and sharp sense of humour, and if you want realistic answers to genuine questions, she will provide them. The appointment is only daunting for the ill-prepared. Anything too trite will be dismissed, any attempt to discover personal details will be neatly side-stepped. It is not unknown for a journalist to be told, 'That is a ridiculous question,' or she will say, 'You're leading onto a rather different sphere,' if you deviate too much from the intended topic.

One area of Princess Anne's private life has recently taken a new turn. From three-day eventer she has turned flat racer, and for once she has not taken exception to the mixture of journalists with this former 'grey area'. Flat racing was a new skill that she has been determined to develop, and she could quite literally have fallen flat on her face in public, but as every race has been heavily sponsored to raise money for her favoured charities she has been happy to receive publicity, even if the end result could turn out to be a sporting disaster. As it happened she turned her first race at Epsom into a personal Derby. For a first-time jockey the experts described the Princess as having all the 'grit and panache of a seasoned veteran'. On her horse Against the Grain she came in a creditable fourth at 11–1. Her trainer, David Nicholson, was impressed with the performance, 'She did everything right. She rode a very smooth race and didn't get flustered. The horse just wasn't fast enough, that's all.' Princess Anne was less convinced. 'I think I'll write that one off,' she laughed, but obviously she had enjoyed this new experience and had acquired a taste for the racecourse. Her ambition was to become the first member of the Royal Family to win a race under Jockey Club rules. Prince Charles has tried and failed, never reaching higher than second place at Plumpton in 1980.

A few months later Princess Anne was racing again, this time as the punters' favourite in the Hayward Pickle Stakes. Although according to her trainer she was technically riding better, she only came in eighth out of 29 horses. Before the race the Princess was offered her own private changing facilities, but refused any special privileges and insisted on getting ready in the communal changing room with the other female participants.

On Tuesday 5 August 1986, on her thirteenth attempt, Princess Anne romped home by five lengths in the Mommessin Amateur Riders' Stakes at the small Redcar seaside track in Cleveland. In just one year she had fulfilled her ambition in a faultless race on Gulfland belonging to Mr. Gavin Pritchard-Gordon, who was obviously delighted about the win. In the winner's enclosure the beaming Princess received a magnum of champagne for her efforts and was given a standing ovation by the crowd. 'I've always wanted to have success,' she said later. 'I enjoy the business of riding out and going to the races and to have a winner certainly makes a difference to the level of enjoyment. It's all down to generous owners who let me ride, and to horses like Gulfland who do not mind being ridden by idiots, or even prefer it.' The Princess laughed, the cameramen took their pictures, both in perfect harmony. A few days short of her thirty-sixth birthday, at last the Princess appeared to have mellowed. Her chance came again in July 1987, when she won the coveted Dresden Diamond Stakes at Ascot riding Ten No Trumps.

At the end of the decade Princess Anne will reach the landmark of her fortieth birthday. The 1980s have seen the Princess blossom from an irritable unfulfilled young woman into a confident, self-assured lady. Her family is now complete with a boy and a girl, her marriage, despite the rumours, is solid in its foundations. In public she is more relaxed than before, the pressures of youth behind her. With increased public awareness and admiration of her work, Princess Anne has a certain aura that puts her in a class of her own amongst royal princesses. The Princess of Wales, the Duchess of York, the Gloucesters, the Kents, are royal ladies who have come from non-royal backgrounds. They are people with whom the girl in the street can identify, but Princess Anne retains the mystery that has long surrounded the Queen and the Queen Mother, an inherent aloofness that sets them apart. Princess Anne has been seen plunging into water at Badminton, covered in mud after riding, at work she has operated a mechanical digger, climbed an oil rig, driven tractors and buses, yet throughout it all retains an unquestionable dignity.

Princess Anne taught herself to type and we are full of praise, but thousands of people are self-taught typists. This irrational placing on a pedestal stems from her birthright. Paradoxically Princess Anne is more 'ordinary' and down to earth than those who have married into the Royal Family and members of the aristocracy. Margaret, Duchess of Argyll, once said to journalist Lynda Lee Potter in an interview: 'I have never cooked. I can't cook. I do not wish to cook,' adding later, 'I would offer you a cup of tea but I'm afraid I can't. My maid isn't here.' The trenchant scribe wrote that the 'mundane chores of day-to-day living have totally bypassed the glorious duchess'. The same cannot be said for Princess Anne who, given the choice, would much rather make the tea herself then sit twiddling her thumbs waiting for a member of staff to serve it.

The atmosphere at Gatcombe Park is relaxed, informal with the air of a country house rather than a royal residence. The house is half a mile from the main road and not visible to the public so that the Phillips family can be 'at home and not very much in evidence'. The perfect setting for an Agatha Christie film, the house has a rambling garden with a folly built by a former occupant. The rooms are homely with a lived-in, comfortable feel. An antique rocking-horse is on display in the large entrance hall, but it has never been out of bounds to Peter or Zara, or visiting children. It was made to be played with, and it fulfils its original purpose, even though today the children prefer live ponies to the wooden variety. Although there is a permanent cook (or semi-permanent, for professionals discover that they can earn far more money in a hotel or private house than in a royal residence and tend to depart swiftly), the Princess is happy to take a turn in the kitchen and since her Save the Children Fund tours has become much more adventurous with her food. At the end of February 1987 the Princess had lunch at an Indian community centre in Leeds. On the menu were samosas, mutton biryani, a dish of rice and chickpeas, followed by sweet sticky cakes. Just in case this did not tempt the royal palate, in reserve they had waiting milder alternatives of egg mayonaise and cheese sandwiches, but Princess Anne tucked into the Indian menu with relish. Not because she did not wish to offend her hosts, but because she enjoys curry and spicy dishes. If friends call in for a light supper they are quite likely to congregate in the kitchen while the Princess produces scrambled eggs. Surprisingly, close friends *do* simply drop in occasionally for lunch or supper. It is difficult for Princess Anne to fit in with their arrangements, but they know when she is free and she likes nothing better than friends ringing up on the spur of the moment and taking pot-luck.

The social circle is naturally small. Royalty choose their friends carefully. People cannot themselves choose to be friends with royalty. It takes a long time to build up a relationship, but once Mark and the Princess find people they can trust, people who will not talk to the press or even socially to colleagues about Princess Anne's private life then they have friends for life. Being friends with the Phillips does not only mean social gatherings at Gatcombe Park, they in turn are quite happy to spend weekends at friends' houses, and at least once a year Princess Anne and Mark will stay with their close companions, the former motor racing champion Jackie Stewart and his wife Helen. Princess Anne it seems is an easy, undemanding guest who helps out domestically and is quite at home in relaxed surroundings. She wants to be treated as a friend rather than a guest, after spending almost her entire working life as somebody's guest.

Those honoured with the hand of friendship are privileged to see Mrs. Anne Phillips, wife and mother. The woman who, under other circumstances, would have been happy to settle in the country with children, horses and dogs, enjoying an active life in sport and country pursuits. It's not that she would shun the glamour and the royal ritual given the choice, she enjoys films, theatre and lively parties, but in an ideal world she would prefer to slip into the stalls unnoticed than in the spotlight of the royal box; she would like to dance the night away unannounced rather than as guest of honour. But, there are compensations and comforts of being royal that she would not deny and would reluctantly surrender. Financially she is secure. If the farm at Gatcombe Park did not pay its way, if Mark's business interests collapsed, the family would never starve. Princess Anne may be careful with money to the point of being thrifty, but financial problems do not hang over her head like the sword of Damocles as with many twentieth-century aristocrats. Although the children's future careers may give cause for concern in the next decade, she can at least provide the best education for them. She may grudge spending money on clothes, but the best designers are at her disposal when she needs them. Horse riding may be the sport of kings, but there is no shortage of horse owners willing to lend Princess Anne a competent horse if she needs one. Travel will never be a problem, with traffic halted along her route if necessary, the Queen's Flight and the Royal Train available to her, and if in the right location the Royal Yacht *Britannia* provides a floating palace on the sea.

Unlike some members of the Royal Family, Princess Anne's endearing quality is that she realises the privileges that she has in life and never takes them for granted. She more than most has seen real unadulterated poverty. Having witnessed the slums, filth and squalor that exists in our own apparently civilised towns, she appreciates the relative luxury that Gatcombe Park affords. This she drums into her own children, who cannot yet understand the horrific sights that their mother has seen and refused to be spared, but she has done her best to instil in them values, and a realisation of the quality of human life. Zara and Peter have not been spoilt, have never had all their own way, have not been burdened down with possessions so great that their intrinsic worth is lost. Manners have been placed higher than money, love ranks higher than material wealth. Conscious of her position, through sheer hard work Princess Anne has attempted to give something back in return for the richness she has received, and it is a return worth its weight in gold.

As a wife and mother Princess Anne has found it hard when work has kept her apart from her husband and children. In some ways she tries to over-compensate when they are together, but angrily dismisses any suggestion that she is over-protective towards her children. They live out of the public eye in the country because that is their home, she insists. She encourages them to live as normal a life as possible, enjoy their friends and school life, because the kind of life she leads means nothing to them and the work she undertakes will not be copied by them. When she is free to spend time with the children, they do everything together. Although there is a nanny to act as a stabilising and practical influence in the children's life, Princess Anne was involved in their early upbringing. Never were they packed off to the nursery and brought out for an hour in the evening as still happens in some country homes. The large attic,

The ninth wedding anniversary family portrait by Norman Parkinson.

Princess Anne and Mark Phillips at work on the farm.

Controversial again, the Princess meets the travellers.

A visit to a sausage factory in Suffolk shows another aspect of the variety of Anne's work.

At the première of a **A Passage to India** *Princess Anne proves that she can still compete in the royal fashion stakes.*

formerly servants' bedrooms, at Gatcombe Park has been converted into the bright equivalent of a self-contained apartment for Peter and Zara. This is where their bedrooms are, there is a playroom, somewhere to do schoolwork, a bathroom, sitting-room and a small kitchen; they are not confined to quarters (unless naughty, when they are smacked and sent to bed, which rarely happens) but they have somewhere that they can call their own and it has given them an early sense of responsibility.

There is today a very small contingent of servants – a butler, who doubles as a valet for Mark Phillips, Princess Anne's dresser for formal occasions, a cook and two daily ladies who come in to clean. 'The servants are in the background always,' says a close friend, 'Anne doesn't ring for the butler or anything like that. The sitting-room is the central gathering place; it's very homely and usually cluttered with toys.' Because the land around Gatcombe is farming land, the Princess has no need to employ a gardener. Neither does she have a chauffeur of her own. The royal cars are housed at Buckingham Palace and chauffeurs are part of the Queen's Household. All those who work on the farm, those who help out in the stables, and the children's nanny, make up the staff (Princess Anne hates the word 'servant', which she finds demeaning) and are all paid for out of the Princess's private money or the income from the farm, as appropriate. The Civil List income is used purely for the official side of life, never private. Ladies-in-waiting are in attendance only on public engagements, if they visit Gatcombe Park it is generally for a social visit, or if it is Princess Anne's base for a particular working day. Leonora Lichfield, ex-wife of royal photographer Lord Lichfield, is perhaps closest socially to the Princess, and is often included in the Queen's private house parties at Sandringham and Balmoral. She and Princess Anne have been friends for many years.

The Royal Family are a very close-knit community and it is only when Princess Anne is with her husband and children or her own immediate relations that she feels totally able to relax and forget about public duties. Although the Queen and her daughter are extremely close today, this has not always been so due to the Princess's rebellious nature. Once at Sandringham the family were getting ready to follow the hounds and Princess Anne announced that she was going to get her dogs. 'Would you fetch mine, too?' asked the Queen. 'Get your own dogs,' snapped the Princess. The Queen was visibly livid. As the Princess has grown older a closer bond has developed, and it is no secret that the Queen has the greatest admiration for her daughter's work. From her mother, Princess Anne has learnt a devotion to duty and the two find it easy to discuss worries and problems with each other. Interviewers have often raised the question of how it feels to have the Queen as a mother, but to Princess Anne she is a mother first and foremost. Being monarch is a secondary role.

It is the father and daughter relationship that she has with the Duke of Edinburgh that is probably closer, as in many families. In temperament the Princess is much more akin to her father. They are fiery by nature, intolerant of incompetence, both love sport, are fascinated by modern technology, and he has encouraged her equestrian activities. The Prince is greatly concerned about the problems of the Third World and is proud of his daughter's achievements in this area. Neither father nor daughter particularly enjoy the pomp and ceremony of being royal. Prince Philip has been known to have a miniature radio and earpiece secreted about his person to discretely relieve the boredom of long formal functions. They both have an overwhelming dislike of the press. When Prince Philip visited Gibraltar to see the famous monkeys, he looked at the press corps surrounding him and asked, 'Which are the monkeys?'

Of her three brothers she feels naturally nearer to Prince Andrew and Prince Edward as they are the youngest, and in many ways in a similar position to herself with which she can identify. She has a close affinity with Prince Charles as they are the eldest and spent ten years together before Prince Andrew's birth, but they are like chalk and cheese in their nature and approach to life. In the press she has apparently branded her elder brother 'a wimp', this could be pure media mythology but the Prince of Wales has a less positive side to his nature and lacks his sister's dynamism and energy. In sport Princess Anne is on a par with her husband, but has always had the edge over Prince Charles. It is probably *because* of the Prince of Wales that Princess Anne has a subconscious desire to succeed. Being the second-born implied second best. By the laws of inheritance Charles will be king and master of all he surveys, while Princess Anne will continue to be pushed further and further down the line of succession. In history second-born daughters had only one role to play, that was to marry into another royal family to join together two great dynasties and allies. In rebellion, if not deliberately, Princess Anne married a commoner. She might say that she did not choose to fall in love with a non-royal or untitled person, but it is typical of her character that she did.

As Anne, Edward and Andrew are all behind Prince Charles, a close bond has grown between them. Today, the position that once irritated Princess Anne is now a source of comfort to her. With mature eyes and hindsight, she sees the pressures that are involved with being 'Number One', the heir to the throne. Freedom is restricted, the expectations greater. This she has been spared. She can serve Queen and country, and when the time comes King and country, in her own way. Had there been any possibility that she might one day inherit the throne there would have been opposition to her marriage.

As the only girl amongst three boys Princess Anne fulfilled a variety of roles. When the Queen was abroad or away from home, she became a mother figure, sorted out squabbles, gave advice, and played games. She also came in for teasing, hair pulling, and was a source of amusement to them at times. Today there is great affection, and often Prince Andrew and certainly Prince Edward feel that they can talk to Princess Anne about a worry more easily than they can approach the Queen or the Duke of Edinburgh. On numerous occasions the diplomatic side of Princess Anne's nature has surfaced and she has acted as peacemaker in family disputes. Prince Charles has frequently irritated his father and in royal circles it is common knowledge that they have had major disagreements that have resulted in the Duke not speaking to his son. It has been Princess Anne who has eventually poured oil on troubled waters.

In early 1987 when Prince Edward decided to quit the Royal Marines after only four months because he found the commando training uncongenial, Prince Philip was angry. Knowing that it would be seen as failure and embarrassment for the Royal Family, his father tried to persuade his son to change his mind and was furious when the Prince disobeyed his wishes. For anyone else it would have been possible to put the experience down to a bad choice and wipe the slate clean, but for the Prince it was high profile news, headlined in the press for four consecutive days.

To get away from the Duke of Edinburgh and to gather his thoughts, Prince Edward turned to his sister and was given refuge at Gatcombe Park. Princess Anne gave her brother full support, applauding his decision to go his own way and not be dictated to by convention. There were, she pointed out, several options open to him. He could return to teaching, something he had enjoyed in

New Zealand; he could take up the director general of the Confederation of British Industry Sir Terence Beckett's offer of work in industry, or he could pursue a career in the arts, either the theatre or broadcasting. It would be new ground for a member of the Royal Family, but whatever path he chooses he can count on her support. She sympathised that the stigma of the Marines episode will haunt her brother for the rest of his life, made all the more difficult by the fact that the Duke of Edinburgh is honorary Captain General of the Royal Marines, but supports the theory that everyone should enjoy their work, just as she finds great rewards from her own.

In 1968 Princess Anne was confronted with the decision that her younger brother has been forced to face up to. What was she to do with her life? Which path did she wish to take? She forsook a university education and the chance of a career to enter royal service. It is a decision that she has not regretted, and she is now firmly established at the top of the royal league of workers. But what does the future hold for the working Princess? Will she continue to take on added responsibilities, or will she slowly reduce the number of engagements as the years roll by and settle for the life of a country landowner's wife?

As someone who is easily bored and needs constant stimulation, it is unlikely that she will relinquish any of her royal duties, using the Queen and the Queen Mother as examples. It seems unlikely too that she will accept any appointments as challenging as her Presidency of the Save the Children Fund, yet there will come a time when something will be needed to fill a gap in Princess Anne's life. By the end of the century Princess Anne will reach a point when Peter and Zara are married and have homes of their own. By that time she will be feeling less able to participate so physically in the sports that she now enjoys. Too young and unwilling to retire from public life Princess Anne will need to find a new function.

Each time that the New Year's Honours List was published, and each time that Princess Anne reached a birthday milestone, speculation began about the possibility of her being created the Princess Royal. At the end of 1986 the *Daily Mail*'s Court Correspondent, Andrew Morton, wrote: 'Princess Anne has bowed to pressure from the Queen and agreed to accept the honorary title of the Princess Royal . . . for years the Princess, who is not worried by titles, fought against the award. But now her close friends say an announcement is "imminent". The most likely time is the New Year's Honours List.'

Similar stories had been published annually for 20 years. The title was always 'imminent', but never arrived. It was something that Princess Anne refused to be drawn on. There had not been a Princess Royal since the Countess of Harewood died in 1965, and to the younger generation the title tends to conjure up the image of a wiry, severe and prudish spinster, or a matronly dowager. Princess Anne falls into neither category, nor have many of her predecessors. Few people of any generation know anything about the title and any notions that there are are misconceived. It has, for example, long been the assumption that the first born daughter of a British monarch is automatically created Princess Royal at birth. This was certainly the belief of Queen Victoria, who was not amused to discover that a Royal Warrant was necessary and that it was not a birthright but a gift. Her daughter, Princess 'Vicky', was actually eight weeks old before she officially received the distinction. When Princess Anne was born in 1950 her mother was heir presumptive, not the sovereign, and as there was already a living Princess Royal there was no question of the title being conferred. Even if the situation had been different, Princess Anne would not have been given the title automatically in the same way that Princes Charles rightfully became the Duke of Cornwall from the moment of his birth.

In the history of the monarchy the title of Princess Royal is a relatively recent rank, being only 350 years old. Since its creation there have been countless elder daughters yet only six Princesses Royal. King Charles I created the honour for his first born daughter, Mary, in approximately 1641, although the exact date is unrecorded. There was no apparent ceremony, and any particulars that might have been laid down would have been destroyed along with other historic records during Oliver Cromwell's dictatorship. With the title came no formal duties, responsibilities or privileges; it does not alter the line of succession; there is no financial inheritance or Civil List increase, and unlike the Prince of Wales, the Princess Royal does not become princess of any territory. The title is nevertheless seen as an honour bestowed by the Monarch on the eldest daughter, often at a period when she has attained the affection of the nation. It is afforded as a mark of respect and a symbol of acknowledgement. Since 1983 there had been calls for Princess Anne to be suitably honoured following the recognition of her working success overseas.

The position of Princess Royal had been vacant for almost a

quarter of a century and ever since Princess Anne's sixteenth birthday there had been pressure on the Queen to grant her daughter the title. There was great speculation that it would be bestowed at the time of her eighteenth and twenty-first birthdays, and again an announcement was expected at the time of her marriage in 1973. Yet Princess Anne did not feel it was a gift that could be taken for granted. Given the choice, it is possible that the Queen would have honoured her daughter sooner, but on Saturday 13 June 1987 the birthday honours list announced that Princess Anne had at long last agreed to accept the title. The news was greeted with universal approval; had it been awarded ten years earlier there would undoubtedly have been criticism. Asked how she felt on receiving the title, Princess Anne answered with magical brevity 'honoured'.

Whether the Princess finally conceded under pressure we cannot tell. Her instincts had always been to gain experience and knowledge before accepting the role. She felt she had to earn the honour and will never accept *any* kind of award unless she feels that she warrants it. There was a time when it was suggested that the Queen might create a new precedent by making her sister Margaret the Princess Royal, someone – like Anne – forced by birth to take second place. But, content now to take on a less active public role, Princess Margaret is happy that her niece has been rewarded.

The only significant change the Princess Anne has had to adopt has been the change of titling. Instead of being officially called 'Her Royal Highness, The Princess Anne, Mrs. Mark Phillips' on every official document, court circular, invitation and plaque, it is now acceptable to refer to her simply as 'The Princess Royal'. For a no-nonsense princess, the new title is probably welcomed for its brevity, although radio and television presenters still have difficulty remembering the change.

As a formal bestowal the title could have been decreed by a Royal Warrant issued under the Great Seal as an official proclamation. For greater pomp a ceremony such as that for the investiture of the Prince of Wales could have been created, but the Queen decided to uphold the twentieth century practice of an Honours List announcement alone. Princess Mary (daughter of King George V and Queen Mary) was created Princess Royal in the New Year's Honours List of 1932, with no further ceremony or seal. She is even today held in high regard by those who came into contact with her for the dignity and vitality she brought to the role that gave renewed spirit to this historic tradition. Princess Anne has an equally indomitable spirit.

How the actual title 'Princess Royal' originated remains a mystery. In Scotland there was a long tradition of calling the sovereign's eldest son the 'Prince Royal', although this practice appears to be verbal rather than by decree and certainly does not appear in any official documentation. Around 1610 a warship was launched and named *The Prince Royal* after Prince Henry, the son of King James VI of Scotland and brother to the future King Charles I. Prince Henry's sister, Elizabeth (later Queen of Bohemia) is sometimes wrongly attributed as Princess Royal by modern historians, simply because she was the eldest daughter of a monarch and not through any concrete evidence. The title almost certainly developed from 'Prince Royal' and was first officially used by Charles I when he wished to give his first-born daughter a distinction. Mary had been weak as an infant, her life in the balance, which built up a close parental bond between father and daughter. When Mary married the Prince of Orange in 1641 she went to live in Holland and to retain her English identity Charles set a precedent by styling his daughter 'The Princess Royal of England'. In later life, during widowhood, having built up a certain enmity with the Dutch, Mary refused to be called the Princess of Orange and insisted on being the Princess Royal.

The history of the Princessess Royal is sporadic with no set pattern or inheritance. After Princess Mary died in 1660 almost 70 years passed before the title was used again; this time, in 1727, it was granted to another Princess Anne. On her death some 30 more years elapsed before George III bestowed it on his eldest daughter, Charlotte, and when she died in 1828 it was not until 1840 that England had a new Princess Royal in Victoria, named after her mother the Queen. Strangely in this century, when we consider the title archaic, there will have been more years with a Princess Royal than at any other period, for when Princess Louise died in 1931, having held the title for over 25 years, it was passed on less than a year later to Princess Mary, who was herself to hold it for 33 years until her death.

As Princess Royal, Princess Anne is now the second lady of the land and ranks as the senior princess second only to her mother. As the years go by it could be that the Queen will feel unable to undertake as many royal duties as she does now, in which case some could be taken over by the Princess Royal, filling the gap that may occur in Princess Anne's later life. Already the Queen has been advised to slow down following a visit to a heart specialist, and she has given up riding on horseback for the Trooping the Colour ceremony, travelling now in a horsedrawn carriage. Already past the normal retiring age for women, the Queen knows that she cannot carry on indefinitely, but her duties could be shared.

Try to ask Princess Anne how she sees her role and she backs away, hating to be pigeonholed and categorised. When one reporter said that it helped with the newspaper headlines, she bounced back with , 'That's *exactly* what I mean!' To those with whom she works to raise money for charity, she is the 'caring' princess who uses her talents to the best advantage. As a skilled sportswoman, she uses the gift at every available opportunity. Sponsored for the Bob Champion Cancer Trust to raise £500,000 the Princess agreed to be one of 250 personalities to ride Grand National winner Aldaniti for one mile on the retired chaser's walk from Buckingham Palace to Aintree on 1 March 1987, arriving on the morning of the great race on 4 April. At Prince Edward's instigation she consented to take part in *It's a Knockout* to raise a further £500,000 for charity. By taking part in just two events, the Princess had helped to raise one million pounds. If that alone were classed as her role in life it would be sufficient. Even she finds it difficult to believe that she is such an inspiration.

Had Princess Anne been born a century ago she could have contented herself with a life in the country with her family and her horses, and seldom have appeared in public. Whether she would enjoy this is something only she can say, having now dedicated herself to a life of service. It is a life that she may not have immediately chosen given the option of any career, but it was a path that lay open to her as a member of the Royal Family and a life that she has come to accept. With a private life at Gatcombe Park and a public life at Buckingham Palace she has been able to draw a clear division between the two. A sensible approach enables her to be wife and mother in Gloucestershire and a princess elsewhere. Whilst respecting and upholding the monarchy she has retained her individuality and her own identity. By retaining this identity she has achieved the respect and admiration of the public. She has matured into a woman who is aware of her responsibilities and has the strength to carry them out, often above and beyond the call of duty. That she has achieved so much in the wake of fierce media opposition and a bad reputation and has emerged as the member of the Royal Family with the most support is due to her own fortitude.

On her first major tour abroad in 1970, Princess Anne followed in the footsteps of Captain Cook on the 200th anniversary of his historic trip to Australia and New Zealand. In 35 days she undertook 235 official engagements, and was in her own words 'flung in at the deep end'. Had her entry into public life been gradual, possibly her approach today would be different. Her first engagements in Britain and abroad were sudden and unexpectedly demanding. Anything since has been easier by comparison.

Today Princess Anne, some 8000 engagements later, has proved her worth, withstood the trials, and displayed the courage and loyalty expected of a Princess Royal. In 1588 Queen Elizabeth I sat astride her horse at Tilbury and proclaimed the immortal words: 'I know I have the body of a weak and feeble woman; but I have the heart and stomach of a king, and a King of England too . . .' They are words that Princess Anne could utter four centuries later and few would dispute her sincerity. She may have a new image but her fighting spirit and uncompromising determination will always remain. She has set a precedent that any princess in the future will find hard to follow.

*E*pilogue

Historians looking back on the nineteen-eighties will undoubtedly class the decade as the most significant in Princess Anne's life. Having made the transition to become one of the most respected members of the Royal Family, it is unlikely that she will regress; in her autumn years she will almost certainly command the same kind of esteem as Queen Mary or Queen Elizabeth the Queen Mother, of whom any criticism is now sacrilegious. After she accepted the title of Princess Royal in 1987, not one lone voice censured the honour, and in a year when the rest of the Queen's children fell foul of the media, the Princess was constantly upheld as an example for them all to follow.

Prince Edward found himself constantly lambasted because of his apparent procrastination in finding himself a career after leaving the Royal Marines. He undertook only 37 official duties, attended 22 dinners and receptions, and spent 20 days abroad in a year when his sister carried out 704 engagements, spending 67 days overseas, longer than any other member of the Family. 'If Prince Edward is not going to pull his weight then he should have his £20,000 Civil List income withdrawn,' declared one senior Member of Parliament, echoing what many had thought, but never said. Prince Andrew received similar criticism for a long absence from his naval career, and Prince Charles suffered many months of speculation about the 'imminent' collapse of his marriage resulting from a six-week separation from his wife and children. Princess Anne and the Princess of Wales may not have a great deal in common, but for once they could compare notes on media attack. 'Forget it,' said Anne philosophically, 'it will soon be yesterday's news.'

In June 1987 the dignity of the Royal Family was allowed to lapse, somewhat misguidedly, in the name of charity. The royal 'It's A Knockout' competition may have raised vast sums of money for four deserving causes, but the idea of allowing members of the Royal Family to become television-game-show contestants for a day was a serious error of judgement, and ultimately the image of royalty suffered. It is said that the Queen will not allow the exercise to be repeated in future. Prince Edward received justifiable denunciation following his petulant display of swearing at the press after the event, and at the end of the day only the Princess Royal came through unscathed and victorious, having won the competition and maintained decorum throughout. Having realised when it was too late that taking part was probably a mistake, it is typical of her character that she remained, in her own words, 'cool, calm and collected', and with a hand-picked team won the games in a suitably sportsmanlike manner.

Away from the fun and games the more serious side of the Princess Royal's life came to the fore at the end of 1987 when she undertook what Buckingham Palace described as 'one of the most adventurous Royal tours yet'. To many in the Princess's homeland the ten-day trip to Korea, Singapore, Thailand, Laos and Burma was just another of the overseas visits that have become such an integral part of her working life, so much so that, although still lauded, they are now almost taken for granted. So successful are her Save the Children Fund tours that we *expect* to see her amongst the poverty-stricken. Yet, this tour *was* different. Not only was the schedule typically heavy, the tropical heat intense, but this time political dangers outshadowed the natural disasters. Laos has been described as the most bombed-out country of the Indo–China War. In London protests were made about Burma's treatment of its ethnic minorities who had fought for the British Commonwealth in World War Two, and marchers displayed placards outside the London Embassy saying 'Princess Royal. Don't dine with murderers'. Leaders of the Kachin and Karen rebel armies wrote to the Queen pleading with Her Majesty to cancel the tour.

Despite the obvious opposition, Princess Anne's advisers now know better than to attempt anything other than laying the facts and objections before her. The Princess saw her role as a 'healer of rifts' and when two successful dummy runs had been carried out by others, her planned tour went ahead. In ten days she visited five countries, undertaking over fifty engagements, doing much to thaw the ice that had formed around the relationship between Socialist Burma, Communist Laos and Britain. In Bangkok she met children at a Save-the-Children-Fund-run school, many the sons and daughters of squatters threatened with eviction. Eviction would destroy the children's homes, families, education and future. Princess Anne persuaded Bangkok's deputy governor, Apron Pukkaman, not to evict any of the families and to keep his bargain, which came as a great relief to the Fund. 'In one hour she achieved what we have been trying to do for years,' said Father Joseph Maier, the project's co-ordinator. 'We have been trying to get that assurance for a long time.'

Through the dusty camps she met thousands of refugees, many who had used her visit as a means of escape, and visited many Save the Children Fund projects. None other than those closest to her were aware that the Princess was suffering from exhaustion and was feeling ill. She had come too far and had too much to achieve to give in. She gave hope to the living and, in a moving ceremony at the Commonwealth War Grave, she respected the dead, laying a wreath to the memory of the 27,000 soldiers who died in Burma. In Rangoon she struck the Peace Bell and was asked to make three wishes. 'We hope she wishes to come back,' said one official. Return she almost certainly will, but we can assume that the Princess Royal's wishes were bound to have been more fundamental.

Exactly two months later, at the end of January 1988, Princess Anne went to the Queen Elizabeth II Conference Centre in London to support a topic much closer to home. A crisis that once out of control could cause deaths on a scale of the Ethiopian famine. By opening the World Summit of Ministers of Health on Programmes for AIDS Prevention, Princess Anne became the first member of the Royal Family to openly involve herself in the AIDS issue, and closely monitors the progress of a cure. It is perhaps not insignificant that when a seemingly insoluble problem occurs, it is Princess Anne who is prepared to take up the challenge. AIDS, like death and poverty in the Third World, cannot be instantly conquered, but somehow she seems to thrive when the odds are stacked against her. This ultimately will give her a place in history.

Appendix I

PRINCESS ANNE FACTFILE

BORN
Tuesday 15 August, 1950 at Clarence House. Weight 6 lb.

CHRISTENED
21 October, 1950 at Buckingham Palace, by the Archbishop of
York, Dr. Garbett.
Names: Anne Elizabeth Alice Louise
Godparents: HM Queen Elizabeth (the Queen Mother)
Princess Andrew of Greece
Princess Margarita of Hohenlohe-Langenburg
Earl Mountbatten of Burma
Hon. Andrew Elphinstone
13 June, 1987 created Princess Royal

MEDICAL AILMENTS
Tonsils and adenoids removed at Great Ormond Street Hospital
(May 1958).
Chickenpox – at Windsor Castle (April 1959).
Whooping cough – at Buckingham Palace (March 1961).
Measles – at Windsor Castle (April 1961).
Ovarian cyst removed in King Edward VII Hospital for Officers
(July 1970).

CHURCH
First attended on Christmas Day 1953 at Sandringham.

BROWNIES AND GUIDES
May 1959
Palace Brownie Pack formed.
July 1959
Enrolled in Pixie Six.
May 1961
Guide meeting of 1st Buckingham Palace Coy.
July 1961
Enrolled in Kingfisher patrol.
June 1962
First camp, for five days in Sussex.
July 1963
Second camp at Maldon Island.

BRIDESMAID
13 January, 1960
Wedding of her cousin Lady Pamela Mountbatten to Mr. David Hicks at Romsey Abbey.
6 May, 1960
Chief bridesmaid at the wedding of Princess Margaret to Mr. Anthony Armstrong-Jones at Westminster Abbey.
8 June, 1961
Wedding of the Duke of Kent to Miss Katherine Worsley at York Minster.
24 April, 1963
Wedding of Princess Alexandra to Mr. Angus Ogilvy at Westminster Abbey.
18 September, 1964
Wedding of King Constantine of Greece and Princess Anne-Marie of Denmark at Athens.

EDUCATION
1955 September
Began lessons with governess, Miss Peebles.
1957–1963
Caroline Hamilton and Susan Babington-Smith joined the Palace class.
In August Princess Anne had a French mistress, Mlle Bibiane de Roujoux, at Balmoral for four weeks.
1959 May
Mlle Suzanne Josseron began regular weekly French lessons at Buckingham Palace.

At Balmoral in August the Princess studied under Lt. Jean Lajeunesse.

1961 October

More serious French lessons, language and culture, became part of the curriculum with Mrs. Untermayer.

1962

Extra history lessons began with Mrs. Garvin, and Latin lessons were introduced, with Mr. Trevor Roberts.

In the summer Princess Anne stayed with the Marquis de St. Genys in France to improve her French language.

1963 (20 September) – 1968 (23 July)

Benenden School, Kent.

Headmistress: Miss Elizabeth Clarke, MA, BLitt.(Oxon), JP.

Housemistress: Miss C. Gee, BA(Bristol), MA(Bryn Mawr, USA).

House: Guldeford.

Dormitory: Magnolia.

1966

O levels: English Language, English Literature (A), French, History, Geography, Biology.

The Princess failed her Latin O level, but did also pass a Royal Society of Arts test in Arithmetic.

1968

A levels:

History (Grade D)

Geography (Grade E)

1968 (October)

Six weeks intensive course in French at the Berlitz School of Languages.

FIRST STATE OCCASIONS

31 October 1967

State Opening of Parliament.

25 July 1968

Buckingham Palace Garden Party.

23 April 1969

State Banquet at Windsor Castle for President Saragat of Italy.

7–10 May 1969

Accompanied the Queen on a State Visit to Austria.

1 July 1969

The Investure of the Prince of Wales, Caernarvon Castle.

DRIVING

Passed driving test at first attempt (17 April, 1968).

FLYING

First flew in a helicopter at Windsor (May 1955).
First aeroplane flight was to Scotland (June 1955).

RIDING

First lessons began in February 1953, with Miss Sybil Smith.
Whilst at Benenden the Princess trained at Mopat House under
Cherry Kendall (Mrs. Hatton-Hall).
From 1968 onwards Princess Anne trained for eventing with
Alison Oliver at Brookfield Farm, Warfield.
Her horses have included: William (roan from Ireland); Green-
sleeves (Welsh mare); Bandit (grey Welsh); High Jinks
(brown Irish); Purple Star (Bay gelding); Doublet; Goodwill.

MARRIAGE

Wednesday 14 November 1973, at Westminster Abbey, to Mark
Anthony Peter Phillips.

CHILDREN

1. Peter Mark Andrew Phillips, born 15 November 1977, at St.
   Mary's Hospital, Paddington, London.
2. Zara Anne Elizabeth Phillips, born 15 May 1981, at St.
   Mary's Hospital, Paddington, London.

RESIDENCE

Gatcombe Park, Minchinhampton, Gloucestershire.

Appendix II

PRINCESS ANNE'S GENERAL APPOINTMENTS

1950   Within hours of her birth Princess Anne was elected the millionth member of the Automobile Association.

1969   Patron of Benenden Ball.

1970   Hon. Member Young Adventure Club.
President of the Save the Children Fund.
Commandant in Chief, St. John Ambulance and Nursing Cadets.

1971   Member of Reliant Owners Club.
Hon. Member of Island Sailing Club.
Patron of the Riding for the Disabled Association.
Hon. Member of Royal Thames Yacht Club.

1972   Hon. Life Member of Flying Doctor Society of Africa.
President of British Academy of Film and Television Arts (BAFTA).
Patron of Jersey Wildlife Preservation Fund.

1974   Hon. Member of British Equine Veterinary Association.

1976   President of The Hunters Improvement and Light Horse Breeding Society.
Freedom of the City of London.
Vice Patron of British Show Jumping Association.
Visitor of Felixstowe College.

Patron of Gloucester and North Avon Federation of Young
  Farmers Clubs.

1977   President of the Windsor Horse Trials.
       Patron of Royal Port Moresby Society for Prevention of
         Cruelty to Animals.
       Patron of the Horse of the Year Ball.

1978   Hon. Member of Minchinhampton Golf Club, Gloucester-
         shire.

1979   Patron of the Royal Lymington Yacht Club.

1980   Patron of All England Women's Lacrosse Association.

1981   President of the Three Counties Show (for 1 year).
       Hon. President of Stroud District Show.
       Chancellor of London University.

1982   Patron of Home Farm Trust.
       Patron of Bourne End Junior Sports and Recreation Club
         (until 1985).
       Patron of National Union of Townswomen's Guilds.

1983   Commonwealth Universities Congress Patron.
       Visitor of the Strathcarron Hospice.
       President of the British Olympic Association.
       Patron of the British School of Osteopathy.

1984   Patron of the Surrey Agricultural County Show.
       Patron of the Spinal Injuries Association.
       Hon. President of Chartered Institute of Transport.
       Patron of the Riding for the Disabled Association (Aus-
         tralia).
       President of the Missions to Seamen.
       Hon. President of the British Knitwear and Clothing
         Export Council.
       Patron of Oxford House, Bethnal Green.

1985   Patron of the Suffolk Horse Society.
       Hon. Associate of the Royal College of Veterinary
         Surgeons.
       Patron of the Butler Trust.
       Patron of the Greater London Horse Show.
       President of the Royal Bath and West Show.

1986   Patron of the Amateur Rowing Association.
        Member of the Beaufort Hunt.
        Hon. President of the Royal Caledonian Hunt.
        Hon. Member of the Sussex Agricultural Society.
        Hon. Member of the Royal Yacht Squadron.

OFFICIAL APPOINTMENTS (*The Services*)

1969   Col-in-Chief 14th/20th King's Hussars.

1970   Col-in-Chief Worcestershire and Sherwood Foresters
        Regiment.
        29th/45th Foot Guards.

1972   Col.-in-Chief 8th Canadian Hussars (Princess Louise's).

1974   Chief Commandant of the Women's Royal Naval Services
        (WRNS).
        Patron of the Association of WRNS.
        Patron of the Army and Royal Artillery Hunter Trials.
        President of the Women's Royal Naval Service Benevolent
        Trust.
        Life Member of the Royal Navy Equestrian Association.

1975   President of the Royal School of Daughters of Officers of the
        Royal Navy and Royal Marines (until 1990).

1977   Col-in-Chief Royal Corps of Signals.
        Col-in-Chief The Canadian Forces Communications and
        Electronics Branch.
        Col-in-Chief The Royal Australian Corps of Signals.
        Col-in-Chief New Zealand Corps of Signals.
        Col-in-Chief Royal New Zealand Nursing Corps.
        Col-in-Chief The Grey and Simcoe Foresters Militia
        (Canada).
        Patron of Royal Corps of Signals' Institution.
        Patron of Royal Corps of Signals' Association.
        Hon. Air Commodore of RAF Lyneham.

1978   Life Member of Royal British Legion Women's Section.
        Hon. Life Member of RNVR Officers' Association.
        Patron The Canadian Forces Communications and Elec-
        tronics Branch Institution.

1981 Commandant-in-Chief Women's Transport Service (FANY).

1982 Col-in-Chief The Royal Regina Regiment.

1983 Col-in-Chief The Royal Scots (The Royal Regiment).
Patron of the Royal Tournament.

1985 Joint President Lowland Brigade Club.

LIVERY COMPANIES

1971 Yeoman of the Saddlers' Company.
Honorary Freeman of the Worshipful Company of Farriers

1972 Honorary Freeman of the Worshipful Company of Loriners.
Freeman of the Fishmongers' Company.

1976 Honorary Liveryman of the Worshipful Company of Farmers.

1979 Honorary Liveryman of the Worshipful Company of Loriners.

1982 Honorary Liveryman of the Worshipful Company of Carmen (Hon. Assistant 1983; Senior Warden 1985).

*A*ppendix III

OFFICIAL OVERSEAS VISITS

1954   Libya, Malta, Gibraltar.

1962   France.

1964   Greece.

1966   Jamaica.

1969   Austria, Norway, Federal Republic of Germany.

1970   Fiji, Tonga, New Zealand, Australia, Federal Republic of Germany, Canada, United States.

1971   Kenya, Canada, Iran, Turkey, Hong Kong.

1972   The Far East, Federal Republic of Germany, Yugoslavia.

1973   Ethiopia, Sudan, Federal Republic of Germany, Soviet Union, Ecuador, Colombia, Jamaica, Montserrat, Antigua.

1974   Canada, New Zealand, Norfolk Island, New Hebrides, British Solomon Islands, Papua New Guinea, Australia, Federal Republic of Germany.

1975   Australia, Federal Republic of Germany.

1976   Canada, Federal Republic of Germany.

1977   United States.

1978   Federal Republic of Germany, Norway.

1979   Portugal, Federal Republic of Germany, Thailand, Gilbert Islands, New Zealand, Australia, Bahamas, Canada.

1980   Cyprus, France, Belgium, Fiji.

1981 Federal Republic of Germany, Nepal.

1982 Federal Republic of Germany, United States, Canada, Swaziland, Zimbabwe, Malawi, Kenya, Somalia, Djibouti, North Yemen, Lebanon.

1983 Netherlands, France, Japan, Hong Kong, Pakistan, Federal Republic of Germany, Singapore.

1984 United States, Yugoslavia, Morocco, The Gambia, Upper Volta, United States, Bangladesh, India, United Arab Emirates.

1985 Federal Republic of Germany, India, Tanzania, Mozambique, Zambia and the Sudan.

1986 Brazil.

1987 Australia, United Arab Emirates, Qatar, Kuwait and Jordan.

Appendix IV

DIARY OF ENGAGEMENTS 1986

The entries here are Princess Anne's official engagements only. There were numerous private functions and unofficial visits to charities that she supports which have not be included.

JANUARY

15 As Chancellor of the University of London, attended a presentation ceremony at the Royal Albert Hall.

21 Attended a fashion show in aid of the Riding for the Disabled Association at the Guildhall, London.

28 As Patron of the Home Farm Trust visited Cherington House, Cherington, Warwickshire, to open the new house and grounds.
In the evening attended the Rededication Service of HMS *Forward* RNR Unit at Birmingham.

30 As Patron of the British School of Osteopathy, visited the clinic and opened a new lecture hall, Suffolk Street, London SW1.

FEBRUARY

6 As Chancellor of London University, visited Lillian Penson Hall of Residence, London W2, for celebration of its 21st Anniversary.

7   Evening: As Past Master of the Worshipful Company of Farriers, attended the Court Ladies Dinner at the Innholders' Hall, London.

10 As Chancellor of the University of London, opened University College's new unit for Endocrinology and Diabetes at the Whittington Hospital, Highgate.
Opened the Associated Islington Health Authority Ward.
Evening: Attended the Sports Aid Foundation Banquet at the Mansion House, London.

12 Evening: Attended the Annual Banquet of the Bristol Chamber of Commerce at the Grand Hotel, Bristol, and received a Land Rover on behalf of the Save the Children Fund.

13 Morning: Addressed the Royal Institute of International Affairs on the Save the Children Fund at Chatham House, London SW1.
Evening: Attended the Westminster Christmas Appeal Trust Reception at MEPC Office, Brook House, London W1.

15 As President of the Save the Children Fund visited Glasgow.
Attended a luncheon given by the Rotary International in aid of the Save the Children Fund, received the Paul Harris Fellowship.
Visited the Lady Muir Youth Project and the Darnley Street Family Centre.
Visited the Save the Children Fund Shop.
Evening: Attended a Fiddlers Rally at the New Scottish Exhibition Centre.

17 As President of the Save the Children Fund visited the Patmore Project, London SW8 and the St. Peter's Children's Centre, London SW11.
Afternoon: As President of the Save the Children Fund attended the Brownie/Guide Tea Challenge Party held at the Savoy Hotel, London.

21 As President of the Save the Children Fund visited the Milestone Intermediate Treatment Project in Sunderland.
Visited Glenhow School, Saltburn by Sea, Cleveland.

23   As President of the Save the Children Fund attended a performance of *Messiah* at the Royal Albert Hall, London.

24   Opened the British Equestrian Trade Association Fair at Sandown Park racecourse.

25   Morning: Addressed the Annual Convention of the Institute of Directors at the Royal Albert Hall, London.
Evening: Attended a dinner at St. Ermin's Hotel, London, with the Chatham Dining Club.

26   Attended a dinner and fashion show at Woburn Abbey organised by the Horse Trials Support Group.

MARCH

4   As Patron of the Home Farm Trust opened an exhibition of craftwork at St. Mary's Tradescant Church, London.
Evening: As Patron of the British School of Osteopathy attended a reception at the Mansion House, London.

5   Opened a new school at Blockley, Gloucestershire, and the North Cotswold Centre for the Physically Handicapped at Bourton-on-the-Water, Gloucestershire.

6   Opened the 'Careers for the 1980s' exhibition at the Bristol Exhibition Centre (morning).
Opened the Linear Accelerator Unit at the Regional Radiotherapy and Oncology Centre, Bristol (afternoon).
Attended a banquet in aid of the Great Ormond Street Hospital for Sick Children, London.

9   As President of BAFTA attended the Crafts Awards Ceremony, Piccadilly, London.

10   Received an Honorary Fellowship of the Royal College of Physicians, after which the Princess attended a dinner at the Royal College of Physicians, London.

11   As President of the British Knitting and Clothing Export Council visited GB Clothing Company, West Yorkshire.

12   Visited Unsted Park Rehabilitation and Medical Centre, Godalming, Surrey (morning).
As Chancellor of the University of London attended a presentation ceremony at the Royal Albert Hall, London.

16   Attended a special evening in aid of the Save the Children Fund at the Savoy Hotel, London.

18   Visited the Fourways Assessment Centre, Tyldesley, Greater Manchester.
Opened Osborne Court, Atherton, Greater Manchester.

20   Morning: As President of the Save the Children Fund visited Hammersmith Gypsy Project, London.
Visited the Southern Regional Office/African Family Advisory Service, Hammersmith.
As Patron of the Riding for the Disabled Association attended a luncheon to receive the 10th Silver Jubilee Saddle from the Worshipful Company of Saddlers, London.
Evening: Attended the London Hospital Medical College's Bicentenary Dinner at the Guildhall, London.

22   As President of the Save the Children Fund attended the Rock Gospel concert at the Royal Albert Hall, London.

APRIL

8   Visited HMS *Amazon* at sea.
Evening: Attended a performance of *My Fair Lady* to celebrate the re-opening of the Everyman Theatre, Cheltenham.

9   Attended the Royal Philharmonic Orchestra's 80th birthday concert for Maestro Antal Dorati at the Royal Festival Hall.

10   As Chancellor of the University of London attended the naming of a Midland Region electric locomotive as part of the University's 150th Anniversary celebrations at Euston Station, London.

11   Took the Salute at The Sovereign's Parade, Royal Military Academy, Sandhurst, Surrey (morning).
As Patron of the National Union of Townswomen's Guilds, attended a Gala Choral Concert in aid of Operation Dhaka at the Free Trade Hall, Manchester.

15   As Patron of the Home Farm Trust opened Orford House, near Bishops Stortford (morning).
Opened the Family Finding Centre, Hertford (afternoon).

16   Attended the Piper Champagne National Hunt Awards, Cheltenham Racecourse, Gloucestershire.

21   Attended the Queen's 60th birthday celebrations.

22   Opened the new Ealing YMCA Hostel, London.

23   As President of the British Knitting and Clothing Export Council, visited the Regent Belt Company, Northamptonshire (morning).
As Patron of the Riding for the Disabled Association visited the Peterborough District Hospital Group, Cambridgeshire.

24   Attended a meeting of the Royal Bath and West and Southern Counties Society at Shepton Mallet, Somerset.

25   Attended the Soroptimist International of Gloucester and District's dinner in aid of the MacMillan Home Care Nursing Service at Gloucester Cathedral.

28   Visited the Farms for City Children Project, Iddesleigh, Devon (morning).
As Patron of the Home Farm Trust visited Rivendell, Chudleigh, Devon, to mark the occason of its completion.

29   Opened the new Institute of London Underwriters Building, London (morning).
As President of the Save the Children Fund attended a fashion show to mark the Golden Birthday of Simpsons, Piccadilly, London.

30   Opened the Housing and Hostel Scheme for disabled people at Eastleigh, Hampshire.
Opened a day centre for physically handicapped children at Cosham, Hampshire.
Evening: Attended a Gala Performance of *La Cage aux Folles* in aid of the Army Benevolent Fund and the Save the Children Fund at the London Palladium.

MAY

2   Visited Southend, Essex. Named a train at Southend Pier. Named a new lifeboat of the Royal National Lifeboat Institution at the lifeboat station. Visited Nazareth House and

opened the reconstructed West Wing. Lunched with the Mayor of Southend.

Opened the new Abbeyfield Home for the Elderly, Billericay.

3–4   Visited Guernsey.

5   As Patron of the Suffolk Horse Society attended the Spring Show, Ipswich, Suffolk.

6–7   As Col-in-Chief, The Royal Signals, visited 21st and 16th Signal Regiments, West Germany.

8   As Chancellor of the University of London, visited the London School of Economics.

Evening: Attended the Annual Dinner of the Chief Constables Club at The Savoy Hotel, London.

9   As Chancellor of the University of London attended Queen Mary College's Thanksgiving Service at St. Michael's Cornhill, followed by a reception at the Drapers' Hall, London.

12   Attended a charity performance of *Chess* at the Prince Edward Theatre, London, in aid of the Stars Organisation for Spastics.

13   As Chancellor of the University of London, presented Purple Awards to sportsmen and women of the University of London at the International Students House, London.

14   As Chancellor of the University of London attended a presentation ceremony at the Royal Albert Hall, London (afternoon).

Evening: Attended the Court Ladies' Dinner of the Fishmongers' Company, London.

15   Opened the new Police Training Centre, Sheffield. Visited Fletchers Bakeries Ltd., Sheffield (morning).

As Patron of the Riding for the Disabled Association, visited the Sheffield Group (afternoon).

16   Presented medallions to commemorate the 20th anniversary of the Winston Churchill Memorial Trust at The Guildhall, London.

19   Presented the annual Pye Television Awards at the Hilton Hotel.

20   As President of The Missions to Seamen visited The Missions to Seamen Clubs at Fowey and Par.
Visited the offices of English China Clays in St. Austell.
Attended a thankgiving service to commemorate the 10th Anniversary of the work of The Missions to Seamen in Cornwall.
Visited the town of Penryn to celebrate the 750th anniversary of the granting of the Royal Charter.

21   As President of the British Knitting and Clothing Export Council, attended their Annual General Meeting, Berkeley Hotel, London (morning).
As President of the Women's Royal Naval Service Benevolent Trust attended the 44th Annual General Meeting in the Carisbrooke Hall, London (afternoon).

22   Attended a banquet of the Royal Academy of Arts, Burlington House, London.

27   As Commandant-in-Chief, St. John Ambulance and Nursing Cadets, attended a Regional Cadet Rally, Preston, Lancs.
Evening: Attended the Four Stars' Golf Tournament Ball at the Guildhall, London.

28   As Col-in-Chief of the Royal Scots Regiment, visited the 1st Batallion in West Germany.

29   As Col-in-Chief, Royal Corps of Signals attended a Cocktail Party and Playing of Retreat by the Royal Signals Band, Shepton Mallet, Somerset.

29–30   As President of the Royal Bath and West and Southern Counties Society, attended the Society's Annual Show, Somerset.

JUNE

3   11.30 am visited Combined Cadet Force Contingents affiliated to The Royal Scots, Edinburgh.
As President of the British Knitting and Clothing Export Council, formally opened their new head office, Glasgow (afternoon).

4   As Patron of the National Union of Townswomen's Guilds, attended the launch of the Diamond Jubilee tapestry, Banqueting House, Whitehall, London.

5   Opened the new Royal British Legion Country Home at Rhaydar, Powys (morning).
    Opened the new coating plant at The Wiggins Teape Group Mill at Ely, near Cardiff, South Glamorgan (afternoon).
    Attended the St. John Evening in aid of Avon County Appeal at the Country Club, Yatton, Avon (evening).

6   Attended the Women's Amateur Athletic Association National Track and Field Championships at the Alexander Stadium, Birmingham.

7   Addressed the Convocation of the Cranfield Institute of Technology on the occasion of their 40th Anniversary at the Cranfield Institute of Technology, near Milton Keynes, Bedfordshire.

9   As Chancellor of the University of London opened the Royal Veterinary College's new equine surgical facilities at Hawkeshead Campus, Potters Bar, Hertfordshire.
    Attended the Vice-President's Dinner of the Incorporated Liverpool School of Tropical Medicine at Baring Brothers Ltd., London (evening).

10 Attended the Three Counties Agricultural Show at Malvern, Worcestershire.

11 Opened the new European Headquarters at Amdahl Corporation at Dogmersfield Park, Witney, Hampshire (morning).
    As Patron of the Riding for the Disabled Association, visited the Andover Group, Hampshire (afternoon).

12 As President of the Save the Children Fund attended the American Junior League of London luncheon at the Grosvenor House Hotel, London.

13 Opened The Princess Anne Wing of the Stroud General Hospital, Gloucestershire.

15 Attended the Prix de Diane-Hermes at Chantilly, France.

18 Visited HMS *Dryad*, Southwick, Hampshire.

19–20   As Colonel-in-Chief of the Royal Signals, visited 11 Signals Brigade participating in Exercise Calm Fence in West Germany and Belgium.

28   As President of the Save the Children Fund attended the Princess Anne Award Ceremony at Sandringham House, Norfolk.

JULY

1   As President of the Missions to Seamen, attended their Annual General Meeting at St. Michael Paternoster Royal, London.

2   Attended a Scottish Design Show and Dinner at the Commonwealth Institute, Kensington High Street, London.

3   Opened the WRNS Exhibition at the Fleet Air Arm Museum, Somerset.

4   Visited RAF Henlow, Bedfordshise (morning).
   As Patron of the British School of Osteopathy attended the annual presentation of awards at the Institute of Civil Engineers, Westminster, London.

6   Attended a polo match at Cirencester Park Polo Club and presented the Cup to the winning team.

9   Attended a garden party at the British Ambassador's Residence, Berne, Switzerland to mark the 40th Anniversary of The British Residents' Association.

12–13   As Colonel-in-Chief of 14th/20th King's Hussars, visited the Regiment at Catterick Garrison, North Yorkshire.

14   Opened the World Water '86 Conference at Olympia (morning).
   As President of the Save the Children Fund attended a lunch given by the Foreign Press Association at the Hyde Park Hotel, London.

16   Attended the National Show and Sale of the Suffolk Sheep Society, Kenilworth, Warwickshire.

17   Attended the Golden Jubilee Celebrations of Corman's Fields playground in the London Borough of Camden (morning).

As Senior Warden of the Worshipful Company of Carmen, attended a Court Meeting and Dinner at the Stationers' Hall, London.

18   Patron of the VIII Commonwealth and International Conference on Sport, Physical Education, Dance, Recreation and Health, opened the conference in Glasgow.

21   Opened a new St. John Ambulance headquarters in Winchester, Hampshire.
(Evening) Attended the Annual Dinner of the Association of College Unions International hosted by the University of London.

22   Took the Salute at a performance of the Royal Tournament at Earl's Court, London.

23   Attended the wedding of The Prince Andrew and Miss Sarah Ferguson at Westminster Abbey, London.

24   Attended a dinner of the Army Benevolent Fund at the Royal Artillery Mess, Woolwich, London.

25   Reviewed the 25th Annual Ceremonial Parade at Ryton Police Training Centre, Coventry.

28   Visited Montrose House, Brodick, Isle of Arran.
Attended the celebrations of the 150th Anniversary of the Arran Farmers' Society Annual Show.

29   As Colonel-in-Chief, The Royal Scots, attended the Laying Up of the Colours of the 7th/9th Battalion in the Canongate Kirk, Edinburgh. Afterwards attended a Regimental Reception in the grounds of Holyroodhouse.

August

1   Opened the 2500th sheltered house built by the Bield Housing Association at Bannockburn, Stirling.
Visited Stirling Enterprise Park and opened the second phase of the John Player Building Development, Stirling.
Visited the Guildry of Stirling and was admitted as an Honorary Guild Brother.

20   Visited the Royal College of Defence Studies, London.

22   As Patron of the 1986 World Rowing Championships,
      attended the Championships at the National Water Sports
      Centre, Holme Pierrepont, Nottinghamshire.

SEPTEMBER

7   Opened the XIV International Congress of Microbiology at
      the Free Trade Hall, Manchester.
      Attended a reception at the University of Manchester.

8   Opened a new junior school at Stonehouse, Gloucestershire.
      Opened the new premises of Mecanaids at St. Catherine
      Street, Gloucester.
      Visited Indalex Limited, Cheltenham, to celebrate their
      25th Anniversary.

10   Attended one day of the Olympic Yachting Association at
      Weymouth, Dorset.

11   Visited Christchurch Hospital, Dorset (morning).
      Opened Blandford Community Hospital, Dorset (after-
      noon).

13   Opened the new National Canoe Slalom and White Water
      Course, Holme Pierrepont National Water Sports Centre,
      Nottingham.

15   As President of the Save the Children Fund, attended the
      Launch of New Industry and Commerce Initiative at Man-
      sion House, London.
      Attended a Launch Luncheon and addressed the guests.

16   Opened the new container terminal at Felixstowe, Suffolk.
      As President of the Missions to Seamen visited the Felix-
      stowe Seafarers' Centre.

17   Opened the North London Business Development Agency,
      London (afternoon).
      Attended the Associated Press dinner, Middle Temple Hall,
      London (evening).

18   Opened Lightfoot House, the new Carr-Gomm Society's
      home, Birmingham.
      Visited HM Prison Winson Green, Birmingham.
      Opened Parklands Housing Society's Sheltered Housing
      Scheme, Walsall.

22   As President of the Save the Children Fund, visited the
      Fund's Traveller Project in Buckinghamshire.

23·   Opened British Aerospace's new A320 Hangar, Filton,
      Bristol.
      Attended a dinner in aid of The Caldecott Community at
      the Banqueting House, Whitehall, London.

25   As Chancellor of the University of London, performed the
      re-opening of Dillons Bookstore, Gower Street, London
      WC1.
      As President of the Save the Children Fund attended the
      film premiere of *Eleni* at the Cannon Theatre, Haymarket,
      London.

27   As President of the Save the Children Fund attended the
      opening concert of the Swindon Festival at Farringdon
      Park, Swindon. Later met local Save the Children Fund
      Branch members.

OCTOBER

1   Opened the new unit of L & K Fertilisers Limited, Sharp-
      ness, Gloucestershire.

2   Attended the South Western Dairy Show.

6   Was admitted to the Court of the Worshipful Company of
      Loriners as an Assistant, Barbers' Hall, London (morning).
      Attended a dinner at the Bank of England (evening).

7   As President of the Save the Children Fund visited the
      Hopscotch Asian Family Centre, London.

9   Opened the new hall at Abbott's Hill School, Hemel Hemp-
      stead, Hertfordshire (morning).
      As President of the Riding for the Disabled Association visited
      the South Buckinghamshire Group, Fulmer (afternoon).
      As President of the British Knitting and Clothing Export
      Council visited Reldan Limited, High Wycombe, Bucking-
      hamshire.

10   As President of the British Knitting and Clothing Council
      visited Corgi Hosiery Limited, Ammanford, Dyfed, Wales.
      As President of the Riding for the Disabled Association
      visited Pembrokeshire 'A' Group, Tenby, Dyfed.

Opened the new plant at Rockwool Limited, Mid Glamorgan.

13   As Chancellor of the University of London launched the 'Science for Industry' Fair at Imperial College of Science and Technology in celebration of the University's 150th Anniversary (morning).
Presented Long Service Badges to Nurses from the Queen's Nursing Institute, Drapers' Hall, London (afternoon).
As President of the Save the Children Fund attended the Musicians Appeal for Famine Relief in Africa Concert, Barbican Centre, London (evening).

14   As President of the Riding for the Disabled Association visited the Havering Group, London (afternoon).
As President of The Missions to Seamen attended a Concert in aid of the Mission, followed by a buffet supper, London.

15   Presented Awards at the Beautiful Britain in Bloom Ceremony at Vintners' Hall, London (morning).
As Chancellor of the University of London attended a tri-service military display at Greenwich Naval College and inspected the University Naval Unit vessel in celebration of the University's 150th Anniversary.

16   Opened The Frank Wise School for those with physical or learning disabilities, Banbury.
Visited Banbury Young Industry Training Workshop.
Visited Lesme Limited and Midlands Mart Stockyard, Banbury.
Opened the new sports centre at Blosham School, Banbury.
Lunched with Cherwell District Council.
Evening: As Patron of the Home Farm Trust attended a reception at Luton Hoo, Luton, Bedfordshire, to launch an appeal for a new home for mentally handicapped adults.

17   As President of the Royal School for Daughters of Officers of the Royal Navy and Royal Marines, opened The Royal Naval Schools' new Gymnasium, called 'Princess Anne Hall', in Haslemere, Surrey.

21   As President of the Save the Children Fund, attended the Fund's AGM at the Royal Albert Hall (9.30 am – 4.00 pm).

Evening: Attended a dinner given by the 1975 Club at the Farmers' Club, Whitehall Court, London.

22   Visited the new showrooms of Swaine Adeney Brigg and Sons Limited, Piccadilly, London (afternoon).
As Patron of the Association of Combined Youth Clubs, visited the Clubs' headquarters and formally opened the Centre to be used as the base for the Manpower Services Community Programme Project, Battersea (evening).
Attended the Annual General Meeting and Presentation at the Mercers' Hall, London.

23   As Senior Warden of the Worshipful Company of Carmen, attended the Court Meeting and was installed as Master of the Company.
Attended a Reception and Court Luncheon at Painter Stainers' Hall, London.
As Chancellor of the University of London visited the Institute of Advanced Legal Studies, Russell Square, London, on the occasion of its 40th Anniversary.

24   Opened Berners Street Hostel for Mentally Handicapped, Birmingham.
Opened the new Infant Department block and Administrative Offices at Yew Tree Primary School, Aston, Birmingham.

27   Attended The Air League Annual Reception in aid of The Air League Educational Trust, Martini Terrace, New Zealand House, London.
Attended a banquet in aid of the Great Ormond Street Hospital for Sick Children, Guildhall, London.

29   As President of the Save the Children Fund attended part of the morning session of the Inland Revenue Staff Federation Executive Committee Meeting (morning).
As Patron of British Executive Service Overseas attended their Annual General Meeting at the Institute of Directors, London (afternoon).
Attended the Central British Fund for World Jewish Relief Dinner, Grosvenor Hotel, London (evening).

30   Attended a reception in aid of TS *Royalist* given by the Sea Cadets at Trinity House, London.

Attended the Association of Livery Masters 1985 Ladies Night Dinner in the Chiswell Street Brewery, London.

NOVEMBER

5   As Chancellor of the University of London opened Wye College new student residence and attended the launch of the College appeal, Ashford, Kent (morning).
Opened the new students' hostel for students of the United Medical and Dental Schools of Guy's and St. Thomas's Hospitals in the grounds of Lambeth Palace, London. Attended a Reception afterwards.

6–7 As President of the Riding for the Disabled Association attended the Annual General Meeting of the Association at the National Agricultural Centre, Kenilworth, Warwickshire.

8   Attended the Royal British Legion Festival of Remembrance at the Royal Albert Hall, London.

9   Attended the Remembrance Day Service at the Cenotaph, London.
Evening: Attended a concert to mark the 40th Anniversary of the opening of the Arundel Reserve at the Chichester Festival Theatre, West Sussex.

10 Visited the offices of the *Lancashire Evening Telegraph*.
Visited Blackburn Borough Council's new Leisure Pool.

11 Attended the Council Meeting for the National Council and Voluntary Youth Services on the occasion of the 50th Anniversary of its foundation, Islington, London.
Lunched at Islington Town Hall.
Visited youth organisations belonging to The National Council for Voluntary Youth Services.

12 Presented the 1986 Structural Steel Design Awards at a luncheon at The Savoy Hotel, London.

13 Opened the new offices of the Chiltern District Council at Amersham, Buckinghamshire.
Opened a Day Care Centre and Short Stay Hostel for the Handicapped at Seeley's House, Beaconsfield, Buckinghamshire.

14   Visited the Royal Army Veterinary Training Centre, Melton Mowbray, Leicestershire to watch the 1986 Farriery Championships and presented the prizes.
Watched equitation training and toured the Veterinary Hospital.
As President of the British Knitting and Clothing Export Council, visited Gloverall Limited, Wellingborough.

15   Attended the Annual Dinner of Royal Lymington Yacht Club as its Patron, Hampshire.

17   Opened the new EBEL Boutique, New Bond Street, London.
Attended a dinner at The Athenaeum, Pall Mall, London.

18   Opened the new WRNS Accommodation Block at HMS *Neptune*, Faslane, Dunbartonshire.

19   As Chancellor of the University of London visited Birbeck College, London.
Attended a dinner given by the Marketing Group of Great Britain, London.

24   Visited Marling and Evans Limited Clothing Mill at Stonehouse, Gloucestershire.

25   Attended a ball organised by St. Loye's College for the Disabled at the Hurlingham Club, London.

26   Opened the first Sheltered/Special Sheltered Housing Scheme to be built by Sedgemoor District Council, Somerset.
Opened the new indoor riding arena at Sandhill Park Hospital, Somerset.

DECEMBER

1   As President of the Royal Agricultural Society of England attended the Cooper Dinner at Claridges, London.

2   Opened the new studio and office facilities at The HTV West Television Centre, Bristol.
As President of the British Knitting and Clothing Export Council visited Mulberry Company Limited, Chilcompton, Somerset.

3   As President of the Royal Agricultural Society of England
    attended the Society's Council Meeting, Belgrave Square,
    London (morning).
    As Chancellor of the University of London presided at the
    Degree Ceremony at the Royal Albert Hall, London (after-
    noon).
    Attended a Thanksgiving Service in celebration of the
    University's 150th Anniversary at St. Paul's Cathedral (ear-
    ly evening).
    As Commandant in Chief of St. John Ambulance and
    Nursing Cadets attended The Order Gala Ball at the Inter-
    continental Hotel, London (evening).

4   As Chancellor of the University of London opened the new
    research facilities at the Institute of Neurology, National
    Hospital, London (morning).
    As President of the Save the Children Fund opened the new
    'Charles of the Ritz' factory, Burgess Hill, Sussex, and
    attended a reception (afternoon).

5   Visited Nottingham.
    Opened the new extension at East Midlands Airport.
    Lunched at The Council House.
    Unveiled statuary in Old Market Square.
    Visited the Save the Children Fund Shop.
    Attended a buffet reception at The County Hall.
    Attended a Gala Evening at the Theatre Royal.

7   As President of The Missions to Seamen attended a charity
    Christmas Concert in the Chapel of the Royal Naval
    College, Greenwich.

18 Attended 'Carols for the Save the Children Fund', Royal
    Albert Hall, London.

Bibliography

ARONSON, Theo: *Royal Family – Years of Transition* (John Murray, 1983).

BLOOM, Ursula: *Princesses in Love* (Robert Hale, 1973).

BROWN, Craig & CUNLIFFE, Lesley: *The Book of Royal Lists* (Routledge & Kegan Paul, 1982).

BURCH DONALD, Elsie (Ed.): *Debrett's Etiquette & Modern Manners* (Debrett's, 1981).

CAMPBELL, Judith: *Anne – Portrait of a Princess* (Cassell, 1970).

CATHCART, Helen: *Anne and the Princesses Royal* (W. H. Allen, 1973).

COLVILLE, John: *Footprints in Time* (Collins, 1976).

COURTNEY, Nicholas: *Sporting Royals Past and Present* (Hutchinson/Stanley Paul, 1983).

COURTNEY, Nicholas: *Princess Anne* (Weidenfeld & Nicolson, 1986).

DAVIS, Reginald & MATHESON, Anne: *Princess Anne – A Girl of Our Time* (Frederick Muller, 1973).

DUNCAN, Andrew: *The Reality of Monarchy* (Heinemann, 1970).

EDGAR, Donald: *Palace* (W. H. Allen, 1983).

FISHER, Graham & Heather: *Monarchy and the Royal Family* (Robert Hale, 1980).

GRAHAM, Tim: *On the Royal Road* (Weidenfeld & Nicolson, 1984).

GRUNFIELD, Nina: *The Royal Shopping Guide* (Pan Books, 1985).

HALL, Trevor: *Royal Family Yearbook* (Colour Library Books, 1983).

HAMILTON, Alan: *The Royal Handbook* (Mitchell Beazley, 1985).

HOEY, Brian: *HRH The Princess Anne* (Country Life Books, 1984).

JAMES, Paul: *The Royal Almanac* (Ravette London, 1986).

JAMES, Paul & RUSSELL, Peter: *At Her Majesty's Service* (Collins, 1986).

KEAY, Douglas: *Royal Pursuit* (Severn House, 1983).

LACEY, Robert: *Majesty* (Hutchinson, 1977).

LICHFIELD, Patrick: *A Royal Family Album* (Elm Tree Books, 1982).

LONGFORD, Elizabeth: *The Royal House of Windsor* (Weidenfeld & Nicolson, 1974).

ROSE, Kenneth: *Kings, Queens and Courtiers* (Weidenfeld & Nicolson, 1985).

RUSSELL, Audrey: *A Certain Voice* (Ross Anderson, 1985).

WARWICK, Christopher: *Queen Elizabeth II* (Webb & Bower, 1986).

ZIEGLER, Philip: *Crown and People* (Collins, 1978).

Donations to the SAVE THE CHILDREN FUND can be sent to:

The Save the Children Fund
Mary Datchelor House,
17 Grove Lane,
London SE5 8RD

10p   buys three doses of polio vaccine or one dose of measles vaccine that will safeguard a child for life.

25p   provides a nourishing meal for a hungry child in Asia.

£1   gives a child in Bangladesh books and pencils for a term's schooling.

£2   provides an in-service training course for a community health nurse in the Gambia.

£5   buys a toy telephone to help in speech therapy for a UK child with language difficulties.

£25   buys a medical kit for a village health worker in Nepal.

£50   provides a set of multi-racial dolls, jigsaws and books for a UK project to promote positive cultural experiences for young children.

£100   buys a set of tools for a workshop to give unemployed British teenagers the chance to learn new skills.

£200   buys a doctor's bag and contents (medical equipment and textbooks).

£250   pays a month's salary for a physiotherapist treating disabled children in Thailand.

£400   buys a village water well.

£500   employs a UK playgroup worker for one morning per week for a year.

£750   buys a 90cc motorbike to enable nurses in rural areas to visit village health workers.

£1,000   sets up a ventilated store, protected against damp and rats, with covered cooking area and fuel-efficient stove, so that a Lesotho school can keep its stocks of food safe for the children's much-needed midday meal.

£3,500   buys a solar-powered refrigerator for storing vaccine.

£5,000   builds a pre-school in Papua New Guinea and covers running costs, including teacher's salary, for the first five years.

£7,500   provides a night shelter for street children and mothers for one year in Sri Lanka.

£10,000   provides the salary of a community worker in the UK for one year to support homeless children and their families in bed-and-breakfast accommodation.

£13,000   gives a Honduran village its own piped clean water supply for drinking, cooking, washing and growing vegetables.

£14,000   buys a minibus to take children from troubled inner-city areas on outings – to the swimming baths, the country-side, their first view of the sea.

Index